5795
90k

Heterick Memorial Library
Ohio Northern University
Ada, Ohio 45810

The New Global Economy and the Developing Countries

To Kieran

The New Global Economy and the Developing Countries

Essays in International Economics and Development

G. K. Helleiner

Professor of Economics,
University of Toronto

Edward Elgar

© G. K. Helleiner 1990

All rights reserved. No part of this publication may be reproduced, stored in a retrieval system, or transmitted in any form or by any means, electronic, mechanical, photocopying, recording, or otherwise without the prior permission of the publisher.

Published by
Edward Elgar Publishing Limited
Gower House
Croft Road
Aldershot
Hants GU11 3HR
England

Edward Elgar Publishing Company
Old Post Road
Brookfield
Vermont 05036
USA

British Library Cataloguing in Publication Data

Helleiner, G. K. (Gerald Karl), *1936–*
The new global economy and the developing countries : essays in international economics and development.
1. Developing countries. Economic development
I. Title
330. 91724

Library of Congress Cataloguing in Publication Data

Helleiner, G. K.
The new global economy and the developing countries: essays in international economics and development/G. K. Helleiner.
p. cm.
ISBN 1–85278–329–X
1. Developing countries – Foreign economic relations.
2. International economic relations. 3. International finance.
I. Title.
HF1413.H45 1990
337'.09172'4–dc20 90–38600
CIP

ISBN 1 85278 329 X

Printed in Great Britain by
Billing & Sons Ltd, Worcester

337.091724
H477n

Contents

Tables

Acknowledgements

I should like to thank several organizations and publishers for their permission to use previously published or forthcoming material. Permission has kindly been granted, as follows:

- *Chapter 1*: Portions originally appeared in 'North–South Relations, Then and Now: 1976–86' in North–South Institute, *Review '86, Outlook '87* (Ottawa, 1987), pp. 15–17; and in 'Conventional Foolishness and Overall Ignorance: Current Approaches to Global Transformation and Development', *Canadian Journal of Development Studies*, vol. X, no. 1, 1989, pp. 107–120.
- *Chapter 2*: Originally prepared as the third annual Timlin Lecture, delivered at the University of Saskatchewan, Saskatoon, 21 March, 1985, and subsequently published both by the University of Saskatchewan in pamphlet form, and in 'The New Global Economy: Problems, Prospects and Priority Research Requirements' in the United Nations' *Journal of Development Planning*, no. 17, 1987, pp. 19–35; parts of it were drawn with permission from an unpublished report prepared for the UN Committee for Development Planning in November 1984.
- *Chapter 3*: Originally appeared in 'The Refnes Seminar; Economic Theory and North–South Negotiations', *World Development*, vol. 9, no. 6, (Pergamon Journals Ltd., Oxford, June 1981), pp. 539–55, and 'Introduction', in G.K. Helleiner (ed.), *For Good or Evil, Economic Theory and North–South Negotiations* (Universitätsforlaget, Oslo, and University of Toronto Press, Toronto, 1982) pp. 1–30.
- *Chapter 4*: Originally prepared for the Third World Foundation, New Zealand House, London, November 1982, and published in Ashok Bapna (ed.), *One World One Future, New International Strategies for Development*, (Praeger Publishers, New York, 1985), pp. 279–91. Copyright 1985 by Praeger Publishers. Reprinted by permission.

- *Chapter 5*: Originally prepared for the United Nations and published, with permission, in 'The Impact of the Exchange Rate System on the Developing Countries' in Sidney Dell (ed.), *The International Monetary System and its Reform, Part II* (North-Holland, Amsterdam, New York, Oxford and Tokyo, 1987), pp. 407–510.
- *Chapter 6*: Originally prepared for the United Nations and published in 'Update' and 'Balance of Payments and Growth Prospects of Developing Countries: A Synthesis', *World Development*, vol. 14, no. 8, (Pergamon Journals Ltd., Oxford, August 1986), pp. 875–908; and in Sidney Dell (ed.), *The International Monetary System and its Reform, Part III* (North Holland, Amsterdam, New York, Oxford and Tokyo, 1987), pp. 961–1004; and in UNCTAD, *International Monetary and Financial Issues for the Developing Countries* (United Nations, New York, 1987), pp. 125–76.
- *Chapter 7*: Originally prepared for the South Commission, May 1988; some paragraphs previously appeared in 'The Question of Conditionality' in Carol Lancaster and John Williamson (eds), *African Debt and Financing* (Institute for International Economics, Washington, DC, 1986), pp. 63–91; in 'Policy-based Program Lending: A Look at the Bank's New Role' in Richard Feinberg *et al.*, *Between Two Worlds: The World Bank's Next Decade* (Overseas Development Council, Transaction Books, New Brunswick and Oxford, 1986), pp. 47–66; and in ' Trade Strategy in Medium-Term Adjustment', *World Development* (Pergamon Journals Ltd., Oxford, forthcoming).
- *Chapter 8*: Originally prepared for the Swedish International Development Agency (SIDA) for a conference on adjustment in Maputo, Mozambique, scheduled for June 1989, but subsequently postponed; portions were also published in 'Stabilization, Adjustment and the Poor', *World Development*, vol. 15, no. 12, (Pergamon Journals Ltd., Oxford, December 1987), pp. 1499–513, and in Richard Bird and Susan Horton (eds), *Government Policy and the Poor in Developing Countries* (University of Toronto Press, Toronto, 1989), pp. 23–48.
- *Chapter 9*: Originally prepared for the Seventh Conference of the International Economic Association, Madrid, 1985, and published in Silvio Borner and Alwyn Taylor (eds), *Structural Change, Economic Interdependence and World Development, Volume 2:*

Natural and Financial Resources for Economic Development (Macmillan, 1987), pp. 445–66.

- *Chapter 10*: Originally prepared for the second biennial conference of economic research institutes, Washington, September 1977, and published in Kimberly Ann Elliott and John Williamson (eds), *Global Economic Problems*, pp. 197–215. Copyright 1988 Institute for International Economics, Washington, DC. Reprinted by permission.
- *Chapter 11*: Originally prepared for a conference in Merida, Mexico in December 1985, sponsored by the University of Toronto, Stanford University and El Colegio de Mexico, and used here with their permission.
- *Chapter 12*: Originally prepared for the Commonwealth Secretariat in 1985, and published, in part, in Vincent Cable and Bishnodat Persaud (eds), *Developing with Foreign Investment* (Croom Helm, 1987), pp. 67–83; and in Sidney Dell (ed.), *Policies for Development* (Macmillan, 1988), pp. 123–53.
- *Chapter 13*: Originally published in Rita Cruise O'Brien (ed.), *Information, Economics and Power, The North-South Dimension* (Hodder and Stoughton, 1983), pp. 28–42.
- *Chapter 14*: Originally published as 'The International Economics of the Information Industry and the Developing Countries' in Robin Murray (ed.), *Multinationals Beyond the Market: Intra-Firm Trade and the Control of Transfer Pricing* (Harvester Press, 1981), pp. 207–22.

Preface

With the exception of the bulk of the first chapter, the material in this volume was originally prepared for use elsewhere. I have enjoyed the opportunity of looking at it again and trying to place it all into some overall context. I should like to thank Edward Elgar who galvanized me into doing so.

The papers were written over the course of the 1980s; but I believe they retain their relevance for the 1990s. Indeed, continued relevance was a prime criterion in the selection of papers for inclusion. I have sought to remove material that is clearly no longer accurate, but have made only limited effort to bring data and commentary fully up-to-date.

In addition to those who commented on earlier drafts (who are mentioned at the outset of individual chapters) and those who have granted permission to reprint (who are acknowledged elsewhere) I should like to thank Rodney Schmidt for his help in deciding what to include.

Gerald K. Helleiner
Big Bay,
Ontario

PART I
Developing Countries in the New Global Economy

1. Introduction: Toward the Twenty-first Century

For nearly 25 years I have offered a postgraduate course at the University of Toronto on 'international aspects of economic development' or, as I sometimes irreverently (and with acknowledgement to E.F. Schumacher) call it, 'international economics as if the developing countries mattered'.[1] There do not seem to be many such university courses at any level in the industrialized countries. Students must pick up what they can on 'my' subject on the periphery of mainstream courses in international economics (most standard textbooks devote one chapter out of 21 to developing country issues[2]) or in the 'international' section (typically accounting for more like 10–20 per cent of total content) of courses on development economics; many universities do not offer the latter. Yet these are matters of very great importance not only for the developing countries themselves but also for an adequate appreciation of the functioning of the global economy.

The importance of international or global influences and opportunities, and domestic policies for dealing with them, is self-evident in all but (perhaps) the largest of the developing countries. Most developing countries have what the literature of international economics calls 'small open economies' – unable to affect international terms of trade, yet with overall economic performance very much influenced by them. Major proportions of total production are exported, and imports of goods and non-factor services usually account for even greater shares of total output. Government revenues are heavily dependent upon taxes levied directly on foreign trade and on trade-dependent sectors. External sources of capital (governmental, private or both) have been of significant importance in most developing countries' investment efforts; recently, as capital has 'flown' external outlets have also provided important investment opportunities for domestic private savers. Imported technology and tastes continue to play major roles in Third World development processes.

This catalogue of important external influences should not be taken to imply that the developing countries are utterly helpless before the power of the global economy or that external forces completely determine their economic fortunes. Purely domestic events, constraints and governmental policies (not least on how to relate to the global economy) dominate external influences over longer-term, and frequently fairly short-term, development as well. Nevertheless, external influences are very important, certainly much more so than in the USA, where most university economics textbooks are still written. Analysis of these matters *is* major subject matter in basic courses in economics as well as in more specialized international economics courses in Third World universities.

It has always seemed to me that the important influence of the global economy upon the developing countries places a special onus upon those concerned with international development *outside* the developing countries to understand how it works. Where possible they can then seek to ease the external constraints imposed on the developing countries and/or expand their opportunities in the global economy by altering their own behaviour or governmental policies. That has been a major rationale for my postgraduate course.

There has gradually been evolving a new reason for Northern concern with the international aspects of economic development in the Third World. Perhaps best epitomized by the OPEC oil price rises and the Third World debt crisis, there has emerged a new perception in many quarters of Northern governments not previously known for their concern with Third World affairs that the developing countries influence the performance of their own economies. The growth of such views has slowed in Northern official quarters in the late 1980s, but it is bound to resume because of the sheer size of the Third World, and because of the emergence, with the effective shrinkage of the size of the planet, of a truly global economy (see Chapter 2). Sometime in the twenty-first century, if not before, it will become *de rigeur* for economists and decision makers to analyse and monitor the macro-economic performance of the *global* economy in more or less the same terms as they assess such performance today within their separate national political units. In order to do this well it will be necessary for Northern, as well as Southern, analysts to understand the interactions between the developing countries and the global economy – interactions which have, until recently, been analytically relatively neglected in the North (see, however, Currie and Vines, 1988). Understanding and managing the global economy involves far more than macro-economic policy coordination among a few major industrialized countries, the subject matter of a burst of Northern international economic research in the 1980s (see, for instance, Buiter and Marston, 1985).

The essays in this volume explore many of what I consider to be the most pressing current issues relating to the place of the developing countries in the new global economy.[3] There is heavy emphasis throughout on what economists do *not* know, and thus upon research requirements. Lest my apparent agnosticism concerning many of the conventional Northern economic wisdoms of the day be mistaken for disapproval of the discipline of economics (or international economics), let me make my position quite clear. I believe that there will always be early limits to the usefulness of either international or domestic policy analysis that is conducted purely in terms of economics. I also believe that members of the economics profession have frequently claimed greater knowledge than they had, not least in the subject matter of this volume. But economic analysis, properly conducted and with the analyst's objectives clearly stated, remains a potentially powerful contributor to social progress, to the Keynesian 'possibility of civilization'.[4] At the very least, as Churchill said of parliamentary democracy, I believe it is better than the available alternatives.

By way of further introduction let me offer some brief comment on four subjects not explicitly covered in the essays that follow: the record of Northern and developing country economic performance in the 1980s; the changing state of North–South relations; the measurement of global economic performance; and the development of professional expertise in economics, and particularly international economics, in the Third World.

ECONOMIC PERFORMANCE IN THE 1980s

During the 1980s, following the most severe recession in 50 years, the major industrialized countries enjoyed the longest sustained recovery in just as long a period. Oil prices returned to more 'normal' levels, and seemed unlikely to be subject again to abrupt major price rises. Successive Western Economic Summit conferences expressed satisfaction with the record of relatively low rates of price inflation and continuing, if somewhat modest, overall economic growth. Unemployment rates were higher than previously in the post-Second World War period – a source of concern to many – but OECD policymakers were typically satisfied that these were an inevitable by-product of labour market rigidities and overall price stability. The only shadows over global economic performance, as perceived in the North, were continued US current account imbalances and, for a time, the threat to the international financial system posed by Third World debt. The US deficit persists, but the Western economies have so far been able to contain its potentially damaging global effects, and there has been some limited progress towards its reduction. At the same time, the major industrialized powers have increased their macro-economic policy coordination and moved towards more effective joint exchange rate surveillance and management. The problem of Third World debt remains, but the major Western commercial banks have rebuilt reserves while reducing their real Third World exposure; the stability of the Western financial system is no longer seen to be at risk from this source. By the end of the 1980s, despite the evident growth in the interdependence of all of the world's national economies there was a growing Northern perception that their own economic performance could, after all, be comfortably 'de-linked' from events in the Third World, much of which was faring very badly.

It is in the sphere of the environment rather than the economy (though these are obviously not totally unrelated) that the North today seems more persuaded of the importance of events in the South to the prospects of the North. The fragility of the planet's ecosystem is now seen, even by otherwise conservative politicians, to require accommodations with the South. The urgent need to control the use of chlorofluorocarbons to protect the earth's ozone layer, the growing concern over global warming, the new perceptions of the role of tropical forests in the preservation of the atmosphere, not to speak of the longstanding issue of global population growth, all point to a need for intensified North–South cooperation in the mutual and global interest. (At the same time, the disposal of Northern toxic waste in financially desperate developing countries looks like becoming a matter for new international concern.) The cooperation of the developing countries in environmental management may have to be purchased by Northern concessions in the economic sphere. North–South economic relations cannot in fact be easily separated from other spheres of North–South interaction.

Economic performance in the Third World during the 1980s varied enormously between groups of countries. The record of economic growth in most of Asia maintained, or even improved upon, the impressive record of the previous two decades. The newly industrializing economies of Hong Kong, Korea, Singapore and Taipei/China continued their previous remarkable rates of growth, slowing only a little at the end of the decade. In South-east Asia, while growth rates generally slowed a little in the 1980s, Thailand emerged as a 'star' performer in the latter half of the decade. Most significant of all, because of their sheer size, growth rates in India, Pakistan and the People's Republic of China significantly improved over their 1970s records (Asian Development Bank, 1989: 178).

On the other hand, economic performance in most of sub-Saharan Africa and Latin America was disastrous. For them, the 1980s have generally been described as a 'lost decade', with per capita incomes declining. By the end of the decade sub-Saharan African per capita income probably averaged only about half that in 1980; and the 1970s had already been a decade of stagnation or decline in Africa. Nor, despite major domestic policy changes, are there many signs of improvement on the horizon: key primary commodity prices are likely to remain weak, the debt–service ratio continues to climb, real capital flows are stagnant, foreign exchange scarcities continue to generate severe underutilization of productive capacity and the skill base remains uniquely underdeveloped. The economic prospect for sub-Saharan Africa looks sombre indeed. By the end of the century, according to current projections, it will have overtaken South Asia as the principal locale for the world's absolute poverty. In Latin America, while incomes also declined in the 1980s, they did not, on average, fall so far; and, of course, they began at much higher levels than Africa's. The losses suffered by urban workers and vulnerable social groups in Latin America during the 1980s were nevertheless unprecedented in severity since the Great Depression of the 1930s. Weak external terms of trade, sharply reduced gross capital inflows, domestic capital flight and an unsustainable burden of external debt (worsened by unusually high real rates of interest) continue to bedevil most Latin American economies. They are consequently struggling with fiscal crisis, low investment rates, rapid or even hyperinflation, political unrest, and a limited prospect of widespread income improvement for some years to come.

It is increasingly evident in the light of such varying experience that major interests within the South diverge. In the run-up to the multilateral trade negotiations under the GATT, for instance, the interests of the fast-growing, middle-income and more trade-dependent developing countries (like Korea and Singapore) clearly diverged from those of the less trade-dependent (like India and Brazil) and small primary exporters (like Tanzania). It even proved difficult to hold all of the South's monetary managers together in approaches to pressing external debt problems. The Cartagena group of debtors in Latin America calculated its interests quite differently from the majority of sub-Saharan African debtors; even such similar debtors as Argentina, Brazil and Mexico had difficulty coordinating their positions *vis-à-vis* commercial creditors. The special attention directed to sub-Saharan African problems in the United Nations and the World Bank group generated visible restlessness among some other developing countries. Ideological, religious, linguistic and foreign policy differences, as always, further complicate coalition formation in the South. The best prospects are therefore for less-than-complete, issue-specific, geographically-based or politically-based alliances rather than for across-the-board Southern approaches seeking to provide all things to all countries. There will therefore be important opportunities for issue-specific coalitions, involving select Northern countries as well as Southern countries, like that of the Cairns Group that has been promoting agricultural trade liberalization in the GATT.

None of this is to suggest, as some Northern commentators do, that 'the South' does not exist – that the developing countries do not now possess sufficient commonality of interest or experience or perception to cooperate at all. The South Commission, composed of eminent Third World personalities searching for ways of increasing economic and other forms of Southern cooperation, has given eloquent expression to Third World perceptions of joint interest.[5] Nor is it to suggest that there might not be substantial merit in renewed North–South dialogue along the lines of the Cancun summit meeting of 1981. Western economic summit meetings do not always, after all, generate major tangible policy changes, but they serve important purposes nonetheless. Even a symbolic recognition that the Western leaders cannot, and do not, speak for the economic interests of the world – their own summit rhetoric notwithstanding – would be useful from time to time. Nor, finally, does it reduce the cogency of the case for an effective Third World economic secretariat – some form of an OECD of the South. As in the North, such a secretariat can be expected to coexist with a variety of other institutions that are more focused by geography, issue, language and so on.

CHANGING NORTH–SOUTH RELATIONS

Against this backdrop, North-South relations altered radically during the 1980s. In the mid-1970s the mood among developing country policy-makers was newly self-confident in international affairs. The previous two decades had seen historically unprecedented rates of economic growth in many of the developing countries, achieved principally through improved mobilization of their own resources. Several newly industrializing countries had broken dramatically into markets for manufactures in the industrialized countries. OPEC's success in raising oil prices through collective unilateral action both inspired other developing countries to seek other possibilities for increasing their take from international exchange and lent credence to sharpened Third World demands for a 'new international economic order' in trade, money and finance.

The industrialized countries were themselves at this time somewhat uncertain in their defence of existing international economic relationships. The Bretton Woods exchange rate regime had broken down; the oil price increase had demonstrated a new vulnerability on the part of the industrialized countries, and precipitated a severe global recession; and new concerns over the environment and the appropriate use of 'common' global resources were widespread. The time seemed ripe for the developing countries to move on from their achievements of political independence and significant self-propelled economic growth towards reforms in the functioning of the international economy. The industrialized countries, uncertain and defensive, seemed able only to slow the pace of international changes which they could no longer fully control. In September 1975, the member governments of the United Nations, in a special session, formally committed themselves to the development of a new international economic order, embracing reforms in international commodity markets, financial institutions and a range of other issues.

Among development analysts and policy-makers in both North and South there had also been a major rethink about the basic objectives of development and the most appropriate policies for meeting them. It was widely agreed that rapid economic growth in many developing countries left far too many people still trapped in what the World Bank described as 'absolute poverty'. Disappointment with the human results of economic progress did not reduce analysts' confidence in their ability to generate development of a more satisfactory kind; rather, the rhetoric and, to some degree, practice of international development shifted towards new objectives and new policies for their attainment. As concern with the distribution of the fruits of economic progress mounted, more international resources and policies were directed to the meeting of basic needs – food, shelter, clothing, health, education, clean water, and a sense of participation.

In the second half of the 1970s there was a robust recovery from the oil price shock and recession of 1973–75. An expanded and seemingly resilient private international banking community was playing a major new role in Third World finance. It was a time of exhilaration and optimism in significant portions of both Northern and Southern policy-making circles both about development and about the prospect of agreed new approaches to the governance of the world economy.

The world of the late 1980s was unfortunately a very different one. Momentum for constructive change in international economic affairs in furtherance of a more stable and equitable global future had disappeared. In much of the Third World previous economic progress was being rolled back. Nervousness and uncertainty about the world's medium-term economic prospects were pervasive. National governments everywhere became more cautious and more inward-looking in their approaches to economic policy. The United Nations and its specialized agencies struggled for their very survival.

All this was the primary fall-out from the global economic recession of the early 1980s – the most severe in 50 years. Primary commodity prices fell to the lowest real levels since the Second World War. Voluntary commercial bank lending to the developing countries virtually ceased. A mountain of Third World debt – much of it unserviceable and selling at heavy discounts in secondary markets – accumulated and still hangs over the international financial system. Economic and social progress in the majority of developing countries came to a halt and, in many, it was put into reverse. In this context, the developing countries' confident pursuit of a 'New International Economic Order' was set aside. Urgent national needs displaced international reformist efforts on governmental agendas. Indeed, the developing countries proved much more wary of rocking the planetary boat than many had predicted. At a time of severe global recession they clearly saw advantage in the preservation and strengthening of such multilateral economic governing mechanisms as there were.

Their appreciation of the multilateral system was undoubtedly sharpened by their need to come to the defence of the multilateral institutions against the assault of newly influential conservative political forces, particularly in the USA and the UK. An insensitive and intolerant ideology of individualism and the 'magic of the marketplace' there generated new cynicism about governments, indifference to poverty, suspicion of international cooperation, and myopia about both global and national prospects. The previous US postwar tradition of 'liberal internationalism', which had nurtured the United Nations and the Marshall Plan, already somewhat tarnished in the late 1960s and suffering further setbacks with the relative decline of US economic power in the 1970s, was in full retreat in the Reaganite 1980s.

These changes in Northern political climates also permeated international development institutions. Despite severe deterioration in the availability of basic needs, market-oriented and 'productionist' ideologies rose into fashion in the World Bank as well as in most official development assistance agencies. Most developing country governments, increasingly desperate for finance, were forced on to the defensive as they searched for acceptable accommodations with the new purveyors of conservative policy conditions in official aid and credit institutions (the same institutions that in the previous decade had castigated them for their insufficient emphasis on basic needs).

A key phrase in the development lexicon of the 1960s and 1970s was 'structural change': this meant positive change in the make-up of poor societies and economies – particularly in their productive structure – that would place them on a more rapid, equitable and sustainable growth path. In the 1980s the talk was instead of 'structural adjustment' - alteration of productive structures in response to the deterioration of the world economic environment and, just as frequently, to the pressure of powerful external actors with their own views as to what most needed reform. Where it still existed in official agencies at all, the humanitarian concern of the 1970s was reduced to a defensive advocacy of 'adjustment with a human face'.

A high proportion of the world's poor, notably those in sub-Saharan Africa and Latin America, at best spent the 1980s, in a 'holding pattern'. In Africa, the progress of a whole post-independence generation was lost and the costs of cutbacks to child health, nutrition and education will be felt for more than another generation.

It is possible, however, that the worst in North–South economic relations is over. As seen above, there is a new Northern awareness of the imperative of global cooperation on environmental concerns. East–West political and military detente offers the possibility (but by no means presumption) of improved global cooperation for peaceful objectives. A new US administration promises a 'kinder, gentler' approach to economic policy, and is visibly more supportive of multilateral institutions. A somewhat slimmed-down United Nations system is winning new support from the formerly centrally planned economies, and greater respect all around. Having failed to deliver the promised goods, the extremist market enthusiasts are repairing to their accustomed and more appropriate relative position in the overall disposition of political influence (Killick, 1989). The World Bank shows a refreshing new humility in the assessment of its own advice and adjustment lending (World Bank, 1988); and both it and the IMF also demonstrate renewed and new concern for the social dimensions of adjustment and the welfare of the poorest and most vulnerable groups in the developing countries. Although Third World debt problems are by no means resolved, Northern governments are no longer so rigid over the prospect of debt reduction. Against all odds, the Uruguay Round of GATT negotiations appears to be achieving progress, even in some of the areas of previously greatest North–South difficulty, such as services trade. There seems a genuine and new international consensus that the problems of sub-Saharan Africa require special international attention. And new technological possibilities in electronics, bio-engineering, and elsewhere offer the prospect of accelerated global progress if only the world can lift itself from the 'rut' into which much of it stumbled during the 1970s and 1980s.

MEASURING GLOBAL ECONOMIC PERFORMANCE

As seen above, the 1980s have seen widely divergent economic performance among different parts of the world. The relatively small proportion of the world's population represented by the annual Western Summit conferences has been doing well (at least in the eyes of the summiteers). At the same time the people of Latin America and sub-Saharan Africa have suffered grievously. How well has the *global* economy performed? Without losing sight of the divergent record of different countries (just as one should not neglect the fact of divergent experience within nations) should there not be an 'aggregate' measure of global economic performance? And, if so, what should it look like?

This question forces reconsideration of the most fundamental elements of current national income accounting – in particular, the question of the weighting system as one 'adds up' the divergent experience. Should one adopt the UN system of 'one country, one vote'? Should one employ something more akin to the IMF/World Bank voting systems within which the USA carries about 20 per cent of the total weight? Or is there another system? To my mind, the most obvious starting-point for measuring the performance of the global economy is one that resembles neither.[6] One should begin with the proposition that each individual on the planet deserves equal weight in the measurement of overall economic progress – a very different methodology from the current national income accounting methodology which assigns equal weight to each dollar earned, regardless of who earns it, thereby implicitly weighting each person's progress by his or her income. As a first approximation, then, one could calculate current global economic growth by weighting each country's (already available) growth rate by its population. It is difficult to understand why some international institution, say the UN Secretariat, is not already reporting some such measure on a regular basis. Those of us who are particularly concerned with the world's poverty problem would assign *higher* weights to progress, or lack thereof, in the lower deciles of the world's income distribution.

The new political concern in the industrialized world with the 'sustainability' of national and, even more, global growth may at last engender some reconsideration of standard Northern measurements of economic performance in another dimension as well. Economists should be joining environmentalists in designing more appropriate macro-economic measures of progress. Concerned in the past to beat back the more naive 'doomsday' models of global resource depletion and to expose the shibboleth of 'zero growth', the economics profession has been rather too casual about some of its own accounting conventions. It should not have been left exclusively to physical scientists, environmentalists and ecologists to worry about 'sustainability'. Even before the Brundtland Commission, increasing concern was expressed in many quarters about the longer-run implications of short-term survival strategies in ecologically fragile parts of the developing world, notably in drought-prone Africa. The short-term cutbacks necessitated by the trauma of the 1980s in most of sub-Saharan Africa and Latin America intensified these concerns. What would be the longer-run consequences of failure to maintain current social infrastructure – roads, buildings, schools, hospitals, and so on – not to speak of directly productive capital stock? And, even more frightening, what would be the longer-run consequence of failure to provide minimal nutrition for pregnant women and children in their crucial early years? Brundtland's concern for the environment expands these questions to the infinitely broader realm of planetary equilibrium. In this sphere of accounting, as well as in that of poverty-weighting or population-weighting of income changes, the lead may well come from the developing countries.

"Sustainability" is certainly not a new issue in traditional national income accounting. The most frequently employed summary indicator is described as *Gross* National (or Domestic) Product for a reason. The GNP (or GDP) is, conceptually, a measure that explicitly abstracts from longer-run consequences of current economic activities. Those who estimate it consciously do *not* deduct the costs of maintaining the current physical capital stock, let alone the human capital stock: That is, no account is taken of 'depreciation'. No self-respecting private company or homeowner would draw conclusions as to successful performance without taking depreciation into account. Indeed, our tax laws frequently invite us to err on the conservative side when doing so. Why do we not then take depreciation into account and record the *Net* National (or Domestic) Product in our growth statistics and international comparisons? The conventional and simple answer is that it is far too difficult. Yet the public – and even some professionals – regard the imperfect measure we have as an accurate measure of 'progress' rather than simply a fairly crude measure of gross economic activity.

There can be little doubt that the data on depreciation are, at present, very weak. To generate such data would, certainly, in our present state of knowledge, require large numbers of fairly arbitrary assumptions. But anyone with more than superficial knowledge of the methodology of national income accounting knows that such assumptions and conventions abound already. Thirty years ago Kuznets asked, for instance, whether it would not be better to *deduct* such expenditures as commuter transport, police services and national defence from the National Product (Gross or Net) rather than adding them in (Kuznets, 1966: 20–6). The treatment of household services and a host of other arbitrarily treated items also continues to delight first year economics students around the world. Attempts must be made to account more accurately for depreciation in the measurement of growth.

In any case, how we measure development, and, particularly, in the current context, how we treat depreciation, is profoundly based upon our value judgments. Our conventional GNP measure reduces all goods and services to a common money numeraire, established by using market prices (or the nearest possible equivalent). But relative prices are themselves highly variable across countries and over time; and they are also dependent, in part, on such matters as government policy and the distribution of income. The employment of market prices thus carries with it the implicit value judgment that prices are appropriate measures of social 'value', and that current government policy and distribution of income are acceptable. These are strong and arbitrary assumptions.

Our twentieth-century market-oriented materialist culture is obviously not the only conceivable way in which human beings may organize themselves or pursue their own welfare. In the traditional culture of many North American native people, for instance, there is a conception of man-in-nature and the need for 'sustainability', which appears fundamentally at variance with traditional economic approaches. In some cultures, land and resources must be left in the state in which they are found, and the interests of future generations – of the rest of nature as well as of humanity – must be respected as a matter of *highest* priority. It is not therefore possible to rationalize the 'mining' of the environment by prioritizing the interests of the current generation over those of future generations. In effect, the *first* claim upon current income is the need to make up for depreciation.

The new concern for 'sustainability' will require the re-examination of the measurement of depreciation and Net National Product (and net capital formation) (Bartelmus, 1987). If reputable scientists believe that we are now running down our assets – polluting the water and atmosphere, exhausting non-renewable resources, reducing forest cover to a degree that engenders soil erosion and desertification – we should surely be accounting for it in our measures of developmental performance. It seems particularly perverse to record as extra (gross) income the expenditures on the inputs we devote to trying to offset some of these effects, as current conventions require. When depreciation is fully accounted for, and deducted from gross measures of production, we are likely to find ourselves, if the Brundtland Commission is correct, doing much less well than we thought, particularly in many of the developing countries. New knowledge of the longer-run implications of nutritional deficiency will probably generate even more depressing conclusions. The high measured growth rates of the 1960s may have been partly illusory, and the current setbacks in sub-Saharan Africa and Latin America are probably far more serious than previously thought.

When we both treat depreciation appropriately and take better account of the distribution of net income gains, we are likely to find the developing world, overall, to have been barely holding its own in the best cases, and moving significantly backwards in all too many others. Quite possibly, we shall be seen to be moving backward at the global level as well. Improved measurement of performance may improve the prospect of real global economic progress in the future.

ECONOMIC ANALYSIS IN AND FOR THE SOUTH

Those concerned with both increased understanding of the place of the developing countries in the global economy and with policies to improve global developmental performance can find new grounds for optimism in the progress of economic analysis in the Third World. Although expertise in economics will certainly not solve all problems (in all too many circumstances it may not even be able to address them) it is important that at the outset of the 1990s there is a new generation of well trained and self-confident economists debating, making policy, and teaching in the universities in the Third World. Already collectively quite strong in many parts of Asia and Latin America, these economists are now emerging in Africa as well. Many of them continue to be 'drained off' by the international financial institutions, the agencies of the UN, Northern universities and other external employers (where, one hopes, they exercise some independent influence and do not themselves simply absorb the dominant world views of their adopted institutions). As more and more acquire higher education, however, increasing numbers are remaining at home or returning to their place of birth.

Their study of international economics and the functioning of the global economy is usually undertaken from a starting-point different from that of the typical Northern economist. Obviously they seek to understand the global economy in much the same way as anyone else, but they also seek, as a matter of high priority, to analyse its impact upon development, and they therefore tend to assess global performance by different yardsticks. It would be difficult, for instance, to find a Latin American economist – whether of the political left, right or centre – who believed that the global economy had been performing well during the 1980s. While few hesitate to criticize elements of their own governments' policies (and here political differences certainly surface) virtually all attribute poor domestic economic performance very largely to external influences and constraints. Nor do members of the new generation of Southern economists always see their domestic policy problems through the same intellectual lenses as Northern colleagues. No longer totally in thrall to the journals and wisdoms of Northern economics, they are constructing or seeking to construct models, approaches and policies that relate to their own particular economic situations. Most seem less concerned with elegance and theoretical abstraction and more concerned with policy relevance. Obviously, since the variety of experience is so great, they do not constitute a rival 'school' of economics. Rather, they are simply characterized by a more practical and more eclectic 'mainstream' orientation. Unlike many of their Northern counterparts, the best economics departments of the South still attract and retain some of the brightest and most socially committed students. As their numbers and their skills expand they may be able to influence the overall global economics profession to move back towards a similar style, away from the sterile scholasticism that has grown in influence in many North American university economics departments.

Needless to say, none are happier over these developments and prospects than the so-called 'development economists' of the North. There has recently been a certain amount of discussion and debate over the fate of 'development economics' in the Northern literature (Hirschman, 1982; Bruton, 1985; Lewis, 1984; Sen, 1983). Seen, appropriately, as economic analysis that relates to and/or is practised in the developing countries (by far the majority of the world's national economies) 'development economics' is alive and well; indeed it has never been stronger. The fact that the *American Economic Review* now publishes very few articles that might be characterized as 'development economics', or that relate to developing countries in any way, says more about the dominant current interests of the American economics profession than it does about the state of economic analysis in the Third World.

The time may be ripe for the creation of a new and high-powered Third World institution dedicated to the teaching of tomorrow's Third World economists and policy-makers in terms of their own, highly varied, needs and likely experiences. The previous Northern monopoly of ideas and postgraduate training facilities in economics and public policy could by now be more effectively challenged. There are scores of strong policy-oriented economic research institutions in the developing countries. There is still a lack, however, of high-level educational establishments capable of competing at the doctoral or postdoctoral levels for the 'best and the brightest' of the next Third World generation with the universities of Europe, North America or, probably increasingly, Japan. As Northern doctoral programmes in economics become increasingly distanced from the pressing problems of the developing countries (and many would say from reality itself), the need for appropriate, and obviously no less rigorous, alternative programmes increases.

Is it not now anomalous that such high proportions of the time spent in advanced (and expensive) education by future Third World decision-makers and educators in economic affairs should be wasted in pointless abstractions and analysis of questions that are only of peripheral importance to them? The point is *not* that the existing programmes in Europe and North America are without value, or that the majority of students undertaking doctoral-level study will not continue to profit from them. On the contrary, these programmes are still the best there are; and in terms of the sheer number of student spaces they offer, they will undoubtedly continue to play a dominant role. It is, rather, that what are currently universally acknowledged to be the best available doctoral programmes could be considerably better; and that determined action in the Third World could probably now improve upon them, most particularly, in my judgement, in the sphere of international economics.

If such an institution were to be launched it would have to be done with great care. It would not be worth attempting at all unless it were done extremely well. It must not offer, or even be seen by any to offer, a 'second-class' degree. It would require the very best available minds, each given sufficient time and sufficient other incentives to deflect them from established careers and other rewarding activities towards the creation of substantially new courses and programmes. It would also require the highest-quality library facilities. It would have to carry full professional credibility from the outset. Even after substantial funding was assured, several years would probably be required to recruit the right people and permit them to prepare the ground for an effective launch. There would inevitably be the usual haggling over location, early staffing, funding, and so forth, and possibly attempts on the part of rival 'schools' of thought to 'capture' the institution. It would thus not only be an enormously ambitious enterprise but also an expensive, difficult and, to some degree, risky one. But might not the prospect of intellectually powerful Southern alternatives to the dominant Northern graduate schools of economics be worth the effort? And if not now, when?

NOTES

1. The subtitle of E.F. Schumacher's bestselling book, *Small is Beautiful*, was 'Economics as if People Mattered'.
2. There is obviously much in the remainder of such textbooks and courses that is as relevant to developing countries as to anywhere else.
3. For papers on some of the neglected issues (for example, Northern protectionism, trade in technology, official development assistance and the place of the least developed countries), most of which are still relevant; see my earlier *International Economic Disorder, Essays in North-South Relations* (Macmillan, 1980).
4. The reference is to the famous toast offered by John Maynard Keynes to the Royal Economic Society: 'to economists who are the trustees, not of civilisation, but of the possibility of civilisation' (Harrod, 1951: 193–4).
5. The Chairman of the South Commission was Julius Nyerere of Tanzania. Its Executive Director was Manmohan Singh of India.
6. I immediately admit to any who should wonder that I make the same points about the measurement of *national* economic performance. It is noteworthy that the most vigorous discussion as to how to measure national economic performance has been conducted in the context of Third World development, rather than in the industrialized world. See, for instance, Chenery *et al.*, 1984, chapter 2. The message seems more likely to register, however, in the context of the development of a new global measure, and in the context of the international political arena within which it will be employed.

REFERENCES

Asian Development Bank (1989), *Asian Development Outlook 1989*, Manila.

Bartelmus, Peter (1987), *Accounting for Sustainable Development*, Department of International Economic and Social Affairs, United Nations, Working Paper No. 8, November.

Brundtland, Gro Harlem et al. (1988), (World Commission on Environment and Development), *Our Common Future*, Oxford and New York: Oxford University Press.

Bruton, Henry J. (1985), 'The Search for a Development Economics', *World Development*, vol. 13, nos 10–11, October–November, pp. 1099–124.

Buiter, H. Willem and Richard C. Marston (eds) (1985), *International Economic Policy Coordination*, London: Academic Press.

Chenery, Hollis, M.S. Ahluwalia, C.L.G. Bell, J.H. Duloy, R. Jolly (1984), *Redistribution with Growth*, London: Oxford University Press.

Currie, David and David Vines (eds) (1988), *Macroeconomic Interactions Between North and South*, London: Academic Press.

Harrod, R.F. (1951), *The Life of John Maynard Keynes*, London: Macmillan.

Helleiner, G.K. (1980), *International Economic Disorder, Essays in North–South Relations*, London: Macmillan.

Hirschman, Albert O., 1982, 'The Rise and Decline of Development Economics' in Mark Gersovitz, Carlos F. Diaz-Alejandro, Gustav Ranis and Mark R. Rosenzweig (eds), *The Theory and Experience of Economic Development*, London: George Allen and Unwin.

Killick, Tony (1989), *A Reaction Too Far, Economic Theory and the Role of the State in Developing Countries*, London: Overseas Development Institute.

Kuznets, Simon (1966), *Modern Economic Growth, Rate Structure and Spread*, New Haven and London: Yale University Press.

Lewis, W.A. (1984), 'The State of Development Theory', *American Economic Review*, vol. 74, no. 1, March, pp. 1–10.

Ranis, Gustav and T. Paul Schultz (eds) (1988), *The State of Development Economics, Progress and Perspectives*, Oxford: Basil Blackwell.

Schumacher, E.F. (1974), *Small is Beautiful*, London: Abacus.

Sen, A.K. (1983), 'Development: Which Way Now?', *Economic Journal*, vol. 93, no. 372, December, pp. 745–62.

World Bank (1988), *Adjustment Lending, An Evaluation of Ten Years of Experience*, Country Economics Department, Policy and Research Series, 1, Washington, DC: World Bank.

2. The New Global Economy: Problems and Prospects

The international economy is in a precarious state. Recovery from the longest and most severe recession since the 1930s has been geographically unbalanced, uncertain in its durability and limited in its capacity to overcome continuing fundamental economic imbalances. Victory over inflation in the industrialized countries has been purchased at heavy cost – in terms of high unemployment, savagely depressed commodity prices and, in the USA, an unsustainable overvaluation of the currency. Few believe that these remedies have permanently or adequately overcome the problem. A massive overhang of questionable debt (both domestic and international) saps confidence in the financial system and limits its capacity to encourage productive new investment upon which sound recovery depends. The manifest failure of macro-economic policy coordination among the major Western powers – with the US budget deficit and the consequent unbalanced monetary–fiscal policy mix, which is usually cast as the principal villain – is a further source of anxiety. International trade and investment, though now rising again, remain threatened by protectionist pressures unprecedented in their ferocity in the past 50 years. High unemployment, rapid technological change and limited willingness or capacity to countenance necessary structural changes seem likely both to limit growth and to buttress protectionist sentiment in the Organization for Economic Cooperation and Development (OECD) and particularly in Europe, at least until the end of the century. Meanwhile, in the developing countries, and particularly in Africa and Latin America, the cost of the major external shocks of the past decade continue to be paid. Collapsed raw material prices, increased prices for inputs, and unusually high real interest rates have necessitated sharp cuts in real wages and farm incomes. In Africa successive droughts have made a bad situation tragically much worse, resulting once again, in C.P. Snow's 'ultimate obscenity': rich people sitting in the comfort of their living rooms watching others starve on colour television. Unfortunately, Sub-Saharan African per capita incomes are likely to continue to decline for the next 10 years and it will be longer still before the depreciating and inadequate infrastructure of roads, equipment, buildings – including schools and hospitals – will be on a stable growth path once again.

To the outside observer of what Barbara Ward has called Spaceship Earth – the proverbial Martian – the global economy would certainly seem to be malfunctioning in major ways: severe macro-economic imbalances, major and seemingly unnecessary inefficiencies and grotesque inequities. But what would surely strike our Martian friends as oddest of all is our apparent failure to grasp the undoubted fact that the 'global economy' has now arrived.

The world has changed in truly fundamental ways since the burst of international institution-building that followed the chaos of the Great Depression and the Second World War. The most important changes are usually summarized in the word 'interdependence', which has already become something of a cliché in the rhetoric of international meetings. Yet we have not sufficiently incorporated it in either our analytical models or our politics.

It was the very success of the world economy in the 1950s and 1960s that brought major changes in its make-up. Revolutionary changes in transport and communications systems, liberalized trading arrangements, the relaxation of foreign exchange controls in most of the industrialized market economies, and other impulses, generated growth in international exchange of goods, services and capital that far outstripped growth in production. Increased interdependence or, as some would have it, 'interrelatedness' was obviously associated with important benefits to individual nations. But it also left national economies much more vulnerable to exogenous influences originating in other parts of the world economy. In particular, domestic incomes and employment became more vulnerable to other countries' trading and industrial policies. International capital flows limited national governments' control over domestic monetary affairs and exchange rates. In some instances, international labour flows also generated new domestic tensions.

The new interdependence or interrelatedness of nations is thus multidimensional. It is not merely, or even primarily, a matter of international trade although the proportion of exports in overall economic activity has risen dramatically since the Second World War – that of the USA has doubled during the past 15 years, and the world's trade interdependence appears now to have reached levels beyond those of the period prior to the First World War, or any period since.

The most significant new element in international exchange is in the capital account of the balance of payments. Billions of dollars of short- and medium-term funds are 'sloshing' about the world's major money and capital markets, wreaking havoc with prospects for independent macro-economic management and stable exchange rates. Open economy macro-economics has now displaced most earlier textbook theorizing about closed economies. (The only closed economy now is that of the planet – and we forget, at our peril, that the global closed-economy 'multiplier' is larger than that which applies to economies with import leakages.) But we do not yet have a firm handle on the substitutability of different kinds of financial assets in different countries and denominated in different currencies, or on how national or global stabilization objectives can be reconciled with the new capital market interdependences, or on the benefits and costs of such proposed remedies as controls over capital movements, regulation of Eurocurrency markets, and the operation of an international lender of last resort.

Labour markets, too, exhibit new interdependence, particularly for the higher skills. Recruitment is now conducted worldwide in many occupations and transnational firms, and domestic labour market segmentation – by age, sex, race, language, and so on – is frequently greater than that found in consequence of national borders.

And employment, trade, investment, and financial issues and policies are themselves linked, one with another, in ways that are much more significant today than they once were. Certainly, trade questions can no longer be considered in splendid isolation from monetary and financial ones. What sense can it make to conduct discussions and negotiations on the servicing of Mexican or Brazilian debt in one institution, while the trading circumstances that may make it possible, or impossible, for them to generate the necessary foreign exchange to service them is discussed in another? The payment of their interest depends on their achievement of trade surpluses. Since there are clear political limits to the degree to which their imports can continue to be restrained via austerity programmes, their exports have to expand. One can, and must, expect increasing Latin market penetration in the North in those products – mainly manufactured – in which they have some comparative advantage. Can these matters be explained to the Northern advocates of anti-dumping duties, countervailing duties, customs slow-downs, quotas and voluntary export restraints? Continuing protectionist measures will guarantee financial disaster! To put it another way, easier financial terms and increased flows for debtor nations will make it easier for workers in our import-competing industries and for advocates of liberal trade policies.

Similarly, US monetary and fiscal policies are today inextricably intertwined with its trading policies. The story is well known – large budget deficits (amounting to a significant proportion of the world's total supply of savings) generating, with current monetary policies, high interest rates; these high interest rates and the prospect of low inflation generating capital inflow to the USA and an appreciated dollar; dollar appreciation, in turn, generating record US trade deficits and unprecedented pressure for protectionism.

The link between trade and direct foreign investment is also a matter of increasing importance as investment decision-making is increasingly globalized. The traditional conceptions of international trade – buttressed by 200 years of economic theorizing – have probably taken us just about as far as we can go with them. Rather than thinking of the micro-level problems of world trade in terms of international trade – that is, as trade between nations – it is time to think of them in terms of global industrial organization.

What is at issue, industry by industry, is the location of new investment, and the incentives to locate in different places, not just policies relating to trade after production begins! Tomorrow's trade is the product of today's investment decisions. The big actors in global industrial organization – in investment and in trade – are governments and transnational firms. Governments now regularly take over, or bail out, large firms, offer a variety of incentives (and sometimes disincentives) to both investment and trade, and develop industrial policies and adjustment policies with varying degrees of success.

Transnationals have internalized and, to some degree, cartelized large proportions of their global trading activity. In the automobile industry, General Motors, Ford and Chrysler each team up with Japanese auto firms and each US firm seeks to influence the interfirm disposition of quotas for the entry of 'their' Japanese products to the US market. Much of international trade is consequently already 'managed' – by both governments and firms.

It seems likely that future international consultations in steel, automobiles, wheat flour, textiles, and so on will take place between governments and transnational firms in sectorally specialized committees that are, in effect, negotiating global industrial policy. Adam Smith, in 1776, in *The Wealth of Nations*, pointed out the risks of such arrangements within nations: 'People of the same trade seldom meet together, even for merriment and diversion, but the conversation ends in a conspiracy against the public, or in some contrivance to raise prices.'

International anti-trust is still in its infancy!

Other markets are also increasingly analysed in global and holistic fashion. The world's interlinked food production and distribution system is a matter of increasing concern as modern communications make the wealthy and well-fed more aware than ever before of the horrors of famine, and generate new political pressures to respond, if not to endemic poverty and malnutrition, at least to intolerable short-term crises. Global market structure and demand prospects in the food sector will inevitably be subject to closer scrutiny than before. On one potentially contentious matter the evidence now seems to be clear – that countries successfully increasing their food (and other agricultural) production simultaneously increase their food imports out of their consequent rising incomes. North American farmers have nothing to fear from efforts to expand Third World agriculture.

In the period following the Second World War, arrangements for political cooperation among sovereign States on matters of economic policy were unable to keep up with the rapid pace of effective economic integration. Trade and capital flows created new and durable private and micro-level links between economies that ran far ahead of intergovernmental macro-level ones. At the same time the economic successes of the industrialized countries other than the USA and many of the developing countries created a much more multipolar world. Political decisions on matters of economic policy that could have wide international ramifications, even if made for purely domestic reasons, were now made in a much wider variety of geographic locations, in a much more decentralized manner. The world economy thus evolved in such a way as to increase both the breadth and the depth of international economic interdependence while, simultaneously, the required political mechanisms for the joint pursuit of previously agreed global economic objectives became ever more complex. The existing multilateral institutions struggled to adapt to the needs of changing world political and economic realities, but their efforts were sometimes flawed and not always very enthusiastically encouraged by national governments.

To this emerging system, already under stress, were then added the major shocks of the 1970s – two major oil price shocks, global price inflation, and two severe recessions. The 1970s also saw rising rates of unemployment in the industrialized countries, and slower overall global growth. These shocks and trends created further strains not only in the world economy but also in the system of multilateral economic cooperation. New problems, new contexts, within which old objectives had to be pursued, and powerful new actors – both governmental and private – further complicated international efforts to restore previous levels of economic performance and overall order.

Ultimately more serious than any of the problems of the international economy so far mentioned (it is still an international one in law, even if a single global one in fact) is the crisis of credibility in the major multinational (global) economic institutions: notably the GATT in trade, the World Bank and International Monetary Fund (IMF) in finance, and the various other economic institutions of the United Nations family. The central intergovernmental pillars of the post-Second World War international economic system are over 40 years old, old enough to be experiencing the usual pains of mid-life – reduced capacity to interact with, and understand (let alone influence), the rapidly changing world around them, a feeling that they are misunderstood, nostalgia for the wonderful years of their youth, creeping arteriosclerosis and other debilitating concomitants of age. Can one reasonably expect that the current creaking institutional machinery will get the world safely through the next 40 years?

The reasons for erosion of confidence and credibility in the traditional forms and institutions of multilateral cooperation are many and various. The great impulse to international cooperation provided by the depression of the 1930s and the Second World War has long since faded away. The economic difficulties plaguing rich and poor countries in more recent years have tended to make them turn inwards, neglecting the international and collective dimensions of the depressed state of the world economy. Some of the most powerful countries, notably the USA, seem to be turning away from previous commitments to multilateralism,and increasingly pursue their interests through bilateral channels. Nor have the international agencies themselves always responded or adapted well to the enormous, almost revolutionary, changes in world conditions that have occurred in the 40 years of their existence or to more recent economic pressures; instead political stalemates and bureaucratization frequently combine to produce a proliferation of irrelevant meetings and reports, to which governments pay less and less attention as they seek to grapple, under heavy pressure, with the realities of an unstable and uncertain world.

The original purposes of the multilateral economic institutions are nowhere in dispute. Efforts at international cooperation in the early postwar years were blessed by a widely shared vision of solidarity and peaceful cooperation in a shrinking world. The General Agreement on Tariffs and Trade (GATT), the World Bank and IMF sought to encourage a liberal and non-discriminatory world – of stability, order and justice in economic affairs – a necessary concomitant of the wider noble aspirations of the founders of the United Nations. It is true that the founding membership did not include large numbers of subsequently independent developing countries, and that the Great Powers exercised dominant influence over their original make-up. But the developing countries later joined in large numbers. In this context, international development came to be seen as a joint and collective responsibility of the international community, even if achievement of agreement on the details of the mandate inevitably involved controversy over national and international responsibilities. Similarly, in later years, a new awareness of the ecological threats to mankind as a whole gave fresh impetus to joint international action to protect the atmosphere, the oceans and biological resources.

Although, today, there is not the unusual vision and determination that characterized the early days of the United Nations, diplomats and statesmen still universally acknowledge the fact of international interdependence and express their belief in effective international economic arrangements that encourage economic growth, macro-economic stability, and development of the poorer parts of the globe. The requirement that a system of independent sovereign states have rules governing national governments' international policies, and cooperative responses to problems of trading and macro-economic policy, is still universally recognized. 'Beggar-thy-neighbour' policies for dealing with domestic economic difficulties, they agree, must still be minimized. Sudden and unexpected policy lurches, with their potential for disruption, ill-considered reaction, and cumulative downward spirals, must be prevented. International crises must be jointly defused and those most vulnerable buffered against their deleterious effects. And agreed means for developing, in an equitable and efficient manner, the global commons – the oceans, space and environment – must be found.

As I have emphasized, the 'international' economy has, to a significant extent, now become a single global economy; and events and developments in one of its parts have ramifications throughout the system. International trade, international monetary arrangements and international development finance are all matters on which a degree of intergovernmental consensus is absolutely essential for a healthy global economy. It is undoubtedly recognized now, as it was in 1944, that, in principle, it is in each national government's interest to support such an international consensus.

Yet where are we, in fact?

In trade, the most fundamental principle of GATT – non-discrimination, unconditional most-favoured-nation treatment for all – is today routinely flouted in practice. The Multifibre Arrangement in textiles and clothing specifically and formally authorizes discrimination against low-income (low-cost) countries and, although that Arrangement, and also its predecessors, were originally temporary measures, they have discriminated for nearly 30 years. Now a host of *ad hoc* industry-specific and firm-specific deals have made further encroachments upon the non-discrimination principle, and frequently on the aspiration toward maximum transparency as well. So-called 'voluntary export restraints' and 'orderly marketing agreements', industrial policies, export subsidies and countervailing measures, are increasingly deployed selectively to discourage the most efficient and the least capable of retaliation. While some still praise the sheer survival capacity of the GATT system, increasing numbers foresee the prospect of continuing disintegration of rules and norms, and the growth of trade disorder. Desperate efforts to re-energize the GATT in the Uruguay Round still risk foundering over (mainly North–South) disagreement as to whether the unfinished business of the past should take priority over widening aspirations in investment, agriculture, services and intellectual property – of particular interest to the USA – for the GATT'S future. If they fail, the USA threatens reversion to bilateral (that is, discriminatory) trade deals with individual allies. Despair over the prospect of further progress within the fully multilateral trading arrangements of the past and the continued growth of discriminatory and *ad hoc* protectionist policy instruments have driven some, including the Canadian government, towards advocacy of special (discriminatory) trade arrangements. The interest of a middle-sized trade-dependent economy like Canada resides overwhelmingly in the strengthening of multilateral rules and dispute settlement mechanisms rather than in bilateral arrangements. The Canadian approach to the USA is a measure of official perceptions of the sad state of the multilateral trading machinery.

In international finance, despite the IMF's admirable and much publicized leadership role in efforts to move through successive international debt crises without undue damage to the global financial system in the early 1980s, its power to perform the functions for which it was established has been weakening. The fact is that the IMF was effectively residualized as a manager of world liquidity during the 1970s. With the resumption of international commercial bank lending, all but the lowest-income, and by definition the least commercially creditworthy, countries became able to finance temporary balance-of-payments problems with greater speed, in larger amounts, and with less 'hassle' over conditions, via the private banks rather than the IMF. This largely demand-determined alternative supply of international liquidity legitimized the declining capacity of the IMF to perform its traditional role as a source of liquidity and surveillance. Its overall resources were not expanded at anything like the rate at which the value of international transactions was growing, let alone at rates sufficient to respond to the fact that these transactions had become subject to much larger relative shocks than at any time since the 1930s. The resultant privatization of international liquidity creation, predictably, proved highly unstable and inequitable. The banks cut back their international lending during the latest recession – at the very time when a socially-oriented liquidity system would have expanded it. Moreover, privatization meant that the poorest countries acquired considerably smaller shares of overall liquidity expansion than was planned for them in the original Bretton Woods arrangements. The international liquidity shortages that resulted in those countries particularly hard hit by the recession, notably the developing countries, have generated acute hardship and an uncalled-for degree of austerity. *Ad hoc* responses to these countries' liquidity shortages have included continued debt rescheduling on the part of banks and governments, and growing resort to various forms of counter-trade, such as barter, that does not rely upon traditional forms of international financing. These solutions are far from ideal and remain extremely fragile; and the IMF is no longer in a position to significantly influence global macro-economic management.

The World Bank was created in an effort to ensure that long-term development finance would flow in adequate volume to those parts of the globe where the returns were high but, because of informational and other imperfections, market incentives were unlikely to generate the socially desirable levels of flow. It was, and is, essentially an intermediary between private capital markets and developing country borrowers. Despite its triple-A credit rating and a long list of available high-return programmes and projects awaiting financing, its borrowing (and therefore lending) is today being limited because of inadequate expansion of its capital base. The US government, seeing the resurrection of international capital markets, apparently believes that there is no longer so much need for the World Bank's intermediation, despite the fact that the private banks and capital markets are manifestly failing to lend in adequate amounts themselves. Nor is direct foreign investment, despite much talk, picking up the slack. The soft-loan arm of the World Bank, the International Development Association, and the International Fund for Agricultural Development – all with remarkably good records of financing productive activities in low-income developing countries – have at the same time experienced even more severe cutbacks in their lending activities in consequence of reduced governmental support. The previous intergovernmental consensus about the need to assist development processes in the Third World and to buffer the most vulnerable against shocks not of their own making seems to be breaking down or may even be in full retreat, although popular response to African famines suggests that Northern electorates may still care.

Governments have responded to the pressures of the past decade in ways they have seen to be politically supportable and economically effective over a relatively short time horizon. In recent years, neither the international implications of domestic measures nor the possible longer-run detrimental effects of actions apparently beneficial in the short term have typically carried much domestic political weight. Macro-economic policies and sector- or industry-specific measures have been undertaken unilaterally, bilaterally, or among small groups of cooperating countries, regardless of wider multilateral forums or agreements. The larger and more powerful the country, the greater its capacity for effective pursuit of its own objectives in disregard of international feedback effects. The most adversely affected by the increasing resort to unilateral, bilateral and small group action, and the decline of multilateralism are undoubtedly the middle-sized and smaller countries. In this, the interests of Canada, the smaller European countries and the developing countries are as one. But all countries are bound to lose from a failure to agree and abide by fully multilateral arrangements for the stabilization and development of the world economy.

The Northern public mood remains overwhelmingly myopic concerning the global economic prospect. Typical responses to the new global economy thus far are frequently reactive and negative ones. Far from responding to its challenges, we often seem to be trying to turn back the clock – to return to less 'dependent' modes, to insulate ourselves from unfavourable external influences, to off load upon non-voting foreigners as many of our domestic problems as we dare. Along that route – travelled also in the interwar years – lies, of course, the potential for international economic disaster. Where each national government thinks only of its own immediate interest there is risk of mutual injury, cumulative downward spirals, and international anarchy.

The multilateral economic institutions that bolstered world economic progress in the 1960s are, today, at best, 'dead in the water'. Many would say they are actually slowly sinking.

What, then, are the essential requirements for multilateral economic cooperation – to encourage more predictable and equitable functioning of the world economy? The primary objective must be to establish or re-establish norms and rules, particularly in trade and in finance, which reduce the prospect of sudden and socially counterproductive policy change. The most fundamental principles that such rules should embody are the traditional ones of non-discrimination and uniformity of treatment. In order to be effective, the details of such rules have to be credible and accepted by all: at present there is widespread perception that they are flouted with impunity by rich countries, both in trade and in finance, and that they are applied with vigour only to the weaker and poorer states. Only if the strong are seen to be ready to subject their policies to the same international scrutiny and discipline as the rest can such rules effectively contribute to multilateral cooperation.

There must also be effective forums for dialogue and information exchange among countries whose approaches and policies may operate at cross-purposes. Present arrangements are widely considered to be unsatisfactory, particularly by developing and smaller countries which tend to be left out of the larger countries' informal networks.

Additionally, and quite distinct from the need for forums for dialogue, is the need for an effective machinery for multilateral negotiation when the time for multilateral negotiation of specific issues arises. Much international economic negotiation is inherently bilateral, but bilateral approaches do not encompass the full range of current global needs. Effective multilateral machinery is required not only for the normal ongoing process of negotiation of international economic issues as they arise – rule construction, dispute settlements and so on – but, more particularly, for the management of major international economic crisis and conflicts.

There must also be intensified efforts to resolve the continued problems in the relationships between powerful multilateral institutions, particularly the financial ones, and their smaller members. In the case of conflicts between a government and the international monetary and financial institutions with regard to the appropriate conduct of national economic policy, there should be opportunities for some kind of hearing or appeal. Procedures for transparent hearings or appeals for smaller countries considering themselves wronged or ill-treated by multilateral institutions would lend the latter credibility and acceptance where their record of objectivity is now significantly in question.

But these are generalities. There are serious negotiations underway today in the GATT; and there are concrete proposals afloat for the launching of extended discussions and negotiations over the future of the international monetary and financial system. The USA ostensibly accords top priority to the GATT round. The developing countries place heaviest priority instead on discussions of the Bretton Woods financial system. Trade, investment and finance are integrally linked, and the multilateral institutions that deal with them all are weakening at the very time when their strengthening would seem more appropriate. Surely some compromises can be found, to permit urgently needed multilateral economic cooperation to be strengthened in response to the new global needs? The vision of effective multilateral economic cooperation, based on concrete need, that drove sovereign states in the 1940s must somehow be rekindled in the more complex and more dangerous circumstances of the 1990s. The risks of failure to achieve it have become very high. Today, as in that earlier period of institution-building, the interest of small and middle-sized powers is particularly clear; and their potential role, as builders of bridges across ideological and political chasms, should not be underestimated. It is time, in the spirit of the original architects of the Bretton Woods institutions, and with the same overall noble aspirations for the new global (rather than the old international) economy, to launch a major fully multilateral review and reconstruction of our global economic institutions. The major agenda items should include:

a) macro-economic policy surveillance and coordination, crisis management, and the exchange rate régime;
b) international liquidity and the role of the IMF;
c) development finance and the role of the World Bank;
d) the trade and investment régime.[1]

Perhaps these suggestions are still too much to hope for. At a minimum, however, we must now come to terms, both analytically and politically, with the new global economy and the interrelatedness of nations within it. Analytically, we must develop the tools of global macro-economic analysis and measurement, while we improve understanding of the new multidimensional interrelatedness that has rendered the traditional assumptions of international economic theorizing obsolete. Patterns of global investment, global market structures and global market segmentation phenomena must be carefully analysed by economic analysts of a more micro-orientation, in much the same way as they currently approach these issues within nations. Here are rich new research agendas for analysts of vision.

And, politically, we must condition ourselves to think more globally, both in terms of longer time horizons and in terms of wider fields of vision. Whether we wish to do so or not, such thought will increasingly be forced upon us by the continued spatial shrinking of our planet and its concomitant new national interrelatedness. It is better to prepare for it, carefully and dispassionately, in order to avoid the shocks, surprises and possible costly policy lurches that could otherwise accompany belated learning processes. We must review both the meaning of national sovereignty in a world of deepened mutual interdependence and the adequacy of our current international economic (and other) institutions for the effective pursuit of global interests. As in the past, we may only come to a full realization of new needs through painful experience. Perhaps disorder in the global economy must increase before political attitudes can change. I pray not. It should surely not be necessary to wait for events to carry the world still further backward before setting out to plan and construct a more satisfactory global future.

NOTES

1. For a detailed exposition of these issues see the report of the group I chaired for Commonwealth Finance Ministers, *Towards a New Bretton Woods* (The Commonwealth Secretariat, London, 1984).

3. Economic Theory and North–South Disagreement*

NORTH–SOUTH DIALOGUE, STALEMATE AND ECONOMIC THEORY

During the course of the 1970s, spokesmen for the developing countries placed a series of proposals for international economic and political reform upon the agenda of the United Nations and its member organizations. Their proposals for a New International Economic Order have been debated at great length at innumerable conferences within the United Nations system and elsewhere, and have been the object of negotiations in a wide variety of different fora. Among other objectives, the proposed New International Economic Order (NIEO) involved: the regulation and stablization of international primary commodity markets and the creation of a Common Fund for this and other purposes; improved access to Northern markets for the exports of Southern countries and appropriate adjustments in Northern economies to facilitate the expansion of Southern shares of global manufacturing industry; international monetary reform; the regulation of the activities of transnational corporations and the creation and enforcement of a code of conduct governing the international transfer of technology; the promotion of economic cooperation among developing countries; increased resource flows to developing countries; and, in general, the alteration of existing institutional mechanisms and structures so as to support the objectives of development in the Third World. Much more than in previous decades, the developing countries' pressure in the 1970s was directed to reforming the institutional framework and the 'rules of the game', both in the private sector and in respect of intergovernmental agreements.

*I should like to thank and absolve from any responsibility for the contents of this paper all those who commented on an earlier draft: H.E. English, Richard Jolly, Alfred Maizels, Gus Ranis, John Sheahan, Frances Stewart, and John Williamson. Special thanks are due to John Cuddy who drafted parts of the middle section: but he, too, must be relieved of any responsibility for the final product.

Although a consensus resolution expressing support for the concepts of the NIEO was adopted by the Sixth Special Session of the United Nations, the countries of the North have never accepted the details of the proposed reform programme. Rather, they have stalled the discussions at almost every turn, giving ground only when – as in the case of the Common Fund – the original proposal had been gradually negotiated into something quite different from that with which the South had begun or when – as in the case of the revised guidelines for the application of IMF conditionality in its upper credit tranche lending policies – they still retained firm control over the institutions and policies at issue. North–South stalemate in the development of the NIEO programme is regarded by many policy-makers in the North as evidence of foreign policy 'success'.

Economic Theory and the Analysis of North–South Issues

North-South debates are conducted primarily in terms of the arguments of economics. While there are unquestionably wider issues at stake in intergovernmental negotiations, and 'issue linkage' among them all certainly exists, the basis questions debated in this sphere of international interaction are economic ones. Those called upon to prepare briefing papers are typically economists, and, when governments have them at their disposition, so are the negotiators themselves.

There are many possible explanations for Northern opposition to the details of the South's proposals in the international economy. Our concern here is with the Northern arguments against it, which have been couched in terms of the language of economics. This chapter attempts to assess the descriptive accuracy of the economic theory employed in the current North–South debates, and the effects of its use for policy prescription. The inherent logic of economic arguments is not at issue; on its own grounds, only in rare instances can it be faulted. Rather, such matters as the suitability of its premises, the relationship of its 'stylized facts' to reality, and its capacity to explain and predict are the objects of our enquiry. A particular watch is kept for gaps and biases which it might be possible to repair. In any such assessment it is virtually impossible to retain total objectivity. The hold of our conceptual frameworks is difficult to break. In the words of John Maynard Keynes, 'The difficulty lies, not in the new ideas, but in escaping from the old ones, which ramify, for those of us brought up as most of us have been, into every corner of our minds' (Keynes, 1936; Preface).

World society and the world economy are highly complex. In order to try to reduce the complex reality to intelligible terms, people construct their own simplified models as to how the world works. Some models are taught in universities' social science courses. Others are developed by formally unschooled men and women who, though they do not call them 'models', nevertheless construct them from their own daily experiences. The former are much more likely to be formalized and explicit in their assumptions; but the implicit model upon which the Third World farmer bases his or her daily decisions may be just as realistic, and sometimes an even better, predictor of events. Underlying 'models' or 'theories' or 'visions' of how the world functions or ought to function play important roles in human behaviour. Religion, ideology, science and culture may all be inputs to individuals' perceptions of the world, together with a variety of individual personality traits, experiences, and hunches. Rarely is anyone so rational and consistent as to be able to relate *all* thought or behaviour to one such underlying model; but some such model does generate presumptions as to how he or she will respond, at least in general terms, to particular situations.

Economics is taught not only as a positive or descriptive science but also as a normative policy-oriented one. By mastering a set of theoretical models, a collection of logical and statistical tools and a certain body of facts and knowledge, the student of economics is encouraged to believe that it is possible to develop economics-based policy recommendations on virtually any subject, whether it is primarily an economic one or not. The structure of modern economic thought is internally consistent, amenable to adaptation in many different directions, and a powerful aid to logical analysis of economic questions. Its very rigour and power sometimes seduce those who employ it into the belief that political balances and compromises, achieved through bargaining processes rather than 'the laws of economics' are contrary to nature and to be deplored.

Economic theory is typically written and taught in terms of a cautious step-by-step approach in which all of the assumptions are carefully specified and all of the resulting qualifications are noted. 'Exceptional cases' are enjoyed and paradoxes abound. On the frontiers of the discipline, vigorous experimentation can be found in the juggling of assumptions, the empirical testing of hypotheses, and the adaptation and improvement of both theoretical and quantitative economic models. Once in the difficult world of policy formation, however, students of economics are prone to forget all the qualifications and assumptions, and frequently apply instead the simplest and crudest versions of the models they were taught, using, as they would put it, only 'the basic principles'. They are not necessarily to be blamed for this. Even eminent theorists have been seen, when pressed, to act similarly in order to be able to reach any real-world conclusions at all.

If this process of bowdlerization takes place, however, and some would argue that it is absolutely inevitable that it does, it becomes crucial to understand the sequences and models through which the subject of economics is typically taught. What are the crude models which are most likely to be retained? What does the loss of the qualifications and refinements do to the reality of the model and its capacity to facilitate understanding? Does the failure to employ the whole range of the relevant literature result in significant error or bias, and, if the latter, does it operate consistently in predictable directions? A further major question – to be addressed later – is whether existing theory, even in its most sophisticated versions, adequately represents or explains the real world.

One of the certain consequences of the use of crude theory is the tendency to apply 'standard recipes' to all situations that appear roughly similar. More generally, it can result in 'knee-jerk' responses and almost 'intuitive' reactions to quite complex phenomena which really require more detailed analysis. The underlying frame of reference sets a 'mood' or a 'tone' to discussion of economic issues.

The 'theory' which lies behind dominant Northern approaches to North–South economic disputes is that of orthodox neoclassical economics. Although the modern literature of economics is rich in adaptations and elaborations of the core of the neoclassical 'paradigm', many of which attempt to bring it into closer touch with reality, it is its 'core' which exercises dominant influence. That core is based upon the assumption of individual, rational, and well-informed actors interacting upon competitive markets in pursuit of their own self-interest. Buyers and sellers do not transact with one another unless there is gain to both parties. From this it follows that the institution of the market is essentially benign in that it permits economic actors to achieve levels of welfare which would have been unattainable in their isolation from one another. It can be demonstrated that, under certain assumptions, the pursuit of individual self-interest will lead to the greatest possible increase in overall welfare, consistent with the requirement that no actor be made any worse off than he was before entering the market. That is, scarce resources are allocated with the greatest possible efficiency among the alternative possible uses which the various market transactors collectively demand. These harmonious results are inhibited only by 'market imperfections', elements of reality which are not in keeping with the assumptions of the model, and cases of 'market failure', which are treated as special cases – exceptions to the general rule. The distribution of income is treated independently of the 'primary' question of allocative efficiency in this approach, although it clearly affects the total composition of demand and is itself affected by the allocation of resources.

Approaching economic problems from a theoretical core of this character accustoms the analyst to treating important elements of reality, such as oligopoly, transnational corporate intrafirm trade, or imperfect and asymmetrically available information, as mere 'wrinkles' on the 'general case'. Similarly, such difficulties of real-world markets as externalities, instabilities, and 'crises' are considered as oddities. The problem is not that there is no literature on these matters (in fact there is a very vigorous one); rather, it is that habits of thought develop which generate simple, and almost subconscious and automatic, approaches to economic issues which (as the relevant theoretical literature demonstrates) are far more complex than the crude core model would suggest. Almost imperceptibly, prisoners of their own paradigm, students of economics risk beginning to regard all governmental policies as 'interventions' likely to impede the harmonious functioning of markets; and to regard the distribution of income (and power) as a matter wholly independent of market functioning, to be handled by separate policies (lump-sum transfers) which do not 'interfere' with markets. Academic economists will instantly deny that they could be so vulgar in their application of their theories. But practitioners, who frequently have neither the time nor the inclination for the pursuit of the finer points of theory, are primarily interested in 'the wider picture'. They need 'rules of thumb'; they read only the conclusions of complex background papers; they must develop a much simplified 'frame of reference' for their daily round of dealing with specifics.

In domestic economic policy, the power of the crude underlying model to influence policy-makers has been tempered by the exigencies of politics. In the modern Western mixed economy there is substantial governmental participation in consumption, production, and rule-making. Governmental policies to influence the distribution of income, the location of industry, the level of competition and the overall behaviour of economic actors are commonplace. Allocative and distributional outcomes are arrived at through a complex mixture of social bargaining, political processes, and markets. Policy-makers employ implicit 'rules of thumb' in which these various influences figure prominently, and economists are frequently derided as 'too theoretical' and inadequately aware of the political determinants of action.

Of course, alternative non-market models of politico-economic relationships have also been constructed. Distribution of wealth and power can be placed, after all, at the very centre of one's concerns, with such questions as allocative efficiency and market functioning relegated to the status of the relatively unimportant 'wrinkles'. It is also possible to focus upon systemic changes and the longer sweep of history, in which case primary focus may be placed upon signs of systemic malfunctioning and breakdown. The 'kneejerk' responses of those whose underlying models are such non-market ones can be every bit as predictable, and their 'recipes' just as monotonously 'standardized', as are those of the Western policy-makers who are here the primary object of our attention.

The nature of the underlying models affects the statistics that are assembled and the bases on which performance is assessed. The way in which the value of production is 'added up' in order to measure the Gross National Product, for instance, is the product of the underlying theory, and the resulting aggregate (GNP) has been enormously influential as a measure of progress. On the other hand, until very recently, statistics of income distribution were virtually non-existent, and assessments of progress on this front consequently almost impossible. It would be difficult not to attribute at least some of this statistical imbalance to the intellectual segmentation of these issues which is found in traditional neoclassical economic thought. Similarly, measures of the degree of market concentration in individual world markets or the degree of internalization of international trade are scarce, whereas data on the commodity composition of national exports and imports are available in enormous detail. Again, this imbalance must be at least partially attributable to the literature's fixation with explaining patterns of international trade, under competitive market assumptions, rather than assessing the distribution of its benefits or its actual overall efficiency.

Wider Northern Perceptions of North–South Issues

The *overall* politico-economic 'frame of reference' which Northern policy-makers employ seems to rest, implicitly, upon the views that:

1. the global economy, run as it is on a more or less *laissez-faire* basis, under the aegis of the Bretton Woods institutions and the GATT, functions reasonably effectively and requires no further 'global management' except when special circumstances so demand;
2. the South is not a sufficiently important component of the global

economy for it to play any greater role in global decision-making than it now does;

3. the most important influences upon Northern welfare are those which are determined by North–North (including East–West) agreements or disputes; and
4. the South can and should therefore be handled – as distribution is handled in traditional market theory – as a separate matter for independent bargaining over distribution, with the clear presumption that how much the Southern 'clients' receive is a matter for the Northern 'patrons'' discretion. (For a lucid summary of these approaches, see Hansen, 1979.)

When, and if, particular parts of the South become sufficiently important through their own efforts, to merit inclusion, they can be admitted to the councils of the North as junior partners, provided that they subscribe to the same rules as all the rest of the members of the 'club'. (The division of the world for analytical purposes into 'the North' and 'the South' is obviously not always the most helpful simplification.) There is no need, in the meantime, to alter the functioning of global markets or other institutions because of the clamouring of the South. Southerners are perfectly welcome to develop their own rules, and to go 'collectively self-reliant', in most areas, precisely because whatever they do is seen to be of such relative insignificance to the North.

This overall perception was clearly shaken in the special case of petroleum and, for a brief period, Third World debt. And some would say that it is also at risk in respect of such issues as population, environment, and nuclear proliferation. But the linkage between these issues and the rest of the NIEO agenda despite strenuous efforts, has still been only imperfectly made. (The most effective recent attempts to draw the arguments in respect of these 'issue linkages' together for Northern audiences are the reports of the Brandt and Brundtland Commissions, but they have not yet registered any palpable impact upon underlying Northern 'frames of reference'.) Beyond the level of rhetoric, most Northern policy-makers do not honestly see any serious link between global prosperity (including their own) and development in the Third World.

As befits a patron when he interacts with his clients, there is a certain sense of *noblesse oblige* in Northerners' approaches to the South. 'More in sorrow than in anger' they must respond to the Southerners' unrealistic representations and explain to them how they have erred in their understanding. There is a certain amount of charade, pretence and hypocrisy in the North's apparent willingness to engage in endless further study of Southern proposals. Already in firm possession of truth and power, they have no intention or need of discovering new truths, least of all from what to them is so unlikely a source. Negotiation and further study permit delay and distract attention from the 'hidden agenda' for international decision-making which is negotiated in private somewhere else entirely. Northerners often genuinely believe that logical and factual errors abound in the details of Southern proposals, and that some of their proposals could therefore be prejudicial to development or inequitable in their distribution of benefits; but it would not and does not matter if they thought that their arguments were faultless. By now, neither side believes what the other side says. The mutual credibility of ostensibly intellectual arguments in North–South debates has been severely impaired.

It is possible to conceive of a 'leap' of perception, following which the world would be viewed quite differently and the impact of all global events upon developing countries (and vice versa) would acquire a new and much greater significance in Northern policy-making. There are sound arguments for Northern moves in this direction in the North's own interests (Brandt *et al.*, 1980; Sewell 1979). One frequently senses that such a leap has already occurred among many members of the North's younger generation. Glimpses of such 'vision' can sometimes be seen in the speeches of Northern statesmen. And it clearly was the hope that such a new vision might be jointly arrived at, and pushed downward upon traditional bureaucrats, that motivated the Brandt Commission's recommendation of a summit conference on North–South issues. Once arrived at, such a new 'frame of reference' could give new meaning to the much abused term of 'interdependence'.

Issue by issue, bargains which take the needs of developing countries into greater account might then be struck. Northern policy 'success' would then no longer necessarily consist of 'talking issues to death' and simply stalling any change. Theorizing about international economic phenomena, whether market or non-market, would then place the implications of events for the economic development of Southern countries at centre stage. But even in such circumstances, the underlying economic paradigms could conceivably still inhibit progress.

Reasonable Objectives for Economic Theory

Clearly, to seek to improve the underlying economic theory of the functioning of the world economy is not to seek to influence next month's policy formation. The objective is much more longer-term. If the pessimists are right, the next several years will be ones during which progress in North–South negotiations will be tortuously slow and most unlikely to produce significant change. When serious dialogue resumes and the potential for change again surfaces, it would be well to have the theoretical ground more adequately prepared than it has been in the past.

One must not, of course, exaggerate the potential power of abstract ideas or underlying 'frames of reference'. If *realpolitik* rules and if the major powers are content to leave the world more or less as it is, no amount of independent academic scribbling, no matter how brilliant, will have the slightest effect upon policy or upon change. Even those most sanguine about the ultimate power of theory and models expect their effects to be apparent only in the longer run (by which time the economists concerned, following Keynes' dicta, will be either defunct or dead). Ideas and frameworks change only very slowly. Moreover, action does not always wait upon theory. Dramatic changes in actual events sometimes produce 'shock' effects in the world of ideas. More frequently, however, changing facts have little short-term effect upon basic models; and it is only a longer-term shift in the accepted model which will generate new behaviour. In the meantime, theory is usually called upon merely to rationalize or legitimize the way in which the world currently works.

ECONOMIC THEORY IN MAJOR AREAS OF NORTH–SOUTH DISPUTE

The developing countries have placed particular emphasis in recent years upon reform in the *institutions* of the international economy – the IMF, the World Bank, the GATT, and so forth – and upon the effects of the 'institution' of the transnational corporation in private markets. It can be argued that institutions do not matter much in the face of the realities of political power and/or market forces. To some degree, these are empirical questions, and are amenable to research exploration, through both historical and cross-sectional comparisons. Why are they not given more attention by Western scholars, particularly those in the Anglo-Saxon tradition? At least in part it is probably, again, because of the relative insignificance of non-market institutions in their theoretical apparatus, in which that of the competitive market is *assumed* to be dominant while all others are assumed to be either constant or irrelevant or both. (There has emerged a literature on the economics of hierarchies and internal organization, as opposed to the economics of markets; but, while it has attracted some of the most powerful minds in the field, it still remains on the periphery of the economics discipline.) On the face of it, the North nevertheless regards the preservation of the present institutional machinery as of very great importance, since it seems to have 'dug in' to defend it.

Indeed, it is quite remarkable that such estimates as there are of the efficiency or redistributional costs to the North of accepting NIEO proposals are all very small. Indeed, some NIEO measures seem likely to involve 'positive sum games' and thus to be positively beneficial to the North. Estimates of the gains or losses to the North from implementing the South's proposals are obviously subject to some dispute; but since even the largest estimates of possible costs to the North are extremely modest in the aggregate, the North's opposition must be based on other considerations. It has sometimes been suggested that Northern intransigence is not based upon the likely short-term costs of the programme, but stems instead from the *fear of losing control* of the entire system. (From this perception flows the implication that too much progress on the part of the South in the assumption of control over the global institutions could result in the North opting out of them in favour of its own independent ones.) Such considerations cannot be easily incorporated into traditional approaches to economic issues. Nor can the alternative prospect of catastrophic 'negative sum' outcomes from continuing international disagreements. But they clearly merit more detailed investigation.

In some instances, traditional theory has run into serious problems in terms either of the validity of its assumptions or its predictive power, or both. The theory of international trade, for example, gives policy-makers little guidance as to which industries they should encourage in order to benefit from the advantages of dynamic comparative advantage, and even less assistance in their attempts to assess the distribution of the overall gains from international trade between the various interested parties. Both rich and poor countries are hampered by the inadequacies of existing underlying trade theory as they grapple with one another and among themselves over industrial promotion and location decisions, relations with transnational corporations, and state trading bargains. In the meantime, traditional free-trade incantations are ritually repeated while policy proceeds independently through a series of ad hoc measures, specific to individual industries and firms, in directions unrelated to any known theoretical map.

In other cases, it seems that theoretical approaches are not in such a state of disarray, but that differences in the importance assigned to different objectives and differences as to the 'stylized facts' of particular cases nevertheless lead to quite different policy prescriptions. Thus, existing macro-models in the eclectic centre of the profession can be employed to generate more or less similar predictions, provided that there is agreement as to the likely size of various key coefficients within the models. The 'structuralist' alternative to traditional IMF analyses of balance of payments adjustment mechanisms rests upon alternative assumptions as to the elasticities of import and export demand and supply, the behaviour of capital markets, the functioning of the price mechanism (in factor as well as product markets) and the like. Differences in policy recommendations also stem from different degrees of emphasis upon the equity of distributional impacts. In such cases, there is greater hope that the sustained application of economic logic and the collection of more relevant empirical material might gradually achieve agreed changes in policy approaches – or so it would appear from the efforts of the Group of Twenty-four to contribute independent high-quality professional assessment to the discussion of IMF policies. This is not to suggest that underlying preconceptions as to the appropriate role of the state, the performance of markets and so on will not continue to lurk behind macro-policy recommendations or that disagreement as to the role of IMF conditionality as against automaticity will disappear. It is only to make the point that there is hope in this area that the ground within which agreement can be reached may be wider than in some other areas in which the underlying theory is inadequate.

In the case of international commodity markets, too, there may be found some rays of hope for achieving a theoretical consensus, although there is none at present. Traditional Northern analyses have been based upon the competitive market paradigm, with modifications considered on a case-by-case basis where 'market imperfections' are particularly blatant. Southern approaches might be characterized as starting from a bargaining or conflict model, more akin to bilateral monopoly or oligopoly/oligopsony theories, with cases of competitive markets treated as the 'imperfect' aberrations from the general case. Both approaches are clearly correct; each in their own 'favourite' cases. There is emerging a relevant literature within the Western tradition which, in effect, is at least partially legitimizing the Southern approach by applying the tools of empirical analysis to particular commodity markets. These theoretical 'bits and pieces' have not yet percolated through to either introductory Western textbooks or Western economic policy-makers, but their volume may already be great enough to permit the thought that the dominant paradigm may yet shift to that of the South, particularly as the debate shifts away from price stabilization issues and towards those of marketing, processing and distribution. At a minimum, it will in future be more difficult to generalize on the basis of the traditional models.

There is a screening and sifting process by which economic analysis of different kinds, reaching different conclusions, moves from those who first prepare it to those who actually employ it in decision-making. Traditions and interests combine to produce biases in the analyses prepared and employed by different institutions and different governments. Authors know what their employers need to hear, and if they do not provide them with what they require, their results may in any case be weeded out. Nor is the professional distribution system neutral. There are instances of quite mediocre papers, sometimes even addressing matters that are not at the centre of dispute, receiving enormous professional and popular attention while others of superior quality languish utterly neglected. One would require the skills of a sociologist of knowledge to uncover all of the reasons for these phenomena. In part, professionals are as guilty as others of seeking out and disseminating the results which their personal backgrounds and experiences lead them to welcome; the footnote references employed by rival protagonists in academic disputes are often disconcertingly lacking in common items. Academics are also inclined to feature the unexpected and counter-intuitive results which, in the case of North–South issues, are more likely to discredit Southern than Northern initiatives. (There are, after all, not many Northern ones, since the North does not seek changes.) There is no doubt that negotiators make extremely selective use of the available knowledge, and some are not above the commissioning of 'independent' studies which 'prove' what is required. There is, in such cases, only a fine line between the provision of information and propaganda.

International Trade in Manufactures

International trade theory has been so refined and qualified in the specialized academic literature of the subject that it has been left with very few real-world conclusions. But, in the world of Northern trade policy-makers, the tenets of static comparative advantage theory and its factor endowment basis remain the touchstone for all debate. 'Free trade' is the standard by which performance is to be measured; and poor countries are to specialize in exports which are intensive in the use of unskilled labour and such natural resources as they may possess. Southern demands in the North–South dialogue in the sphere of trade in processed and manufactured products are generally couched in terms of the same simple paradigm of liberal trading that Northern spokesmen and the GATT secretariat espouse; above all else, the South seeks reduced Northern protectionism against Southern manufactures. But the South's own performance often fails to square with these same principles of theory.

Southern pressure for reduced protectionism is clearly not part of a call for structural reform in the international economy but simply a call for the translation of the conclusions of orthodox trade theory into Northern freer trading practice. Whether the specific targeting of the share of global manufacturing which is to be located in the developing countries by the year 2000, as found in the Lima programme of UNIDO, is any more than the necessary consequence of the fairly orthodox policies which the South is pressing must be a matter of judgement; but it could easily be largely interpreted in such moderate terms, rather than, as is more usual, as a call for massive market intervention. There are, nevertheless, theoretical grounds for the developing countries' adoption of more aggressive industrialization strategies within their own economies than free trading principles would imply.

Fully consistent with their use of the orthodox liberal paradigm in the sphere of international trade is the South's position on the regulation of restrictive business practices at the international level. Principles and rules, or codes governing anti-competitive practices including those engaged in within transnational corporations, are very much in the spirit of the GATT paradigm even if they are being developed primarily under UNCTAD auspices. Provisions of this kind were found in the original Havana charter for the International Trade Organization, and many Northern policy-makers have genuinely regretted that they were not included in the GATT.

In the real world of international trading practice, many of the assumptions strictly required for the policy conclusion that 'free trade is best' are, of course, violated. Among the factors that must vitiate the conclusions of the simple trade models are: scale economies; market concentration (oligopoly and oligopsony); intrafirm trade; significant transport costs; state trading; product differentiation and non-price competition; unequal technological capacities; costs of adjustment as between different productive structures; imperfect information; and existing tariff and non-tariff barriers. Among the profoundly important structural features of international trade in the 1970s and the 1980s is the dominant and rising role of transnational corporate activity. The developing countries have been particularly concerned with the implications for them of this particular institution for global management, within what are ostensibly 'free markets'; their pressure for 'liberal' trading is directed no less at the North's transnational corporations than at Northern governments.

The construction of development-oriented industrial policy, whether in rich countries or in poor, proves to be extraordinarily difficult in such a 'second'- or 'third-best' world. Particularly troublesome has been the handling of 'learning' effects. While it is relatively easy to identify the major 'losers' in which a country is relatively inefficient, it is extremely difficult to determine those industries in which one may best *acquire* a future comparative advantage. How, then, is one to decide upon a rational and globally efficient allocation of the world's industry? The simple static Heckscher–Ohlin formulations, based upon relative factor endowments, simply do not carry one far enough. If productivity improves with experience, early-stage protection of apparently unsuitable industries or firms may be sensible in the longer run. If such learning is industry-specific it also would seem to call, all else being equal, for industry specialization rather than diversification in the industrial sector. The implications for trade policy, and for development impacts, of a theory which builds upon the assumption of industrial learning differ sharply from those of the 'standard' model. Whereas the latter suggests that all developing countries with a labour surplus should specialize in labour-intensive industries, the former implies that, as experience and scientific and technical resources differ among countries, so does the capacity to 'learn' through different kinds of industrialization. Thus countries which are further along in their capacity to learn will benefit from different industrialization strategies; and, in the short to medium term, their pursuit will probably open up even wider gaps between them and less fortunate developing countries.

The more effective incorporation of scale economies – as well as learning effects – into the modelling of international trade will also significantly influence the theory's policy implications. Since the gains which can be realized through increasing returns to scale, where they exist at all, can be expected to dwarf those attributable in traditional theory to marginal reallocations of production and consumption, it follows that in many industries 'big is beautiful'. Scale economies may be found in information processing, financing, marketing and distribution, and research and development, as well as in production. From theories building heavily upon the fact of scale economies and learning effects one may derive the conclusion that trade should be 'free' and conducted overwhelmingly by very large trading units, whether private or public.

Where comparative advantage is diffused or unclear, and information is imperfect, such underlying theory could imply that large size or specialization are what matter most. It may be preferable quickly to specialize in *something* rather than endlessly arguing the relative merits of alternative industries on the basis of benefit–cost calculations of dubious reliability. Technological characteristics may provide as good a set of 'rules of thumb' for the selection of new industries as any other – for example, 'appropriateness' of products, potential for learning effects, availability of scale economies, and so forth. The truth of the matter is that, although such an approach may seem a counsel of despair and an invitation to planning approaches asserting that 'anything goes', knowledge of the roots of future relative industrial efficiency remains remarkably scant. All of these considerations also have obvious relevance to schemes for South–South industrial cooperation and joint industrial planning.

These scale and learning effects are among the underlying theoretical explanations for the rise of transnational corporations and state trading in international exchange. The selective promotion of freer trade by Northern policy-makers has amounted, in substantial degree, to the encouragement of the growth and geographic interpenetration of Northern-based transnational corporations. Theory has lagged considerably behind practice in this realm. If the allocation of resources both within and across economies, the determination of patterns and prices in international trade, the burden of adjustment to recession or other global shocks, and other such major issues are to be substantially affected by the managerial decisions of large transnational firms rather than through the interplay of market forces, then more theory relevant to their decision-making processes is required. Attempts must be made to model the interactions between large transnational corporations and large (primarily Northern) national governments, and the implications of their behaviour and their bargains for smaller actors. For this purpose, it would seem fruitful to draw much more upon theories of industrial organization, managerial decision-making, and bargaining and game theory, rather than to attempt to patch up existing trade theories with altered assumptions as to factor mobility, factor-intensity characteristics, and the like. (Certainly the assumption of internationally immobile capital is, in any case, no longer tenable.)

It can be argued that the growing and interacting roles of large governments and large firms in international production and exchange can render much more plausible the eventual introduction of the international taxation systems, which, if properly constructed, could help to overcome some of the problems which transnational corporate activities now create. As the importance of these issues continues to mount, transfer price manipulation and arguments over the disposition of total tax revenues could be eased by international tax regimes which should now increasingly be explored by fiscal theorists rather than just by tax accountants and lawyers.

A further issue arising for Southern trade policy-makers in the context of such amended theories of international trade is the future productivity of the strategy of 'export-led' growth. If learning effects dominate both in the industrial development process and in the determination of dynamic comparative advantage, then specialization for export either because of factor endowment advantages or because of scale economies may, or may not, be the optimal policy. In a world of slower Northern growth, greater numbers of developing countries coming onstream with industrial exports, transnational corporate control of much world trade, and protectionism in those sectors in which transnationals are weakest, export-oriented industrialization in the South may either bog down in worsened terms of trade or achieve success only at the cost of increasing transnational corporate control of the Third World's national economies. For many developing countries, no less important than the terms of GATT bargains or Northern governments' trade policies will be those of the daily bargains to be struck with the foreign firms which produce or market their manufactured exports. For the purposes of understanding or influencing such bargains, either with private actors or over the size and terms of quotas and marketing agreements to be negotiated with foreign governments, theoretical underpinnings remain slight indeed.

It would seem that 'conventional' economic analysis is potentially much richer than the caricature of it generally presented in policy-makers' speeches to buttress free-trade anti-*dirigiste* positions, but that a 'revised theory' is not yet sufficiently integrated to form a coherent whole which would be immediately relevant to North–South trade negotiations or policy formation. Moreover, the potential richness derives much less from theoretical refinements of the neoclassical model of international trade than from the insights offered by resort to industrial organization, learning, and bargaining theories. The integration of these theories with international trade theories, incorporating the many qualifications necessary for realism, is perhaps the most formidable task now on the agenda for future research.

International Primary Commodity Trade

Primary commodities have frequently been central to North–South negotiations. One of the cornerstones of the NIEO was to be the Integrated Programme for Commodities, including the Common Fund – the former a giant stabilization and development programme for 18 commodities of special export interest to the developing countries, the latter the central financing institution which would tie the various commodity programmes together into a cross-subsidizing package.

Although price stabilization objectives were by no means universally regarded as the most important ones in the commodity sphere, negotiations came to centre upon them. A substantial body of neoclassical literature existed, demonstrating that, under particular assumptions, price stabilization would be good for the world as a whole but harmful, in terms of income effects, either to producers as a group or consumers as a group, depending upon whether price instability originated from shocks on the demand or the supply side. An additional strand of this literature demonstrated, again with carefully stipulated assumptions, that the stabilization of prices would stabilize or destabilize the incomes of the producers as a group, depending upon whether price instability originated from the demand or the supply side. The complexity of the issues is illustrated by the fact that, under the assumptions typically employed, the same circumstances that would achieve income increases for the producers as a group through price stabilization would destabilize their total incomes. Considerable attention was paid in Western capitals to the studies which demonstrated these results, and Northern governmental positions on the Integrated Programme, the Common Fund, and individual proposed international commodity agreements appeared to have been influenced by them. The ambiguities and trade-offs implied in these results created occasions for endless debate, and called into question the wisdom of the South's pressures for price stabilization on the ground that it frequently might not serve the South's own interests.

Unfortunately, the 'results' of the theorizing described above are misleading. They are extremely sensitive to the detailed assumptions of the underlying models, as has been carefully demonstrated by further theoretical analysis which has continued within the neoclassical tradition from which the original models sprung. The range and implausibility of the assumptions required to arrive at conclusions which have been cited in innumerable Northern policy position papers are truly breathtaking. They include particular specifications of both demand and supply functions (they must both be linear); particular kinds of demand and supply shocks (they must be additive and not multiplicative); instantaneous reactions of supply and demand to price alterations; and complete stabilization of prices at a fixed price equal to the mean of the prices which would have prevailed in the absence of intervention. Modification of any of these assumptions in order to approximate reality more closely or simply to test sensitivity, results in the collapse of the widely cited conclusions. These qualifying theoretical contributions have not yet significantly penetrated the Northern policy-makers' perceptions. Needless to say, none of these theoretical contributions questions the underlying model of free and competitive markets, which is required to permit the employment of supply and demand functions as representations of reality in the first place. Nor do they address the *real* problem of 'market failure' created when speculation and panic buying and selling in commodity markets generate periodic 'crises', which must somehow be 'managed'.

Whether these debates over the effects of price stabilization were of much real significance to the commodity negotiations is, in any case, an open question. Certainly, whenever possible, negotiators pick and choose among available sources to find 'objective' sources of support for positions which they have already reached on totally different grounds. In at least one instance during the 1970s (the copper negotiations), one set of Northern negotiators discarded the (public) results of the very econometric modelling exercise they had earlier insisted upon when it failed to yield the expected, and 'required', conclusions.

At real issue are, typically, such matters as the interests of producing and trading firms of different nationalities, strategic interests in supplies, concerns over the eventual effects upon the level of prices and the size and allocation of export quotas. In the longer run, ownership and control of processing, marketing and distribution are clearly much more important concerns than price stability. Northern policy-makers' direction of attention to the theoretical issues surrounding the effects of price stabilization deflected it away from these more fundamental questions. They were, and are, able to do this at least in part because general knowledge of the actual structural characteristics of commodity markets is still so scant. Most commodity markets are characterized by a high degree of concentration on both the buyers' and the sellers' sides. Many are highly segmented in their structure with intrafirm trade within transnational corporations, state-to-state trading arrangements, long-term contracts among private and state transactors, and 'free' residual markets all operating simultaneously. Sufficient proportions of world commodity trade are 'managed' either by private or by state actors as to make nonsensical the exclusive resort to models that imply only atomistic and competitive participants on free and unfettered markets – the models that still dominate Northern policy-makers' presentations and apparent perceptions.

Southern approaches to commodity questions are based less on detailed knowledge about the actual functioning of markets than on a fairly crude perception that prices are set on the basis of bargaining and conflict rather than through neutral and impersonal free and competitive markets. Their paradigm is quite different from that which Northern spokesmen employ, and in this instance it is often at least as accurate. Both Northern and Southern spokesmen can point to specific instances in which their own simplified 'model' best describes reality. While it may be difficult to agree on which is more *generally* accurate, it should by now be possible to build a middle-ground theoretical structure which eclectically takes both market and bargaining approaches into account.

To adopt, even in part, a bargaining model of the determination of international commodity prices is to resurrect the controversial issue of the developing countries' terms of trade and the possibility of indexing their export prices to the prices of their imports. Even in the citadels of market orthodoxy, domestic agricultural prices are determined by political processes as well as by purely market forces. Such possibilities can be realized regardless of the make-up of the developing countries' export or import bills; but, because of the Prebisch–Singer theoretical backing from which the proposals originally sprang, they have been couched in terms of linking the prices of primary product exports to those of manufactured goods imports. That such 'stabilization' of certain relative prices (actually, the proposals were intended merely to set a floor to real commodity prices) can have allocative effects is beyond dispute. What exactly they would be depends upon a host of assumptions as to governmental policies and private responses. Conventional economic theory has been employed to demolish the proposals for the international indexation of primary commodity prices on the grounds of their inefficiency effects. Possible social 'inefficiency' has never been, however, a significant element in the striking of bargains over domestic distributional questions. The basic irrelevance of such considerations in bargaining situations was demonstrated in the 1970s by the widespread Northern interest in quite similar proposals for the stabilization of the petroleum price. Once again, conventional economic theory has little contribution to make to the analysis of bargaining.

What is sorely lacking from the underlying theory of North–South trade, either in primary commodities or in manufactures, is an adequate explanation (or controversially, justification) of the distribution of the gains therefrom. The Prebisch–Singer analysis attempted to analyse it through the concept of the terms of trade, and thereby addressed the effects of changes through time. Emmanuel has based his analysis upon the international immobility of labour and focuses upon labour's entitlement to equal remuneration for equal productivity, regardless of its location.

Neither have proven persuasive or sufficiently rigorous to have been incorporated into the central 'core' of trade theory, although both clearly have an enormous intuitive appeal. Here is another rich area for theoretical exploration. In this connection, the incorporation of transnational corporate activity into the relevant models, as was suggested above, would seem to call for new concepts of the terms of trade which are based upon national 'retained value' from exports, rather than conventionally measured prices for export products.

International Monetary Issues

Those engaged in current North–South debates over international monetary issues, while they may argue over the finer points, all understand and employ basically the same underlying economic models of macroeconomics and balance of payments adjustment. There is neither a paradigmatic clash, as in the case of commodity market analysis, nor rampant confusion and massive dissonance as between theory and practice, as in the case of trade in manufactures. What is at issue is, fundamentally, the distribution of financial power and control, and the objectives of development policies. At a more prosaic level, there are also often differences as to the 'stylized facts'.

Developing countries, as poor countries faced with current account deficits that are not always of their own making, seek monetary reforms that will ease their balance of payments financing difficulties. They seek greater symmetry of balance of payments adjustment responsibilities, so that countries in surplus and reserve currency countries share short- and medium-term adjustment costs. They seek greater resort to SDRs as the source of international liquidity expansion and greater shares of their distribution, in order to acquire a higher proportion of the seigniorage from 'money creation' which at present accrues to reserve currency countries and gold producers and holders. Not surprisingly, they also seek greater influence and voting power within the IMF in order to push the reforms which they favour. The most important immediate source of North–South disagreement is over the terms of developing countries' access to international finance, and specifically to the resources of the

IMF. (Since commercial banks and aid donors may await the IMF 'seal of approval', much more than IMF lending may be at stake.) The 'conditionality' question involves disagreement as to:

1. the appropriateness of the present degree of conditionality in IMF lending; and
2. the terms of the conditions which it typically imposes.

In the first instance, the developing countries view the IMF's approach as excessively rigid and excessively influenced by the assumption that balance of payments difficulties are the product of domestic monetary mismanagement; where balance of payments deficits are the product of external shock rather than of domestic mismanagement, there should be a *prima facie* case, they sensibly argue, for unconditional balance of payments support. This is particularly evident if these external shocks are temporary ones, and not necessarily those of only a year or two's duration; but, even if they are permanent and long-run adjustment is necessary, IMF support should be assumed to be readily available to assist the process. The principles governing such low-conditionality balance of payments support have already been recognized in the IMF's compensatory financing and oil facilities. At present, the availability of low-conditionality financing is inadequate; the result is resort to private banks, expensive suppliers' credits and/or inappropriate deflation.

Second, when the IMF makes recommendations on domestic policies, it has frequently carried with it the biases described above as implicit in conventional neoclassical theory: it over-emphasizes market measures and downplays the influences (real or potential) of such institutions as the state or the transnational corporation, and it does not overly concern itself with the distributional implications of alternative macro-economic policies. Nor does it consider, though this is a matter of wider global concern, the need to maintain longer-run development momentum in the poorer countries. It has therefore tended to apply a fairly standard set of policy prescriptions to *all* countries: reduced government expenditures (particularly cuts in social service spending, food subsidies, and wages, since these are both more visible and more politically acceptable to many governments than cuts in defence budgets or civil service salaries), higher tax rates, domestic credit ceilings and higher interest rates, liberalization of exchange controls and devaluation, all of these to be applied relatively quickly in a 'shock' rather than a 'gradualist' manner.

This uniform deflationary package may be quite appropriate to some circumstances, but is most unlikely to be appropriate for all. A powerful and theoretically rigorous 'structuralist' critique of the IMF's standard package has now been constructed. It addresses the impact upon income distribution, total aggregate demand, inflation, growth and the balance of payments, and concludes, on the basis of assumptions which are not implausible (notably as to elasticities of demand and supply, pricing systems, wage-setting mechanisms, determinants of investment and capital flows) that the IMF package can be counterproductive in the short to medium run; and that the longer run in which events might improve is not guaranteed ever to materialize (Taylor, 1988). The critique of the IMF package is not a critique of adjustment policies themselves (although in popular discussions these matters are sometimes confused), but of the particular package which typifies the IMF approach. Revisions of IMF guidelines for conditionality suggest that at least its Executive Board, if not yet all of its operative personnel, now recognizes that the nature and timing of adjustment programmes must be tailored more closely to fit the circumstances of particular countries. The elaboration of 'better' policy packages is still in its infancy and deserves further study.

The distinction between finance for purposes of balance of payments adjustment and finance for development is not always an easy one to draw. It is particularly difficult when recessions are longer-lasting and when there are major shocks, such as oil price increases in oil-importing countries or severe deterioration in export prices, which require long-term adjustment. In such circumstances, balance of payments finance for the purpose of 'riding out' longer storms or for easing the process of structural (supply) adjustment begins to merge into development finance. When the IMF offers longer-term adjustment loans and the World Bank offers structural adjustment loans, both are employed for essentially the same purposes.

In the 1970s there was a sharp increase in the relative importance to the developing countries of private money and capital markets. Commercial banks operating in the Euro-currency markets channelled very large sums to the more creditworthy developing countries. The criteria for the allocation of these resources, as derived from standard portfolio theory and applied by unregulated private banks, deviated significantly from those which the international community might apply if it controlled the disposition of those resources; among other reasons, this is because the objective function in that community's decision-making does not, as does the private portfolio theory, ignore income distribution. Thus, in particular, practically all of the money lent by the Euromarket to the Third World went to the middle-income countries, and none to the poorer ones. As in all asset markets, changes in investors' expectations, which themselves are vulnerable to the herd instinct, can generate significant 'lurches' into and out of particular kinds of lending, with the result that the amount and composition of commercial bank lending to particular developing countries is inherently unstable. At the same time, the concentration of these banks' lending on so few countries, and the sheer magnitude of the resources so channelled, eventually brought problems for the whole international financial system when some of the 'select' countries proved unable to service debts, causing some of the banks themselves to risk failure. Here, accepted Western macro-economic theory, combined with knowledge of the developmental effects of income distribution, indicated strongly, long before the debt crisis arose, that the view held by many in the international financial community that the private capital markets could handle such recycling well was seriously in error. Deserving of further theoretical exploration are the implications of regulation (in order to reduce the moral hazard problem) as against *laissez-faire* policies in international financial markets for the interests of the developing countries.

None of the above monetary disputes cause great anxiety to orthodox theoreticians or to the policy-makers who negotiate these North–South issues. The discussions proceed on the basis of models which are broadly intelligible and acceptable to both sides. Disagreements are either the result of differences in judgement as to the 'stylized facts', in which case they can presumably be resolved by further detailed research and analysis, or the product of underlying conflict over the international distribution of income and power. In the latter case, again, a theory of bargaining is required for a more complete understanding as to what is actually taking place.

RECOMMENDATIONS FOR FURTHER RESEARCH AND ACTIVITY

The growing interdependence of national markets for goods, services, technology, capital and some kinds of labour have increasingly limited the capacity for national sovereign governments to pursue fully independent policies. Just as the various actors within nations are interdependent and governments have been created for the purpose of assigning and enforcing rules which are in the social interest, so at the international level there is a growing need for a global manager to 'rein in' independent national actors, including governments, on the world stage. (And just as, at the national level, governments are pulled and hauled in their policy formulation by special interests of divergent power, so it would also undoubtedly be in the case of any global authority.) 'International economics' must be replaced by 'global economics' in theoretical analysis. Ultimately we are likely to acquire more effective global government, which can then employ it. The transnational corporations and, to a much lesser extent, the international trade union secretariats are already conducting their activities on a worldwide basis – with effects that are still quite imperfectly understood. It is ironic that while governmental activities have steadily grown at the national level in the mixed economies of the post-Second World War period, and this growth has generally been considered to be legitimate, there has been no corresponding expansion of governmental activity at the global level, where unrestrained market forces and the law of the jungle still seem to be considered more legitimate than any threats on the part of global authorities to national sovereignties. Economic theorists and modellers must surely now begin to apply their general tools of analysis to the problems of the one 'closed economy' which, until interplanetary travel opens up, still remains that of the entire world. Only when national policy-makers begin to employ such comprehensive 'frames of reference' in their own decision-making can one expect to find international issue resolution on the basis of higher global interests. Existing attempts to model the entire world – in the UN, the World Bank, the OECD, the ILO, and the Bariloche Foundation, for instance – are still fairly crude, mechanical, and apolitical.

In the shorter run, there is a great need to improve theoretical understanding of the individual economic issues in North–South disputes, and to raise the quality of the economic analysis which is brought to bear upon them. In this chapter, attention has been particularly focused on the shortcomings of the economic models implicitly or explicitly employed by Northern negotiators. It would be ridiculous to attempt to argue that only the North's negotiators have been biased in their use of available theory, or that their implicit models are more rigid or crude than those of others. Nor, despite their obvious efforts to propagate their views, are Northern policy-makers disproportionately guilty of conscious or unconscious propagandizing. On the contrary, it is the very 'liberalism' and catholicity of Western traditions that facilitates criticism of the way in which its policy-makers employ their knowledge. But there can be no doubt that in the North–South arena, the North has considerably more than its share of the 'good lawyers'. Academia, the media, and government spokesmen have together so swamped the advocates for the South with their (too crude) arguments that they have created a climate within which Southern arguments are almost automatically ascribed to 'unreason' or 'bad economics'; they are assumed to be 'illegitimate' almost as soon as they are made, and it becomes a Northern sport to see who can first firmly prove them so. The transnationalization of knowledge through postgraduate training, scholarly journals and the press furthers the legitimization of Northern positions, and extends even into the academic institutions and governmental offices of the South. Intellectual hegemony may be no less powerful, enduring, and ultimately defensive of privilege than any other kind.

Much of the economic analysis employed in the backing of particular cases *is* complex. The North has an enormous supply of academic and other professional talent for the purpose of making its case, or at least legitimizing it – far larger than that available to the policy-makers of the South. Whether the most important case-makers are lawyers or economists, the South is clearly *always* at a major disadvantage. As the late Carlos Diaz-Alejandro once vividly put it, it is often possible for Northern policy-makers to denigrate well-informed and cogent Southern arguments with statements which amount to saying, 'Hocus-pocus; mumbo-jumbo; therefore you are wrong'. If what we are observing is essentially a bargaining relationship rather than a search for truth, there must be a presumption that, to the extent that arguments play any role at all as against the realities of power, the outcomes will be consistently skewed against the least prepared. Both the search for balance in knowledge and sympathy for the underdog should generate far more professional effort to pick holes in Northern rather than Southern arguments, even if it does not pay as well.

Such questioning of orthodox paradigms as there has been tends to appear either in specialized professional journals with small circulations, or in the 'radical' literature, neither of which are read by policy-makers. The markets for intellectual fare – to use neoclassical terminology – are highly segmented ones; and, as usual, such market imperfections generate social inefficiency. It is not possible to prescribe an alternative core model to which all 'right-thinking' analysts should immediately shift, for it does not exist. But it is important to address the deficiencies in the current dominant models, note their disproportionate influence, and call for attempts at reform. One must attempt somehow to integrate more effectively the better and more relevant 'bits and pieces' on the frontier or the periphery of economic theory into the relevant 'core' approaches. In short, one must do whatever one can to reduce the dogmatism of the intellectually untravelled.

In areas where there is disagreement as to the 'stylized facts' there is an obvious need for the careful assembly of more detailed information. This may be a particularly fruitful area for collaborative North–South research which, as has been seen, may yield especially high returns in the sphere of commodity market functioning and balance of payments adjustment in different types of developing countries.

The task of building new theory is not an easy one. Nor have attempts to prescribe approaches to the development of knowledge ever been very successful. But dissatisfaction with what one has can be a powerful motivator; at present, it is still much more widespread in the South than in the North. The world now badly needs more economists and others working to improve existing theories of the functioning of the global economy, and to disseminate more effectively the full range of such knowledge as already exists.

REFERENCES

Brandt, W. *et al.* (1980), *North–South: A Programme for Survival*, Cambridge, Mass. and London: MIT and Pan.

Dell, S. and R. Lawrence (1980), *The Balance of Payments Adjustment Process in Developing Countries*, New York: Pergamon Press.

Hansen, R.D. (1979), *Can the North–South Impasse be Overcome?*, Overseas Development Council, Development Paper 27, November.

Keynes, J.M. (1936), *The General Theory of Employment, Interest and Money*, New York: Harcourt, Brace and Co.

Sewell, J.W. (1979), 'Can the North Prosper Without Growth and Progress in the South?' in Martin M. McLaughlin *et al.*, *The United States and World Development, Agenda 1979*, New York: Praeger.

Taylor, L. (1988), *Varieties of Stabilization Experience. Towards Sensible Macroeconomics in the Third World*, Oxford: Clarendon Press.

4 Prospects for Increased South–South Economic Cooperation

INTRODUCTION

Arguments for increased South-South economic cooperation do not depend upon the state of the world economy. Overcoming the historical legacy of biased trading infrastructure, communications systems, and credit systems, and countering the gravitational pull of the first comers on the world industrialization scene have been legitimate aspirations, if not the object of much effective policy, for some time. Whether or not the North is experiencing booms or depressions, there will be a need for detailed thought and policy prescription on the means for economic cooperation among developing countries in various spheres and geographical areas.

Slowdown and turbulence in the Northern market economies in the 1970s and 1980s *have* generated new interest, both in the North and the South, in the possibilities of finding a new source of stable global growth in the South. The vast underexplored and underdeveloped resources, the untapped human potential, and the degree to which existing knowledge has not yet been applied there, all suggest that there may exist a 'new frontier' in the South that could impart a new dynamic to the overall growth of the world economy. This potential is a 'supply-side' one, not a matter of international Keynesian 'quick fixes' for temporary inadequacies in Northern aggregate demand, such as some continue to suggest as remedies for the world's immediate problems.

Within the South, this new interest has taken the form of increased discussion of South–South cooperation. The talk now is less of 'collective self-reliance' than it is of an independent 'engine of growth'. If the Northern 'engine' is slowing down, as Sir Arthur Lewis put it (1980), can the South still use trade as an engine for its own development? *Must* the South adjust to Northern slowdown by making cutbacks in its own investment programmes and growth, and suffering the increased urban unemployment and reduced utilization of capacity that such cutbacks imply?

This chapter considers the case for increased South–South economic cooperation in the context of the current international disorder and the sombre prospects for Northern economic growth. It is sceptical about the *degree* to which the current state of the world economy has altered the basic arguments for increased South–South cooperation, but nonetheless offers some novel suggestions as to how such increased cooperation might be achieved. It sees major possibilities for a coordinated Southern push for major reviews of the international trade and monetary systems, in which, paradoxically in view of the debates of the 1970s, the South may legitimately and self-interestedly champion the traditional principles of the postwar international economic order.

NORTHERN SLOWDOWN AND SOUTHERN GROWTH PROSPECTS

It may be best to begin with some summary trade information. Between 1963 and 1977, the North (and the capital-surplus oil-exporting countries in the 1970s) accounted for *increasing* proportions of Southern exports of manufactured goods, the most dynamic part of developing country exports. This was also true of NIC exports, which account for most of the South's such exports. The North and OPEC even accounted for an increasing proportion of Southern (and NIC) exports of capital goods. Opposite trends were encountered in the case of Southern primary products, increasing proportions of which were directed to Southern, and particularly NIC, markets. Manufactures grew so fast in the Southern export bill, however, that despite these trends in market shares, they accounted for an increasing share of *total* South–South trade and of Southern exports to the NICs (Havrylyshyn and Wolf, 1981).

When Northern demand for Southern manufactures fell off, between 1973 and 1980, in response to slower growth and/or increased protectionism, these trends were reversed. Non-oil Southern exports to the non-oil South and to the oil exporters grew considerably more rapidly than those to the North, both in primary products and manufactures, even though these Southern markets were still much less important overall than those of the North (Goldstein and Khan, 1982). During the recession of the early 1980s and thereafter, South–South trade, particularly in Latin America, suffered more severely than North–South trade. What difference then, does slower Northern demand expansion really make for Southern growth?

There is a school of thought, centred in the World Bank, that argues that the main determinant of developing country export success is supply-side export promotion policy, not demand influences. This school also argues that export growth is strongly associated with overall economic growth. The link between Northern growth (which works upon the demand for Southern exports) and Southern growth is therefore tenuous, it is argued; and as developing countries grow and increase their overall flexibility, this link is weakening. While allowance is made for the specifics of particular products and markets, the general line is that, with or without Northern recession, export promotion of the traditional sort is still the best way to stimulate growth (Riedel, 1984).

The problem with such advice, which downplays the importance of the demand side in assessing export prospects, is that it is based upon country prospects rather than global ones. It is logically deficient because of the fallacy of composition. What may be true for one country may not be true for all (Cline, 1982). If the global prospects were not a problem for country-level behaviour during a period of rapid growth, they are still not a problem for any single country in a period of recession for basically the same reason. Differences in the global rate of growth alter the seriousness of the implications of the fallacy of composition; they do not significantly alter the policy advice one would dispense to individual countries singly. Northern growth *does* matter to Southern export prospects. Other things being equal, the same export volumes pushed upon more slowly growing markets will result in worsened terms of trade.

That said, one must not overemphasize the importance of Northern growth to the prospect for Southern growth, and therefore for Southern trade policies. It is easy to exaggerate the importance of Northern growth for Southern development prospects. A detailed study of 1973–80 experience (Goldstein and Khan, 1982) made, among others, the following relevant points:

- The impact of Northern growth upon Southern exports varies greatly depending upon the commodity, the greatest effects being registered upon products with a high income elasticity of demand (including many manufactures); this impact is not always overriding, particularly at the level of individual exporting countries where supply-side constraints or policies may be dominant determinants of export performance.
- The link between Northern growth and imports from the South is considerably tighter than that between total Southern exports and

Southern growth; many other influences operate upon Southern growth, particularly in the low-income countries and the net oil exporters.

- The link between export volumes and GDP growth has been strongest in the case of major exporters of manufactures (and middle-income oil importers) and it is stronger over longer periods than it is for short periods – for example, year to year.
- Links between Northern and Southern growth rates appeared to *strengthen* in the 1970s, both because of a stronger link between Northern growth and Southern exports and because of a stronger link between Southern exports and Southern growth; this is attributed to the increased importance of manufactures in Southern exports, their higher income elasticity of demand in the North and their greater growth spin-offs in the South.

This study argued that:

> ...a relatively high degree of integration with the world economy carries both benefits and costs. Relatively high sensitivity of domestic growth with respect to industrial country growth is beneficial when industrial countries grow rapidly and costly when they grow slowly. ...Turning inward as a response to projected slow industrial country growth rates might reduce the short-run fluctuation in non-oil developing country growth rates but would also likely reduce the medium-term level of their growth. (Goldstein and Khan, 1982: 39)

Need there be such a trade-off? First, *is* there a significant growth pay-off from 'outward orientation' (somehow defined, and this definition may be important)? Second, if there is, are there *alternative* strategies for maintaining the degree of outward orientation necessary for growth other than the crude Northern orientation that has characterized the past?

It seems safe to say that the largest developing countries, notably China and India, are less likely to be affected by Northern slowdown. At the same time, they will find it easier than other countries to develop their own indigenous engines of growth. Were it not for their previous high degree of foreign borrowing (another dimension of outward orientation), the same might have been said for Brazil, Mexico, Indonesia, and perhaps some of the other middle-income newly industrializing countries; even now, setting debt-servicing obligations aside (about which more later), many of these countries can be categorized as 'potential self-starters'. The history of Latin America in the 1930s suggests that such countries, even at considerably more modest levels of income, are able in some circumstances to forge development strategies that are considerably less dependent upon the world economy. There *is* some choice in these matters.

There have been large changes in the degree of trade dependence in individual countries over time. Between 1960 and 1980 the average middle-income oil importing developing country increased its export share of GDP from 14 to 22 per cent. Clearly the degree of 'outward orientation' in recent years has been greater than historical norms. It may be, as is customarily said within orthodox circles, that this increased outward orientation is associated with very good growth performance. But the direction of causality in this relationship is by no means clear. Moreover, the association is not present for the poorer developing countries. In any case, the effects of export problems upon growth have been particularly severe, according to the above study, in the middle-income and manufactured exporter categories of developing countries. It is *not* evident that this is merely a short-run problem.

The key questions now are:

- What is the potential for inwardly oriented growth (not necessarily more inwardly oriented than before) in the larger developing countries, and are strategies to this end likely to generate more rapid and/or more reliable growth?
- Which, if any, countries that have now reached the threshold of size that would permit them sensibly to shift to more inwardly oriented development strategies might have the potential for more rapid and/or reliable growth?
- What are the potential benefits and costs to *all* parties, and particularly the largest countries, from increased cooperation with one another in such international exchange as they undertake – that is, a redirection of their exchange away from traditional directions and toward one another?
- What are the options for the smallest and poorest developing countries in a world of slowed Northern growth? Might they do better for themselves by reorienting their international exchange toward the countries that are expected to expand more quickly? What are the costs and benefits of such a reorientation?

PROSPECTS AND POLICIES FOR INDEPENDENT SOUTHERN GROWTH

If one believes that exports impart a particular thrust to Southern growth, and markets in traditional outlets do not look buoyant, one may seek exporting activity of new kinds and/or to new markets. Alternatively, one may seek to keep activity growing by disproportionately expanding non-export activity and thus reducing the relative importance of trade in the overall economy. Both approaches may be combined by expanding South–South trade, so that individual countries' exports are sustained but the place of total Southern trade with non-Southerners is reduced in overall Southern economic activity.

The prospect for developing and maintaining an independent growth momentum outside the traditional 'centres' must rest upon the coordinated action of a significant number of large and/or middle-income countries. Some of these countries could 'go it alone' to a significant degree, but the task will certainly be easier if it is undertaken jointly. The key players are China and India. Also of potentially great importance are such countries as Indonesia, Brazil, Nigeria, Mexico, the Philippines, Thailand and Korea.

In the first flush of newly acquired access to international money and capital markets, it was understandable that these developing countries were usually reluctant to risk 'sullying' their prospects by involvement in joint borrowing with others over whose subsequent behaviour they had no control or whose creditworthiness was already more suspect. In the current much more difficult circumstances, however, when bank lending to developing countries has already been cut and is likely to be considerably more cautious in the future, there may be virtue in resurrecting the prospect of multilateral bond flotations or bank borrowings, both for already established regional institutions such as the development banks and for new projects or programmes yet to be created, not least those associated with the expansion of economic ties among Southern nations. Joint approaches to borrowing might also increase the possibility of innovations in respect of the character of the financial instruments involved, altering the way in which risks are shared in particular.

Discussions of South–South trade cooperation have traditionally been couched in terms of preferential import tariffs, common markets, and customs unions. In this respect, as in so many others, Southern problems have been seen through the prism of Northern experiences and literature. It is now time for these discussions to shift to the possibility of preferential export subsidies. The promotion of 'infant-industry exports' may be a particularly effective way to hasten the development of international competitiveness, provided that such learning as occurs is truly incorporated within the technological base and/or the human capital of the exporting country rather than being absorbed only by foreign corporations. Westphal notes that most of Korea's exports

> ...are produced by wholly local firms. Selectivity in respect of the industries to be promoted may be crucial to the success of growth strategies, with the degree and nature of selectivity varying with country size, level of development. ...The selectivity with which infant industries are promoted appears to be of far greater consequence than the relative magnitude of the effective incentives initially granted to them. (Westphal, 1982: 268)

There is therefore a case for the subsidization of exports on a selective infant industry basis, whatever one may think of the orthodox case for subsidizing them across the board to offset the anti-export bias in typical industrialization programmes.

Strictly speaking, export subsidies are prohibited under GATT. Codes relating to them have been agreed, authorizing the levying of countervailing or anti-dumping duties if they cause or threaten 'material injury' in the importing country. There are many points at which these codes are still very vague and subject to interpretation by the importing country. Moreoever, many developing countries have not signed these codes and their application to an exporting country is conditional upon its having accepted the codes. It seems likely, then, that the North will increasingly resort to these instruments of protection – with or without the appropriate determination of 'injury' – against Southern exports that are perceived as subsidized, even though these 'subsidies' may simply compensate for overvalued exchange rates, cascading tariffs in the importing country, or other distortions.

However, under existing conventions, there is no need for such countervailing duties to be imposed if the export subsidies in question are acceptable to the importing country, as they may be if that country does not possess the relevant import-competing industry or has agreed to cede its market to the exporter in question. There is a reasonable prospect, then, that some subsidized Southern manufactured exports will face offsetting duties or the prospect of such duties in the North but *not* in the South. Preferences may consciously be accorded by Southern exporters to Southern importers; but they may thus also fall out of the existing rules of the international trading game. Southern exporters to the South face competition from Northern exporters of the same products. In some instances, Northern exporters are already limited in the extent to which they may subsidize their exports by the terms of the OECD agreement as to minimum interest rates to be charged on export credits. Southern exporters are not bound by any such limits on credit terms. It remains to be seen whether Northern countries are prepared to compete in other dimensions of export subsidization with each other and with Southern exporters in the South. There may be advantages, then, in encouraging Southern penetration of Southern markets via the active extension of subsidies by the exporting countries (conceivably similar to those they would like to have on exports to the North were they were not subject to countervailing duties, but also possibly higher).

The burden of the cost of any trade diversion that results from such export subsidies falls upon the (subsidizing) exporting country, which is the gainer from whatever scale economies, learning effects and externalities the expanded exports are supposed to be generating. In this way, the problem of persuading Southern importers to buy from more expensive Southern suppliers, which has been the bane of Southern trade cooperation schemes focusing upon preferential tariffs, is to some degree overcome. Where subsidized Southern exports compete with local Southern industries, the importing country may, like any other country, impose countervailing duties if it feels 'injured' thereby. A superior response would still frequently be 'market swapping' agreements that permit scale economies to be realized where they exist. As in the case of import substitution, selective infant industry protection is likely to be cheaper if countries can agree with one another as to some industrial allocations. These 'market swapping' arrangements can be assisted by the development of joint productive enterprises, Southern transnationals, and by state trading and governmental procurement policies.

One must not get too carried away with the short to medium-term potential for reliance upon expanding Southern markets as alternatives to Northern ones. Table 4.1 shows the relative dimensions of import purchases by various countries and country groups and their relative importance in Southern exports in 1980. Particularly for the middle-income countries, markets in the developing countries are still of limited significance (about 30 per cent of the total). Nevertheless it is the margin that matters. The potential is illustrated by the fact that China has been importing less from the rest of the world than Hong Kong. Population growth is faster in the South. Moreover, for many Third World exports, including many primary products and traditional early-stage manufactures, income elasticity of demand is higher in the developing countries than it is in the industrialized countries, so that even with equivalent rates

Table 4.1 Measures of relative market size, 1980

	1980 Merchandise imports ($ millions)	% of total	Destination of 1980 Exports: By Low-income Countries %	Destination of 1980 Exports: By Middle-income Countries %
China	19,550		—	—
India	12,858		—	—
Hong Kong	22,413		—	—
Singapore	24,008		—	—
Mexico	19,517		—	—
Korea	22,292		—	—
Brazil	25,000		—	—
Total of all low- and middle-income	430,397	21.6	40	30
High-income oil exporters	60,328	3.0	5	2
Industrial market economies	1,362,479	68.3	51	64
Nonmarket industrial countries	140,727	7.1	4	4
Total	1,993,931	100.0	100	100

Source: World Bank, *World Development Report*, 1982, pp. 124–125, 130–31.

of growth in population and per capita income, markets can be expected to grow more quickly in the South. If Southern growth *can* acquire a momentum of its own, to some degree independent of that of the North, as has been suggested, growth itself may also be more rapid in the South than in the stagnant North. Income elasticity information obviously will be among the inputs to policy-making as to the industries chosen for selective encouragement in infant industry exporting to the South.

The poorest and smallest of the developing countries are likely simply to direct their trade wherever it is most favourable in static terms. They are too small and, in the case of most, too trade-dependent to develop much growth momentum independently of the growth performance of trading partners. As they develop their marketing and trading infrastructure and, in some cases, their export subsidy programmes, they must calculate the marginal benefits and costs. If the growth and growth prospects of the larger and middle-income developing countries improve, they will redirect more of their exports to them, as to some degree they already have done. If the newly industrializing countries liberalize their import regimes, either generally or preferentially in their favour, such a redirection will be so much the greater. These countries will benefit from *any* increases in external growth, whether in the North or the South, but are themselves unable to exert much influence on overall Southern growth performance.

What might thus be hoped for is an expansion in the NICs' share of the poorer and smaller countries' imports, including those that are externally financed. More Northern official development assistance to the poorest countries that is not tied to procurement in the donor country, including IDA lending, might be spent productively in sourcing from developing countries in the future. But such a redirection of their import purchases should be the result of competitiveness and not generate worsened terms of trade for the poor. One way in which this process might be helped along, and Southern solidarity more convincingly demonstrated, might be for the better-off Southern countries consciously to assist the poorest. This could be achieved through official development assistance – perhaps with a targeting system based upon the principles of progressive (per capita) income taxation, in which proportions of GNP ranging upward to 0.7 per cent are prescribed – and the application of a GSP-type (generalized system of preferences) tariff preference system for the poorest. (It would be appropriate to develop a preferential scheme for the poorest that met all of the well known objections concerning rules of origin, upper limits, exceptions, and so on, and thus constituted a model for the rest of the world; but this may be too much to hope for.)

SOUTHERN APPROACHES TO GLOBAL ISSUES

As far as global and North–South issues are concerned, the developing countries should speak for some of the fundamental principles of the old international order, regardless of what they may feel about the desirability of a new one. In the sphere of international trade, the growing resort to bilateralism, non-transparency, and ad hoc measures not covered in the GATT, and the evident decline in the effectiveness and credibility of the GATT, have generated a 'crisis of confidence' in the existing trade order.

The principal losers from the new complexity and obscurity of trade-inhibiting measures – bilateralism and discrimination in their application and the disrespect for rules and dispute settlement procedures – are the smaller and poorer countries. The South can plausibly join the smaller industrialized countries in a major push for the 're-creation' of an effective international trade organization based upon the original and fundamental principles of the GATT system: non-discrimination, predictability, transparency, and multilateralism (Diaz-Alejandro and Helleiner, 1982). Rather than abandoning the GATT, as some from the 'GATT-is-dead' school recommend, the world could and should build upon its experience and staff as it develops structures that incorporate the activities of other UN agencies in a more universal, credible, and ultimately more effective trade body. It is anomalous that, while the World Bank has a professional staff of about 2,600 and the IMF about 1,600, GATT and UNCTAD together probably employ fewer than 300 on world trade questions. The South should be pushing hard for negotiations leading to a new world trade secretariat and a system of rules that will permit the old-fashioned virtues of comparative advantage to work on their behalf. The South is likely, for a change, to have the weight of Northern professional opinion working with it on a push of this kind.

While the GSP should not be dropped unilaterally, it certainly might be traded – without great loss to the South – for tangible progress toward a system that generates less discrimination, and more predictability, transparency and order; the South should now develop genuine counter-proposals for the future of 'special and differential treatment', the treatment of the least developed in the trading arena, and the problem of 'graduation'. (The logic of the graduation issue would seem to call, for instance, for the simultaneous graduation of NICs from the Multi-Fibre Arrangement's applicability and the GSP.) At present, the South is behaving in the reactive mode that has typically characterized Northern responses to Southern proposals, rather than trying constructively to search out possible alternatives to the North's suggestions and/or unilateral actions on graduation.

In finance and macro-economic management too, the developing countries are emerging as the principal defenders of the major original principles and more recently agreed adaptations of the Bretton Woods institutions. It is they who call with the greatest vigour for the strengthening of the IMF through adequate quota expansion; the centreing of the international monetary system upon SDRs rather than upon gold, national currencies and commercial bank lending; measures to reduce the volatility of exchange rate charges; and increased coordination and cooperation in pursuit of the IMF's primary objectives of maintaining employment and growth both nationally and internationally. The existing international monetary system does not remotely resemble Keynes' and White's original vision. Nor does it take account of the careful reform-oriented deliberations of the Committee of Twenty in the early 1970s. It is surely time for a major review of the international monetary system's capacity to perform the tasks required of it – a review that ought to be coordinated with that suggested above for the institutional machinery governing world trade. Once again, a push for such a general review is likely to carry the weight of substantial professional support in the North.

Needless to say, the manner in which Southern proposals for reviews of the trade and monetary institutions are presented will be important to the way in which they are received. It may be that suspicions are already so great that any Southern push of this kind will be viewed with great scepticism in the North. It should be possible, however, for the South to 'take the high road' and call for a return to original principles and adherence to already multilaterally agreed decisions, rather than calling for a 'new order'. For the present, an appropriate rebuilding of the GATT and the IMF would represent significant and effective advances for the South (as well as for the world).

While advocating this multilateral and non-discriminatory system, the South should not hesitate to threaten discriminatory arrangements – both formalized and informal – at the North's expense. Some of these possibilities were discussed above. Collectively, the South's trade is already sufficiently important to the North for it to be employed as a bargaining tool; this is particularly the case for manufactured goods trade, where Southern imports from the North are a multiple of Northern imports from the South. It is not necessary for the entire South to combine in this respect; it would be sufficient for a few NICs to band together and, where appropriate, play individual Northern countries off against one another.

What are the prospects for the long-discussed Third World Secretariat? It seems that, for the forseeable future, it may not be possible to create such a body with the full support of all members of the Group of seventy-seven. Does this dim prospect really matter?

In the first place, information networks and informal exchange have undoubtedly been expanding among key Southern decision-makers and professionals. More importantly, there remains great potential for Secretariat-type cooperative ventures among more limited numbers of people and countries. It is now time to move forward with a limited version of the proposed Secretariat, allowing those who want to participate to move, and perhaps to demonstrate its possible usefulness (or even to induce the more reluctant to join simply to avoid being left out). This could be achieved by a modest start with a high-powered staff in a particular location, along fairly traditional lines, although this approach has not worked too well thus far. Alternatively, a beginning might be made by utilizing part of the time of individuals holding line positions and convening regular meetings of the group on a rotating geographic basis. This might amount to very little more than the systematization of some of the present informal arrangements among key Southern officials and policy-makers, together perhaps with increased technical backup. To be workable, a Southern movable 'think tank' of this type would be fairly limited in number (say a total of 20, with perhaps an average attendance of 15), and the commitment of its members (both the individuals and their governments) to it would have to be real and unconditional. It might function, at least in part, by using materials from other international bodies as major bases for discussion.

REFERENCES

Cline, William R. (1982), 'Can the East Asian Export Model of Development be Generalized?', *World Development*, vol. 10, no. 2, February.

Diaz-Alejandro, Carlos, F. and Gerald K. Helleiner (1982), *Handmaiden in Distress: World Trade in the 1980s*, Ottawa: North–South Institute; Washington, DC: Overseas Development Council; and London: Overseas Development Institute.

Goldstein, Morris and Mohsin S. Khan (1982), 'Effects of Slowdown in Industrial Countries on Growth in Non-Oil Developing Countries', IMF Occasional Paper 12, Washington, DC, August.

Havrylyshyn, Oli and Martin Wolf (1981), 'Trade Among Developing Countries: Theory, Policy Issues, and Principal Trends', World Bank Staff Working Paper no. 479, August.

Lewis, W.A. (1980), 'The Slowing Down of the Engine of Growth', *American Economic Review*, vol. 70 no. 4, September.

Riedel, James (1984), 'Trade as the Engine of Growth in Developing Countries, Revisited', *Economic Journal*, vol. 94, no. 373, March.

Westphal, Larry E. (1982), 'Fostering Technological Mastery by Means of Selective Industry Promotion' in M. Syrquin and S. Teitel (eds), *Trade, Stability, Technology and Equity in Latin America*, New York: Academic Press.

World Bank (1982), *World Development Report, 1982*, Washington, DC

PART II
Developing Countries in the Global Financial System

5. The Impact of the Exchange Rate System on the Developing Countries*

INTRODUCTION

It is generally agreed that the Bretton Woods adjustable peg system of exchange rates was no longer sustainable under the conditions of the 1970s. The increased size and mobility of liquid capital at this time brought out the inherent brittleness and susceptibility to crisis of postwar international monetary arrangements. The post-1973 exchange rate régime differs from the adjustable peg system primarily 'by the greater frequency of exchange rate changes, by the larger share of the external adjustment burden that is assigned to the exchange rate, and by the absence of a publicly declared target rate' (Goldstein, 1980: 1). While the post-1973 system of managed flexibility of exchange rates, formally authorized by the Second Amendment to the Articles of Agreement of the IMF in 1978, may have somewhat eased medium- to long-run balance of payments adjustment among the major industrialized countries, new and, to some extent, unforeseen problems have emerged in its functioning. Particularly required is a careful assessment of the implications for developing countries of the workings of the new more flexible exchange rate regime.

In assessments of alternative exchange rate regimes it is important to distinguish between: (a) the effects of longer-run realignments of currency values over time, which can occur under any realistic exchange rate

*Many people had a hand in the preparation of this report. The project was originally conceived and organized by Sidney Dell. The authors of several country studies which were prepared in connection with this project have contributed significantly to its content: Peter Ady, Edmar Bacha, Charles Harvey, Alberto Jimenez de Lucio, V.R. Panchamukhi, Delisle Worrell. Very useful comments on earlier draft material were made by Edmar Bacha, Alec Chrystal, Carlos Diaz-Alejandro, Sidney Dell, Chandra Hardy, Roger Lawrence, Lance Taylor and John Williamson. Research assistance was provided ably by Xolile Guma and Damas Mbogoro. Above all, David Brodsky and Gary Sampson of the UNCTAD Secretariat, should share the credit for such originality as this report may possess. None of the aforementioned is to be implicated, however, in its contents. The responsibility now rests exclusively with me.

system; and (b) the effects of floating exchange rates themselves. It is unfortunately not possible to state definitively that longer-term realignments are totally unrelated to the exchange rate regime; advocates of more stable exchange rates frequently argue, for instance, that floating rates reduce monetary discipline and thus contribute to more divergent and higher rates of inflation and, hence, to currency realignments. Arguments can also be heard to the effect that the floating rate regime is partially responsible for slower rates of growth in output capacity, a deterioration in the terms of the unemployment–inflation trade-off, and slower realized growth. In the absence of counter-evidence demonstrating what would have occurred if rates had not floated, these issues cannot be resolved conclusively. Recent surveys conclude, in any case, that international monetary arrangements cannot be assigned any more than a marginal role in any of these macro-economic questions (Williamson, 1979; Goldstein, 1980). Our attention is confined to an analysis of the effects of the floating exchange rate system on the assumption that global macro-economic developments and longer-run currency realignments are not significantly affected by it. This approach implies that its prime concern is with the short-run and medium-term exchange rate instability which characterizes the current floating exchange-rate system; at some points, however, longer-run issues are nevertheless addressed, since they cannot be evaded.

This focus of the analysis is not to be taken as reflecting a view that longer-run currency realignments are relatively unimportant. On the contrary, discussions with monetary policy-makers in the developing countries revealed that, typically, they were more concerned about the longer-run changes in the values of major currencies, and particularly that of the US dollar, than they were about the shorter-term fluctuations which were the primary object of our enquiry. Not only are the longer-run realignments of the major currencies of crucial significance for developments in the global economy but, at the national level also, in the developing countries as elsewhere, longer-run exchange rate policies and regimes, together with other balance of payments policies, are likely to be of greater importance to overall development patterns than are the effects of short-term exchange rate fluctuations.

The most troublesome feature of the post-1973 exchange rate regime is unquestionably the greatly increased 'turbulence' – erratic short-term instability – of foreign exchange markets. There has been a significant increase in short- and medium-term nominal and real exchange rate *instability* in the industrialized countries. Between June 1973 and February 1979, the average absolute percentage change in pound, franc and mark rates *vis-à-vis* the US dollar exceeded 2 per cent per month, more than twice the average rate of monthly change in wholesale and consumer price levels, and much more than twice the monthly changes in relative price levels (Frenkel and Mussa, 1980: 374–5). This instability has been erratic and unpredictable; it seems unrelated to the longer run requirements of balance of payments adjustment, and is therefore frequently described as 'overshooting'.

Flexible exchange rates, it was thought, ought to permit quicker exchange rate responses to international differences (or more accurately, inconsistencies) in inflation rates, as well as to structural changes of various kinds. It seems, however, that deviations from purchasing power parity have been significantly *greater* in the floating period than in the 1957–72 period of adjustable pegs, and these increased deviations are primarily the product of sharply increased variance in nominal exchange rates, with sluggish price changes, rather than of increased differentiation of inflation rates (Genberg, 1978: 260). Not only have short-run fluctuations in exchange rates been unrelated to those in relative national price levels, but 'changes in exchange rates over longer periods of time have frequently been associated with large cumulative divergences from relative purchasing power parities' (Frenkel and Mussa, 1980: 375; see also Isard, 1977; Genberg, 1978, Krugman, 1978, Kravis and Lipsey, 1978, Kenen and Pack 1980, for empirical confirmation).

It is true that the required longer-term adjustments in exchange rates are now achieved more gradually than hitherto, and that the periodic speculative crises of the adjustable peg system are no longer observed. But large short-term fluctuations – far beyond the requirements for current account adjustments and reflecting, above all, the continuing importance of large short-term capital flows responding to changing expectations as to political events, inflation rates, exchange controls, and ultimately exchange rates themselves – have reduced enthusiasm for the new regime's possible accomplishments. Contrary to some expectations, these fluctuations have not gradually declined as the markets became more accustomed to the new, more flexible exchange rate regime. It seems that the stabilizing role which many observers expected short-term capital flows to play only appears at the outer limits of a very wide 'band' of short-term fluctuations around the trend, and sometimes only following governmental intervention. As one analyst put it, 'banks and other private risk-bearers were unwilling to take over the function previously carried by central banks under the system of pegged exchange rates: that of guaranteeing a range for the exchange rate for any length of time' (Black, 1977: 176). There have been no serious efforts as yet to grapple with the continuing problem of short-term international capital flows 'sloshing' between currencies in enormous volumes.

The foreign exchange markets now appear to be just as inevitably turbulent as other asset markets, such as those for stocks or commodities. Indeed financial analysts have been calling attention to the growing link between speculation in commodities and that in foreign exchange; commodity traders now must assess the short-term changes and expectations for major currency values as well as the real prospects for commodities, and investors of liquid capital may find commodities no less appropriate a short-term investment than financial assets denominated in volatile currencies. There are no effective equivalents in international currency markets for the regulatory agencies which oversee particular national stock or commodity exchanges, limiting the degree of price change permitted within given periods, suspending trade for particular items in unusual circumstances, and policing certain 'rules of the game'. Governments can and do intervene in currency markets, but there are no established rules for their conduct and there is potential for different governments acting at cross-purposes; the IMF has been authorized to exercise surveillance over exchange rates but it has little policing power except in respect of its poorer members. Small wonder, then, that 'floating' has led to substantial turbulence in exchange rates.

On the face of it, then, there has been little success in attaining the internationally agreed objective of avoiding erratic and excessive exchange rate fluctuations, or at least moderating them when they are not the product of underlying economic conditions. Disruptions and instability in underlying economic and financial conditions can, of course, never be totally eliminated, and the post-1973 period has been one of considerable international economic disorder. But 'orderliness' of markets – whether money, bond, commodity, or foreign exchange – can be achieved with varying degrees of success and, in this case, it is generally agreed that success has been limited.

Developing countries' terms of trade (and overall income) *are* more unstable, on average, than those of richer countries (Branson and Papaefstratiou, 1980: 53). At the same time the costs of such instability are presumably greater, however they are measured, in developing countries than they are in richer countries. This chapter shows that, contrary to earlier assessments (for example, Cline, 1976), the costs of the instabilities of the present international exchange rate regime bear especially heavily upon the developing countries. For the major industrialized countries to return to the adjustable peg regime is not now a feasible option even if it were considered desirable. It may well be that there were alternative exchange rate regimes, involving crawling pegs or reference rates or purer floating, which were just as 'realistic' as the adjustable peg system which was abandoned or the 'managed float' which followed it. But the only two regimes for which there exists firm evidence are the two actually experienced. It is not therefore very fruitful to debate further the academic question as to what might have been in a variety of hypothetical worlds and thus to determine in some philosophical sense whether or not the degree of turbulence in foreign exchange markets under the managed float has been 'excessive' (for example, Frenkel and Mussa, 1980). Rather, since it is undeniable that there has been a quantum jump in the degree of short-term exchange rate instability in the post-1973 period, it is important to ascertain whose interests have been most affected by it, whether there have been significant costs imposed, and, if so, how governmental and inter-governmental policies might now reduce them. It will be argued that, given the 'flexible' character of the present exchange rate regime, measures to create a greater degree of exchange rate 'order' and measures to reduce the costs of such disorder as remains have now become urgent matters for policy-makers' attention.

EFFECTS OF INCREASED EXCHANGE RATE INSTABILITY ON DEVELOPING COUNTRIES

Fluctuations in effective exchange rates which are the product of instability of foreign currencies can obviously complicate macro-management in developing countries. If they are large enough, and if there are price or nominal wage ratchets operating, they may even generate more rapid domestic price inflation, and hence depreciation of the domestic currency *vis-à-vis* its peg currency and the possibility of further inflation in an upward spiral. But any such effects are difficult to verify, and there is no consensus as to their importance, even in the developed countries where there have been attempts at doing so empirically. On other costs of exchange rate instability, however, there is much wider agreement.

In the careful words of the 1978 Annual Report of the IMF:

> The short-run fluctuations in exchange rates in recent years have ... caused problems for the less developed countries, despite the fact that most of them continue to peg their exchange rates. For those countries that peg to a single currency ... greater exchange rate variability between the intervention currency and other currencies is likely to result in an increase in variability in both the

> country's effective exchange rate and in the local currency price of its imports and exports. Increased short-run fluctuations among the major currencies also may mean that a less developed country's exchange rate (vis-à-vis countries with which it does an important part of its trade) responds to factors more closely associated with the external position of the country issuing its intervention currency than to its own domestic or balance of payments needs. Some less developed countries have attempted to minimize these problems by switching from a unitary peg to a peg based on a basket of currencies, but many countries find this solution administratively inconvenient, particularly when there is a single dominant currency used in trade and exchange transactions ... The increase in exchange rate fluctuations has also caused problems of portfolio management for the less developed countries. ... While the fluctuations in exchange rates have diminished the store-of-value function of some of the major currencies, the rise and variability in import costs have led to a demand for higher and more assured levels of reserves. Those less developed countries that peg to a single currency whose future value is uncertain may therefore face the dilemma that they need to hold larger working balances in that currency, yet they may also wish to diversify their reserves. (IMF, 1978: 39–40)

Again,

> ... greater unpredictability of import prices and export receipts in both the short run and the intermediate term ... has made it more difficult for both the public and private sectors to plan their activities, manage their finances, and choose between import suppliers. Moreover, the greater unpredictability of exchange rates in the intermediate term has complicated the task faced by many less developed countries in the management of both their foreign reserves and their external debt. (IMF, 1979: 42)

All in all, the new exchange rate regime increases the need for rapid information acquisition and analysis, and places a premium upon quick responses and flexibility in production, trade and finance. It therefore places those least endowed with these capacities at a new relative disadvantage – notably poorer countries and smaller firms. These issues will be addressed under the following headings:

1. Trade Effects – level, pattern, and terms;
2. Financial (or Portfolio) Effects – foreign exchange reserve and debt management.

Trade Effects

Level of trade

Increased variability of exchange rates, all else being equal, will increase the risks involved in international trade and, through its effects upon domestic prices, in particular types of domestic production and consumption – notably tradable goods and services. It might be argued that more flexible exchange rates, particularly in periods of crisis and extreme uncertainty, substitute for other impediments to the free flow of international trade (exchange controls, trade barriers, and so forth) – that is, that other things are not equal – but this possibility is difficult to take seriously as a general description of likely alternative events throughout the floating period. Assuming some degree of risk aversion, there ought therefore to be some reallocative effects. These may include diverting production away from exports with their increasingly uncertain prices, and towards non-traded products; possibly import substitutes, prices for which are less influenced by these new uncertainties; and, similarly, diverting consumption away from imports and towards non-traded products and, perhaps, exportables.

The various devices which may be employed by international traders to protect themselves against foreign exchange risk, which are generally less accessible to those in developing countries (as will be seen below) are, in any case, not without costs. Even when the increased short-term exchange risk of the post-1973 period is effectively covered there still ought to be anti-trade effects arising from the increased risks. Other things being equal (and, as noted, they might conceivably not be), increased exchange rate fluctuation and uncertainty should thus work towards the emergence of more 'closed' national economies, reduced international trade and therefore, most would argue, reduced overall efficiency at both the national and global levels. Even without risk aversion, increased instability of prices muddies the signals upon which efficient resource allocation must be based, and is thus likely to lower overall economic efficiency. Some argue that increased uncertainty as to the permanence of exchange rate changes makes trade and investment responses more sluggish. To the extent that reallocations actually take place in response to price signals – and this will depend upon expectations as to the permanence or transitory nature of changes in them – the increased instability of the prices of tradables will generate increased pointless resource reallocations, (because they are soon to be reversed), although, in the structurally more rigid developing countries, the resulting misallocation may be less than in more price-responsive economies. There may also be disruptions in trade and production as a consequence of decisions taken in anticipation of short-run changes in exchange rates, whether or not they actually occur (Richardson, 1978). There are thus clear social costs from the increased uncertainty of prices for traded or tradable goods – taking the form of less efficient allocation, excess frictional costs, or the opportunity cost of the resources involved in the arrangement of cover against risk.

While all analysts agree on these likely effects, such effects are not in fact easy to verify empirically. So many other factors have been in motion during the post-1973 floating rate regime that one simply cannot isolate the effects of increased exchange rate instability alone upon levels of international trade. For many, the extra exchange risk or costs involved in covering against exchange risk seems miniscule in comparison with the other determinants of production, trading and investment activities.

From the evidence, it is not clear that, in the *aggregate*, the turbulence in foreign exchange markets has actually significantly affected international trade or investment. Both econometric tests and surveys of businessmen in industrial countries suggest that they have been able to adapt to the new circumstances without cutting back on international activity (IMF, 1979; 37).[1]

Large internationally diversified corporations are unlikely to be bothered very much by the short-term volatility of the various currencies in which their international activities are denominated. Their accountants and foreign exchange specialists can easily hedge their positions in each currency if they choose to do so. Indeed, through the familiar process of leads and lags in commercial payments they can and do take positions in individual currencies. Many respondents to a survey of multinationals carried out by the Group of Thirty stated that it is worth their while forecasting exchange rates since they believe they can often do so more accurately than the forward markets (whether they actually can do so is another matter entirely); they therefore engage in 'selective hedging' (Group of Thirty, 1980: 48–9). By so doing, they sometimes *create* exchange rate fluctuations or 'lead the market'.[2] Thus it should not come as a surprise that this survey of approximately 20 large and sophisticated multinational industrial corporations revealed that their managers do not believe that floating rates have 'materially impeded international trade or investment' (Group of Thirty, 1980: 6). The general view was that floating rates 'had not appreciably raised the costs of conducting business internationally' (Group of Thirty, 1980: 45), although some respondents mentioned increased costs of hedging, increased management and staff time devoted to foreign exchange matters, and so on. There is some evidence that risk-bearing is compensated by price changes without significant changes in trade volume (Hooper and Kohlhagen, 1978).

For the developing countries, however, the presumption as to the negative effects are much stronger. How important these increased exchange rate risks are to particular transactors depends upon the currencies in which their international trade is denominated. Clearly, those in the USA incur low and fundamentally unchanging exchange risks because of the dollar's use in the denomination of international trading and financial contracts. To the extent that their international transactions are denominated in other currencies they also would benefit in the same way when their value is fixed in terms of the US dollar. The international transactions of the developing countries, on the other hand, are denominated in internationally acceptable currencies, and only rarely in their own.

> For trade between the developed and developing countries, very little pricing is done in LDC currencies. In some cases, involving primary products, dollars or sterling are used; but in most others, the currency of the developed country trading partner predominates. (Magee and Rao, 1980, 370–1)[3]

It follows that, except in the cases where there is a rigid peg maintained with the currency in which trade is denominated (or where real exchange rate stability is maintained), a much higher proportion of their nationals' transactions is subject to exchange risk than is the case in industrialized countries, where at least some trade (usually exports) is typically denominated in the home currency.

The currency in which international trade is invoiced is currently very much a matter of relative bargaining strength. The burden of exchange risk is as much a part of the total 'price' of exported or imported goods and services as the unit price at which the transactions are recorded.[4]

Generally, there is today a tendency for goods to be invoiced in the currency of the exporter in OECD trade (Carse, Williamson and Wood, 1980; Magee and Rao, 1980:370; Van Nieuwkerk, 1979; Basevi *et al.*, 1980).[5] This has been particularly the case with differentiated manfactured products, such as machinery and equipment, where exporters possess greater market power (McKinnon, 1979). Exchange risk is thus pushed upon weaker trade partners, and in particular on developing countries. While manfactured goods prices are usually set in terms of one of the two currencies of the transactors to a bargain, in many circumstances – particularly in primary commodity markets – a vehicle currency, usually the dollar and sometimes still the pound, is employed instead (Magee and Rao, 1980). As exchange risks have increased, they are likely to have been shifted disproportionately upon those least able to bargain; in the case of North–South trade, that is, on the developing countries.

While one would expect disincentives to trade and the other possible costs of increased exchange rate instability to be greater for smaller firms and smaller countries, this has not as yet been generally verified by empirical testing. Most tests of the effects of exchange rate instability upon trade volume have been inconclusive. However, scattered findings, exist to the effect that instability in either real or nominal exchange rates has been correlated with reduced trade in a number of specific, usually semi-industrialized, developing countries (Bautista, 1980: 79–80, 83; Rana, 1979; Coes, 1980; Behrman, 1976: 185–8; Diaz-Alejandro, 1976b: 64–9).

Fluctuating exchange rates may also influence developing countries' trade in less direct ways. By encouraging developed countries to maintain relatively free trade and payments systems, the floating rate system was at first generally expected to be beneficial to the developing countries relative to conceivable alternatives (for example, Diaz-Alejandro, 1976). But, in practice, these very real potential advantages have been somewhat eroded in recent years as protectionism – particularly against developing countries' manufactured exports – has grown and controls upon private lending to developing countries are threatened. In the sphere of trade, it is even argued that the floating rate regime has reduced the predictability of the protectionist effects of import tariffs and therefore, together with other probably more important factors, has increased governmental proclivities for the use of quantitative controls over imports instead (Nowzad, 1978: 932; Frank, Pearson and Riedel, 1979: 49); these are typically more costly and socially undesirable for both the exporting and importing countries. There is also some evidence, though it has not been systematically assessed, that there may be a tendency for protectionist pressure during temporary periods of exchange rate appreciation to reach levels sufficient to generate new trade barriers which are not then subsequently removed: a 'trade barrier ratchet' effect.

Pattern of trade

All else being equal, one would expect trade patterns, as well as trade levels, to be influenced by the degree of exchange rate instability and uncertainty experienced in different directions of trade. Thus, in a world of fluctuating exchange rates there should be a tendency for countries to trade more in currencies which are relatively stable *vis-à-vis* the home currency than in those which are not. Generally speaking, and particularly where their import trade is concerned, developing countries' trade with developed countries is denominated in the currency of their trading partners; trade among developing countries is typically denominated in third currencies (dollars, francs, and so forth) as well. The implication is that, other things equal, developing countries can be expected to divert their trade toward the countries to whose currencies their own currencies are pegged – when they are pegged, that is. Thus, dollar-pegging countries can be expected to increase the share of their trade which is dollar-denominated and thus which is with the USA; franc-pegging countries may be expected to do likewise in respect of franc-denominated trade and trade with France. Clearly, there is potential for a cumulative self-reinforcing process here; countries are motivated to peg their currencies to those of their principal trading partners, and having done so, they are motivated to trade with these countries even further. When the major currencies float *vis-à-vis* one another, there can therefore be a tendency for Northern-based currency and trading blocs to strengthen, with all of their attendant disadvantages.

Empirical tests of such influences upon developing countries' trading patterns have been inconclusive (Dychter, 1979; Greene, 1980). In recent years a variety of other influences have dominated exchange rate instability as determinants of trade patterns: for example, longer-term competitiveness as indicated by changes in real exchange rates; market access; credit availability; multinational firms' activity in trade; aid flows; national diversification objectives; altered purchasing or marketing practices and so on. While in future periods pegging practices can still influence trading patterns on the margin, their influence is probably relatively small.

Similar arguments apply to financial relationships, for which the data are no more conclusive. The issues surrounding these relationships are considered in the discussion below of reserve and debt portfolio management.

Terms of trade

There is by now ample evidence that domestic currency prices do not instantaneously alter in response to exchange rate changes; that is, purchasing power parity does not hold in the short or medium run, and at the micro-level, the so-called 'law of one price' is frequently broken (Isard, 1977; Kravis and Lipsey, 1978; Genberg, 1978; Richardson, 1978; Bautista and Riedel, 1980). That being so, exchange rate alterations can and do alter the real prices for individual countries' exports and imports, *beyond* the periods for which contracts have already been concluded. When prices are set in the major trading countries' currencies, as they generally are, depreciation in the value of the currency in which a small country's exports are denominated (say, US dollars) in relation to those in which its imports are established (say, Japanese yen or Deutschemarks) implies an unexpected and involuntary deterioration in its terms of trade. Increased instability of key currency exchange rates therefore implies increased instability in developing countries' terms of trade, at least for those countries in which exports and imports are denominated in different currencies. Obviously, there are usually other far more important influences upon short-term instability of developing countries' terms of trade; on the other hand, exchange rate fluctuations can cause significant effects by themselves.

If exchange risk diminishes importers' demands or exporters' supply, there may be consequent compensating price effects; there is evidence of such price 'compensation' for risk-bearing in US international trade, even though, because of short-term inelasticities of foreign supply and demand, there is no apparent effect of exchange risk upon trade volume (Hooper and Kohlhagen, 1978). Where developing countries possess market power – say, in some exports – one might expect, on this basis, some increase in export prices to offset any declines in trade volume. But individual developing countries are usually price-takers, not only in their imports but also in their export trade, and most of their exports are, in any case, highly inelastic in their supply, so that favourable changes in their terms of trade in partial compensation for increased exchange risk are exceedingly unlikely.[6]

Financial Effects

Foreign exchange reserve management

Field investigations for this paper confirmed the frequently expressed view that the increased short term instability of exchange rates has created difficulties for the managers of foreign exchange reserves and public debt in developing countries. Even in the more advanced of these countries, the necessary financial experience and expertise for effective portfolio management was frequently found to be lacking. In the smaller countries, with a few fortunate exceptions, these problems have been particularly serious. Scale diseconomies in the management function and the infeasibility or expense of acquiring up-to-the-minute information in these countries increase the difficulty of achieving effective managerial responses to short-term changes; and these countries are usually in any case particularly deficient in the relevant expertise. The risks in the financial sector can be regarded as the product of nominal, rather than real, exchange rate fluctuations.[7] In some countries, substantial losses have been realized on foreign exchange reserve accounts for several years in succession.

The post-1973 'managed' floating rate regime has left opportunities for monetary authorities to intervene in various ways in foreign exchange markets, even when they are not seeking to peg the value of their currencies. Contrary to some purist academic expectations there has therefore been a continuing foreign exchange 'management' role and a continuing need for foreign exchange reserves. In any case, many developing countries continue to peg the value of their currencies in terms of others. Indeed, the increased variability of developing countries' receipts and payments which is implicit in the increased variability of effective exchange rates would require, assuming unchanged demand and supply functions, higher reserves in order for currency-pegging countries to achieve the same domestic macro-economic objectives (Williamson, 1976: 79). In practice, however, any such increased reserve requirements would seem to be very small. This conclusion derives both from theoretical analysis (Williamson, 1976) and empirical testing (Heller and Khan, 1978). The latter found that non-oil developing countries' reserves were actually higher in the post-1973 period than would have been predicted by a demand function estimated from the pre-float period, but that reserve holding behaviour did not alter in a statistically significant manner.[8]

Rough rules of thumb for reserve management can be devised and have sometimes been applied; currency composition of reserves can be related, for instance,to that of the import bill or the external debt or projected deficits, or some combination thereof. There have certainly been systematic patterns and changes over time in the composition of foreign exchange reserves, and these are related to the choice of peg, trading patterns, and longer-run exchange rate prospects (Heller and Knight, 1978). There is obviously a need for more developing country expertise in this area. Careful analysis of the relative merits of alternative rules of thumb for utilization by those whose limitations in managerial capacity are likely to continue could also be productive (see Ben-Bassat, 1980). There is also obvious merit in attempting to pool expertise and information systems among the smaller countries, perhaps on a regional or sub-regional basis.

Debt management

Similar issues arise in respect of the problems of debt management. The currency composition of debt is much more likely to be the product of chance than is the case with reserves. While much of the developing countries' debt is fairly long term, the servicing is ongoing and gives rise to recurrent short-term payments obligations; increases in short-run exchange rate in stability therefore imply increased risks in this sphere, just as in trade and reserves.

At present, the foreign exchange risk inherent in all external finance is forced almost exclusively on to the borrower. Bilateral lenders, with very few exceptions, lend in their own currencies; financial institutions such as the World Bank and Eurocurrency banks match assets to liabilities in each currency.

Even in otherwise ideal circumstances, countries borrowing externally must expect to take *some* risk. Except for the larger and more commercially creditworthy, however, the developing countries have very little control over the extent or the precise character of that risk. Its management is made especially difficult for the smallest and least 'creditworthy' countries – the majority of developing countries – by such factors as the following:

1. For them, the currency composition of the external debt at any one time is given and cannot normally be altered – that is, finance is not normally available to them to refinance external debt in different countries.
2. These countries normally cannot choose which currencies to borrow except on a very long-term basis by shifting trade, aid and financial relationships.
3. In relatively small countries, single externally financed projects can be large enough to have a significant, or even dominant, effect on the country's external debt, so that if such a project is financed in a single currency the country can be dangerously exposed to adverse movements in that currency.

These difficulties are worsened when a country gets into balance of payments difficulties, as many developing countries have done in recent years. Countries faced by a sharp deterioration in their balance of payments are likely to borrow more externally, and, because long-term external finance on soft terms cannot normally be increased suddenly, borrow on harder terms. At the same time, they are in a weaker position to choose which currencies to borrow (except, to some degree, in terms of the currency mix of payments arrears); indeed they frequently have no choice at all. Thus, in the crisis of financing a deficit in order to keep the economy going, they are less likely even to consider the currency of new loans. As a result, the currency composition of the external debt of a poor country which has been or is going through a balance of payments crisis is likely to be largely accidental rather than the result of financial planning.

While the currency composition of the total external debt obviously matters, it is rather the currency composition of each year's debt service that is relevant to short-run policy and practice. The latter tends to be dominated by short-term debt unless a country has been fortunate enough to borrow abroad exclusively on concessional terms. There are such countries, but balance of payments crises tend to push countries into rapid accumulation of short-term debt; so countries with debt service problems are also likely to be those which have recently and rapidly, without adequate opportunity for careful planning, acquired a great deal of short-term foreign debt. These problems arise whether short-term debt is acquired because of an adverse shift in the country's terms of trade, or because of the launching of questionable and inappropriately financed projects at a faster pace than the country can manage or afford, or because of some combination of the two.

There is a striking shortage of international, and sometimes even national, statistics on the currency composition of foreign debt and foreign debt service, implying a general lack of awareness of the problem. Private or multilateral facilities for avoidance or spreading of currency risk in external borrowing or for refinancing inappropriate currency mixtures of debt, have only just begun to appear.

THE MANAGEMENT OF EXCHANGE RISK IN DEVELOPING COUNTRIES

Instability and uncertainty in respect of exchange rates, both nominal and real, have increased significantly in the developing countries under the new international floating-rate regime. Increased instability and uncertainty as to the values of the major world currencies have created *new* risks, and therefore costs, which are the product of external forces entirely outside the control of developing countries' national economic policy-makers. These externally originating risks are *additional* to those major ones created by export commodity price fluctuations (the product of fluctuations in foreign demands and supplies), changes in import prices, technological change, shifts in the expectations or preferences of foreign private and public owners of capital, and uncontrollable influences over domestic export supplies. The latter remain overwhelmingly the most important sources of 'shock' and risk in the macro-economic management of the developing countries (see UNDP/UNCTAD, 1979). Increased foreign exchange risks are nevertheless, by themselves, potentially important influences upon welfare, allocative decisions and development. It is therefore important to consider the possible means for protection against them and/or their possibly deleterious effects.

If anything, governments and private decision-makers in developing countries, at lower levels of income and wealth, have reason to be more risk-averse than those in richer countries. It is ironic that they nevertheless have less adequate means of protecting themselves against risk. Already frequently buffeted by primary commodity price fluctuations, unstable weather and their domestic economic effects, they can also expect to encounter more difficulties than their counterparts in more fortunate countries in covering themselves against exchange risk in a world of turbulent exchange rates. This is not merely because of their disadvantages in respect of relevant information or predictive ability; these can, after all, at least in principle, frequently be purchased from specialists.

So far as private firms in developing countries are concerned, there may not be any forward market facilities available to them. By and large, the developing countries have still

> ...not yet been integrated in international forward markets: with . ... few exceptions (e.g. the Mexican peso] . . ., the currencies of these countries are only quoted and traded abroad on an ad hoc basis. There is but little interest in them, since they are rarely used in international payments. Moreover, in certain cases the major multinational banks tend to be sceptical regarding existing

> exchange rates and apprehensive that, owing to restrictions applied, they might be unable to cover their transactions (Gerakis and Danker, 1977: 29; also see Miller, 1975)

The IMF reported in 1973 that their needs

> may require development of forward market facilities that are now non-existent or rudimentary in many less developed countries, either through provision of new services by their own financial institutions or through improved access to forward market facilities in the main financial centres, or both (IMF, 1973: 32)

The provision of forward cover to private traders is also likely to serve the national interest, both by 'improving the signals' for private decision-making and by protecting the real value of the nation's foreign exchange earnings. Where international trade is undertaken by government-owned corporations, the latter factor is obviously the dominant one. Seven years later, forward facilities, while, 'appreciably improved', according to some (Gerakis and Danker, 1977: 1), were still inadequate in most developing countries. Where central banks have 'made markets' – more usually for exporters where they can sometimes provide hidden subsidies, than for private importers – they have themselves obviously been faced with new exchange risk problems in the management of their expanded portfolios. Where they have not, and where private market facilities are permitted, they have frequently been inhibited from developing by inadequate telecommunications, shortages of local expertise and remaining exchange controls.

At the end of 1979, of the 116 developing countries and territories for which the IMF annually reports information on exchange arrangements, only 25 were reported as having forward facilities (IMF, 1980). A few others, like Bahrain and Hong Kong, not specifically mentioned in this respect in this source, also had forward markets. These varied widely in institutional arrangements, maturities covered, types of transactions for which cover was permitted or provided, foreign currencies for which rates were quoted, bid-ask spreads, and the role of the monetary authorities. The most extensive official forward operations reported are probably those of the Reserve Bank of India which offered forward cover to 'authorized dealers' in four currencies (US dollar, pound sterling, Deutschmark, and Japanese yen) and Asian monetary units, for periods up to 12 months (six for Deutschmarks and yen); and, since mid-1974, 'in respect of specified capital and producer goods, for periods up to ten years from the date of conclusion of the export contract' (IMF, 1980:191). Coverage in the IMF

Report is not uniform and may well be incomplete; one study estimated that forward facilities were actually available in 1977 for as many as 40–45 developing countries (Gerakis and Danker, 1977: 30). But it appears safe to say that the majority of the developing countries, and particularly the smaller and poorer ones, do not have forward facilities of any description. Even those that do have them often have very limited coverage; and there is no information as to the extent of usage of these facilities in developing countries.

The particular problems encountered by the weaker developing countries' governments and central banks in covering themselves against substantially increased short- and medium-term exchange risk, and therefore in providing cover for their citizens, have not always been fully appreciated although most would recognize that exchange risk is more costly for some transactors than for others. Where there is a need to cover an exposed future (short-term) position in particular national currencies, there is generally the possibility of resort either to forward markets, or to the spot markets in foreign exchange, together with international borrowing and lending opportunities (financial hedging). This route is an easy one in the industrialized countries where the foreign exchange and security markets are most developed, and the foreign exchange controls least limiting. For a number of reasons, however, developing countries are in a relatively disadvantageous position in respect of operations in this market.

Bid–ask spreads, which are generally believed to have risen since the world moved to floating exchange rates (McKinnon, 1979: 21–2) and which rise further in times of particular turbulence (Gerakis and Danker, 1977: 21), vary with the customer and with the maturity. They are lowest, and the cost of forward cover is therefore the lowest, for customers who are the best credit risks (due to the lesser risk that the transactor will not be there at the date of maturity), whose transactions are the largest, who generate the most ancillary business, and who are the best informed about the market; according to the Group of Thirty's survey, international oil companies can get 'interbank spreads or even better' (Group of Thirty, 1980: 20). Similar generalizations can be made about the cost of acquiring insurance against foreign exchange risks through various bank-arranged insurance schemes. Thus, small private firms and small developing countries' governments, as those with the least creditworthiness, smallest transactions, least ancillary business prospects, and least information, are those likely to incur the highest charges for protecting themselves against foreign exchange risk.

In developing countries' trade with developed countries there are likely to be further costs because of the typically longer duration of the period between contract and delivery for which forward cover is required (see Carse *et al.*, 1980:89). Spreads rise markedly with the length of the forward contract, and forward markets thin out dramatically for maturities beyond those typically required for the finance of intra-OECD trade (usually six months). It is also likely that the 'offer risk' period – that between the offer and the contract, frequently more than three months in the experience of Federal Republic of Germany exporters (Gehrmann *et al.*, 1978:83) – is longer for developing countries; and for that there is generally no means of covering at all. There is evidence that, in recent years, the availability of forward cover for periods of over one year has been further reduced as some of the smaller London banks which specialized in this portion of the market have been unable to handle the increased risk (Group of Thirty, 1980:4). 'Longer dated forwards in some currencies are still obtainable for five and even ten years, but not easily and only in limited amounts' (Group of Thirty, 1980:35).

In short, financial markets have not provided the breadth or depth of forward facilities that their more enthusiastic supporters expected. Exporters in many industrialized countries (and a few less developed ones) can purchase long-term insurance against exchange risk from governmental export credit agencies; but such facilities are obviously not open to 'outsiders'.

As has been seen, crucial to the burden of exchange risk is the currency denomination of commercial and financial contracts. Generally contracts in North–South transactions are denominated in the currency of the relevant Northern transactor, with the result that exchange risk is pushed entirely upon the Southern party to the contract.

The unit of account in international trade *may* be arranged so as to achieve a fairer distribution of exchange risks by such devices as contractual provision for price changes in response to subsequent exchange rate changes, the splitting of the price into two (or more) separate currency components, the use of an agreed third vehicle currency (or, in earlier days, a 'gold-clause'), flexibility as to the date of payment, or the use of an artificial basket currency unit. In some cases, local traders are provided with transactions entirely in their own currency by foreign buying or selling agents who, in effect, for what may be a stiff price, manage their exchange risks for them. While data on the prevalence of these arrangements are imperfect, such devices do not so far seem to have been of great relative significance in developing country trade. Their prospects may be greater in cases of large, longer-term contracts – particularly those with an element of political content.

While there are some developing countries which are firmly within the dollar or franc monetary areas in the sense that most of their trade in both directions is denominated in one currency, for the majority of developing countries, export prices are fixed in terms of far fewer currencies (usually predominantly in US dollars) than are their import prices. The pricing of their exports in terms of some composite unit of account which better reflects the structure of their payments obligations, commercial as well as financial, would certainly ease their problems with increased exchange risk.

Similar innovations in international financial accounting could ease some of the problems of exchange risk in developing countries' debt and reserve management. For instance, the World Bank introduced an exchange risk pooling system to reduce what had been an arbitrary and capricious distribution of exchange risks among its borrowers (World Bank, 1979: 28–9). This had resulted from the fact that, although loans were denominated in US dollars and interest rates on these 'dollar' loans were uniform, borrowers actually received *currencies* in accordance with the chance circumstances of the Bank's recent borrowings and the decisions of its portfolio managers; servicing obligations were then incurred in the borrowed currencies, regardless of subsequent alterations in exchange rates, and the Bank also determined the order in which these currencies were to be repaid. The Bank thus not only passed all of the exchange risk on to its borrowers but also did so in a peculiarly erratic fashion. Particularly in the case of smaller countries, where a 'natural pooling' through large or repeated borrowings could not take place, the degree of one country's exposure in any one currency could be high. Indeed, where the Bank lent to development finance companies or agricultural credit institutions which themselves on-lent their funds, without accepting any exchange risk, the sub-borrowers could not even know in advance what currency their borrowing was going to be in; understandably, this made them unwilling to borrow through these channels. The Bank took steps in 1979 toward meeting the requirements of the latter sub-borrowers through a prior commitment that half of the funds would always be in US dollars, with the other half in yen, Deutschmarks or Swiss francs. During 1980 the Bank introduced a currency pooling system which, while not lowering overall risks, at least shares them equitably among the Bank's borrowers. The system involves providing the same basket of currencies to all of its clients.[9]

This current pooling arrangement does not *reduce* overall exchange risk for borrowers; it merely *spreads* more equitably among the borrowing countries that risk which flows from the Bank's own management practices and the course of international financial events. An obviously simpler means of spreading, and even reducing, risks for borrowers, and potentially reducing effective interest rates as well, would be the total conversion of the World Bank – both its borrowing and its lending – to an SDR basis. IMF accounts and lending are already denominated in SDRs. Virtually identical comments apply, *pari passu*, to the activities and possibilities of the regional development banks.

CONCLUSIONS AND POLICY IMPLICATIONS

The post-1973 exchange rate system of managed floating for the world's major currencies has been characterized by substantial increases in short-term exchange rate instability for the vast majority of countries and, in particular, for most developing countries. This new and, to some extent, unexpected turbulence in foreign exchange markets is manifest in measures of instability of both nominal and real effective exchange rates. While the 1973–79 period has been one of considerable international economic disorder in other respects, this increased exchange rate turbulence can safely be regarded as the product of the new exchange rate system. The demerits of the previous adjustable exchange rate peg system, particularly that of periodic crises fuelled by speculative capital flows taking advantage of the speculators' knowledge of a one-way option for rate adjustments, have evidently been replaced by the problem of exchange-rate turbulence, the product of the conversion of currency markets into just another set of asset markets on which private expectations and speculative enthusiasms establish short-term prices.

While the major currencies float, most developing countries are forced, by the character of their economies, to continue to peg their currencies in terms of some external standard – either a foreign currency or a basket of foreign currencies like the SDR. Increasingly, they have chosen to peg to baskets rather than to individual currencies, but there remain substantial numbers of dollar- and franc-pegging countries. Pegging to an external standard in the new exchange rate system implies continual changes in effective exchange rates, both nominal and real, which are purely the product of fluctuations among foreign currencies, and which are therefore unlikely to be correlated in any way with the needs of the local economy.

An overwhelming majority of developing countries have experienced increase in such externally caused effective exchange rate instability during the post-1973 period – some of substantial dimensions. Moreover, they would have experienced such increases regardless of their choice of peg.

Externally caused exchange rate fluctuations are by no means the most important of the external 'shocks' which generate problems for macro-economic management and development in developing countries. Nor has it even been possible to estimate with any precision the cost in terms of resource misallocation, the terms of commercial or financial exchange, overall welfare, or increased exchange rate fluctuations in the developing countries. (This deserves more detailed country- and industry-specific research.) It is nevertheless possible to say that the post-1973 exchange rate system has certainly not, as some observers have suggested, been without cost to the developing countries.

Apart from the domestic effects of increased exchange rate uncertainty, imperfections in international financial markets have always made it both more difficult and more costly for traders and financiers from developing countries to cover themselves against foreign exchange risk. There is a clear presumption that the increased foreign exchange risks under the post-1973 exchange rate regime have been passed disproportionately on to the developing countries.

For these reasons, there must be considerable unease over the functioning of the present international exchange rate regime. It has unfortunately not yet been possible to approach the objective of 'an exchange rate regime which, while flexible, is capable of promoting adequate stability' (Group of Twenty-four, 1979: III, 2b). Increased flexibility of exchange rates has been achieved; stability has not. Some reforms of the current exchange rate regime which would be in all countries' interests could be particularly beneficial to the developing countries. To the extent that the developing countries are disproportionate 'losers' from short-term exchange rate turbulence, they would be disproportionate 'gainers' from measures which achieve smoother changes in exchange rates and fewer disruptions and less disorderliness in foreign exchange markets. This is not the place for another exposition of the various proposals intended to achieve these ends (for example, short-term capital controls, crawling pegs, reference rates, and so forth) which have been in circulation for years. Renewed efforts, however, to address these issues more successfully do seem now to be called for. Also of both general interest and particular interest to developing countries would be measures to increase the depth and breadth of forward markets, a matter which has so far received remarkably little attention from the IMF or its individual members.

On some matters, the developing countries not only have an interest but also some independent capacity to implement reform. Particularly useful to the smallest and poorest developing countries, but also to the Third World as a whole, would be the increased use of basket currencies, notably the SDR, in commercial and financial contracts. It is noteworthy that another report to the Group of Twenty-four, on alternatives for monetary reform (Williamson, 1987), reached parallel conclusions.

While each individual country should be studied in detail there may be a number of instances in which particular developing countries could reduce the extent of externally caused effective exchange rate instability by altering their currency peg, usually to the SDR or some other basket of currencies. Fluctuations among the developing countries' own currencies would obviously be minimized if they all chose the same basket to which to peg, and, though not optimal for all countries, the SDR could be a convenient basis for such policies. The merits and demerits of joint developing country pegs to the SDR deserve more study.

In the meantime, it is clear that the developing countries, particularly the poorest of them, could benefit from increased research and technical assistance in several areas in which the post-1973 exchange rate system has generated new difficulties for them. Financial management capacity in many countries has not kept up with the increased complexity of foreign exchange markets, although the new communications technologies ought to make it possible for them at least to acquire more efficiently the relevant information for better management. The development of better information systems and suitable 'software' for better reserve and debt management in the developing countries should therefore be a matter for urgent attention. The functioning of forward markets and other means for covering foreign exchange risk, both at national and international levels, has not been carefully studied from the standpoint of the needs and possibilities of developing countries, either individually or as a group. Data on the currency composition of developing countries' assets and liabilities, and external trading arrangements, are still woefully lacking. In these areas, the IMF should be urged to expand its activities, and the central banks of the developing countries should consider, through their joint organizations, the possible advantages of collective research, information collection, and action.

NOTES

1. The overall empirical evidence is surveyed in Artus and Young, 1979: 681–4. One recent study of 16 advanced countries did, however, uncover some statistical evidence of a negative correlation between capital formation and exchange-rate volatility (Kenen, 1979: 41–2).
2. While changes in their asset preferences may generate exchange rate fluctuations, these companies' own intrafirm goods flows are unlikely themselves to react significantly to such fluctuations.
3. Detailed data on the currency composition of developing countries' trade are rarely available; such information as there is often either originates with developed country trading partners or is quite impressionistic.
4. In principle, there exists a set of national currency prices which could exactly offset the exchange risks perceived by 'the average' risk-averse trader in invoicing in terms of each of them (Rao and Magee, 1979: 64-5); in practice, however, prices are established via a variety of other influences, unrelated to exchange risk, and this equilibrium set is unlikely to be found.
5. Occasionally, however, as has been the case of the Federal Republic of Germany, the strong prospects of the importers' currency generated exporter preferences which coincided with importers' preferences for the use of their own currency (Gehrmann *et al.*, 1978:85).
6. While longer-run currency realignments cannot be blamed primarily or, many would say, at all upon the more flexible exchange rate regime, there is evidence that, in recent years, their particular direction, specifically the declining value of the US dollar, in which much developing country export trade is denominated, imposed transitory but nevertheless serious terms-of-trade losses upon many developing countries. Each of a sample of 11 developing countries in a recent study, in which prices in vehicle currencies are assumed to be independent of exchange rate changes, experienced terms-of-trade losses *because of exchange rate changes* between 1970 and 1979, with the deterioration concentrated in the 1971–74 and 1977–79 periods (Bautista and Riedel 1980). Some of these estimated losses may only be 'theoretical' in that they depend on fixed trade patterns. If trade flows were altered in response to the new structure of incentives, losses would obviously be lower; but trade patterns are usually fairly slow to alter, and probably this is especially so in less developed countries, in the face of longstanding customer relationships, long-term ties of ownership, uncertainty and limited information and/or scanning capacity. Although in some cases these estimated losses were quite large (in Thailand, Indonesia and Colombia the terms of trade were estimated as deteriorating by over 10 per cent because of exchange rate changes), they were nevertheless dwarfed by other influences upon the terms of trade.
7. For a more detailed exposition on exchange risks in financial markets, see Wihlborg, 1978.
8. There were also other factors tending to raise their reserve requirements, notably the requirements imposed by Eurobanks on their developing country borrowers and the increased instability of primary commodity and key developing country import prices.
9. The possibilities of differential interest rates and of changes in currency allocations were also considered (World Bank, 1979: 28–9).

REFERENCES

Artus, Jacques R., and John H. Young (1979), 'Fixed and Flexible Exchange Rates: A Renewal of the Debate', *IMF Staff Papers*, vol. 26, no. 4, December.

Basevi, G., Cecci, G. and Steinherr, A. (1980), 'Exchange Rate Changes and Their Effects on International Trade: Empirical Studies of the Italian Experience', *Review of Economic Conditions in Italy, Banco di Roma*, no. 1, February.

Bautista, R. (1980), 'Exchange Rate Adjustments and Export Performance under Generalized Floating: Comparative Analysis Among Developing Countries', mimeo.

Bautista, Romeo, M. and James Riedel (1980), 'Major Currency Realignments and the Terms of Trade in Developing Countries', mimeo, World Bank, May.

Behrman, Jere, R. (1976), *Foreign Trade Regimes and Economic Development: Chile*, New York: Columbia University Press for National Bureau of Economic Research.

Ben-Bassat, Avraham (1980), 'The Optimal Composition of Foreign Exchange Reserves', *Journal of International Economics*, vol. 10, no. 2, May, pp. 285–95.

Black, Stanley W. (1977), *Floating Exchange Rates and National Economic Policy*, New Haven and London: Yale University Press.

Branson, William H. and Louka T. Katseli-Papaefstratiou (1980), 'Income Instability, Terms of Trade, and the Choice of Exchange Rate Regime', *Journal of Development Economics*, vol. 7, no. 1, March.

Carse, Stephen, John Williamson and Geoffrey E. Wood (1980), *The Financing Procedures of British Foreign Trade*, Cambridge: Cambridge University Press.

Cline, William R. (1976), *International Monetary Reform and the Developing Countries*, Washington, DC: Brookings Institution.

Coes, Donald V., (1980), 'The Crawling Peg and Exchange Rate Uncertainty' in John F. Williamson (ed.), *Exchange Rate Rules The Theory, Performance and Prospects of the Crawling Peg*, London: Macmillan, pp. 113–36.

Diaz-Alejandro, Carlos F. (1976a), 'The Post 1971 International Financial System and the Less Developed Countries' in G.K. Helleiner (ed.), *A World Divided, The Less Developed Countries in the International Economy*, Cambridge: Cambridge University Press.

Diaz-Alejandro, Carlos F. (1976b), *Foreign Trade Regimes and Economic Development: Colombia*, New York: Columbia University Press, for National Bureau of Economic Research.

Dychter, Aron (1979), 'Flexible Exchange Rates and the Less Developed Countries' Direction of Trade', PhD dissertation, George Washington University.

Frank, Isaiah, Charles Pearson and James Riedel (1979), 'The Implications of Managed Floating Exchange Rates for U.S. Trade Policy', *Monograph Series in Finance and Economics*, New York: New York University, Graduate School of Business Administration, Salomon Brothers Center for the Study of Financial Institutions, Monograph 1979–1.

Frenkel, Jacob A. and Richard M. Levich (1977), 'Transactions Costs and Interest Arbitrage: Tranquil versus Turbulent Periods', *Journal of Political Economy*, no. 85, November–December, pp. 1209–26.

Frenkel, Jacob A. and Michael L. Mussa (1980), 'Efficiency of Foreign Exchange Markets and Measures of Turbulence', *American Economic Review*, vol. 70, no. 2, May, pp. 374–81.

Gehrmann, Dieter, Hans-Eckart Scharrer and Wolfgang Wetter (1978), 'Currency Risk Cover – An Enquiry among German Firms', *Intereconomics*, nos. 3–4, pp. 82–7.

Genberg, Hans (1978), 'Purchasing Power Parity under Fixed and Flexible Exchange Rates', *Journal of International Economics*, vol. 8, no. 2, May, pp. 247–76.

Gerakis, Andreas S. and Debora Danker (1977), 'Forward Markets: A Review of Theory, Practice and Recent Developments', International Monetary Fund, Departmental Memorandum, DM/77/11.

Goldstein, Morris (1980), 'Have Flexible Exchange Rates Made Macroeconomic Policy more Difficult?: A Survey of the Issues', International Monetary Fund, Departmental Memorandum, DM/80/9.

Greene, Benjamin B., Jr. (1980), 'Currency Blocs and the Direction of Trade', mimeo.

Group of Twenty-four (1979), *Outline for a Program of Action on International Monetary Reform* (Belgrade).

Group of Thirty (1980), *The Foreign Exchange Markets Under Floating Rates.*

Heller, H. Robert and Khan, Mohsin, S. (1978), 'The Demand for International Reserves Under Fixed and Floating Exchange Rates', *IMF Staff Papers*, vol. 25, no. 4, December, pp. 623–49.

Heller, H. Robert and Knight, Malcolm, (1978), 'Reserve-currency Preferences of Central Banks', *Essays in International Finance*, no. 131, Princeton University.

Hooper, Peter and Kohlhagen, Steven W. (1978), 'The Effect of Exchange Rate Uncertainty on the Prices and Volume of International Trade', *Journal of International Economics*, vol. 8, no. 4, November, pp. 438–512.

International Monetary Fund (1973), *Annual Report*, Washington, DC: IMF.

International Monetary Fund (1978), *Annual Report*, Washington, DC: IMF.

International Monetary Fund (1979), *Annual Report*, Washington, DC: IMF.

International Monetary Fund (1980), *Annual Report on Exchange Arrangements and Exchange Restrictions*, Washington, DC: IMF.

Isard, Peter (1977), 'How Far Can We Push the "Law of One Price"?', *American Economic Review*, vol. 67, December, pp. 942–8.

Kenen, Peter (1979), 'Exchange Rate Variability, Measurement and Implications', Research Memorandum, International Finance Section, Department of Economics, Princeton University, mimeo.

Kenen, Peter and Clare Pack (1980), *Exchange Rates, Domestic Prices, and the Adjustment Process*, Occasional Papers no. 1, New York: Group of Thirty.

Kravis, Irving B., and Robert E. Lipsey (1978), 'Price Behaviour in the Light of Balance of Payments Theories', *Journal of International Economics*, vol. 8, no. 2, May, pp. 193–246.

Krugman, Paul (1978), 'Purchasing Power Parity and Exchange Rates: Another Look at the Evidence', *Journal of International Economics*, no. 8, pp. 397–407.

Magee, Stephen P. and Rao, Ramesh K.S. (1980), 'Vehicle and Nonvehicle Currencies in International Trade", *American Economic Review*, vol. 70, no. 2, May, pp. 368–73.

McKinnon, Ronald, I. (1979), *Money in International Exchange, The Convertible Currency System*, New York and Oxford: Oxford University Press.

Miller, Richard H. (1975), 'Forward Exchange Facilities in Developing Countries', *Finance and Development*, vol. 12, no. 1, March, pp. 12–15.

Nowzad, Bahram (1978), 'A Note on Some Possible Implications of Sequential World Monetary and Trade Reform', *World Development*, vol. 4, nos. 10–11, October–November, pp. 919–27.

Rana, Pradumna Bickram (1979), 'The Impact of Generalized Floating on Trade Flows and Reserve Needs: Selected Asian Developing Countries', PhD dissertation, Vanderbilt University.

Rao, Ramesh, K.S. and Stephen P. Magee (1980), 'The Currency of Denomination of International Trade Contracts' in R.M. Levich and C.G. Wihlborg, (eds), *Exchange Risk and Exposure, Current Developments in International Financial Management*, Lexington.

Richardson, J. David, (1978), 'Some Empirical Evidence on Commodity Arbitrage and the Law of One Price', *Journal of International Economics*, vol. 8, no. 2, May, pp. 341–52.

UNDP/UNCTAD (1979), *The Balance of Payments Adjustment Process in Developing Countries: Report to the Group of Twenty-Four*, Geneva: UNDP/UNCTAD Project INT/75/015.

Van Nieuwkerk, Marius (1979), 'The Covering of Exchange Risks in the Netherlands' Foreign Trade', *Journal of International Economics*, vol. 9, no. 1, February, pp. 89–93.

Wihlborg, Clas (1978), 'Currency Risks in International Financial Markets', *Princeton Studies in International Finance*, no. 44, Princeton, NJ: Princeton University.

Williamson, John (1976), 'Generalized Floating and the Reserve Needs of Developing Countries' in Danny M. Leipziger (ed.), *The International Monetary System and the Developing Nations*, Washington DC: Bureau for Program and Policy Coordination, Agency for International Development, pp. 75–86.

Williamson, John (1979), 'World Stagflation and International Monetary Arrangements', mimeo.

Williamson, John (1987), 'International Monetary Reform: A Survey of the Options' in S. Dell (ed.), *The International Monetary System and its Reform, Part I*, Amsterdam: North-Holland, pp. 227–78.

World Bank (1979), *Annual Report*, Washington, DC.

6. Balance of Payments Experience and Growth Prospects of Developing Countries*

INTRODUCTION

Growth-oriented adjustment to balance of payments difficulties has acquired a long overdue respectability in international financial circles. After US Treasury Secretary James Baker's speech at the annual joint meetings of the IMF and World Bank in Seoul in October 1985, in which he highlighted the need for developing country debtor nations to grow out of their problems (and to receive increased external finance to assist in the process), 'traditional' demand-oriented approaches have been noticeably less emphasized. New prominence has been assigned to programme lending, geared to medium- and long-term developmental objectives by the World Bank. The Managing Director of the IMF, newly emphasizing the importance of the *form* that adjustment takes rather than merely 'adjustment' for its own sake, has proclaimed the Fund's interest not only in growth-oriented adjustment but also in the protection of vulnerable groups' basic human needs, or what has elsewhere been termed 'adjustment with a human face' (Jolly, 1985). Rhetoric still runs ahead of actual policy changes in these matters but these shifts in conventional and official 'wisdoms' concerning adjustment processes and policies in developing countries are nonetheless of profound potential longer-run significance. Had they materialized a little earlier, much underutilized productive capacity and suffering in developing countries might have been avoided. If they can be translated into improved external assistance – in the forms of both appropriate resource flows and better advice – they may be able significantly to ease remaining current adjustment problems and, perhaps

*This synthesis draws heavily on empirical analysis undertaken by Luiz Avila and Edmar Bacha. I am grateful to Eric Helleiner and Ruth Hussman for research assistance. I alone am responsible, however, for the content of this chapter.

even more important, help prevent the recurrence of needless waste and suffering in the future.

This chapter originated as a paper in late 1982 following Group of Twenty-four discussions of the likely longer-term implications of then current adjustment programmes and policies. It was evident, even then, to many developing country policy-makers that effects of the second (post-1979) severe external shock upon their fragile economies so soon after that of the 1973–75 oil price increase – cum-recession were likely to be severe, not only immediately but also in more fundamental and longer-term ways. Substantial longer-term structural changes – reduced import coefficients and increased export competitiveness – would obviously be necessary and were, to some degree, already being pursued; but they required both more time and more resources than were likely to be available. Without them the stricken developing countries would be driven to cutbacks not only in already meagre consumption levels (where, indeed, political circumstances made them possible at all) but also in the very investment programmes that were ultimately the sole route out of their balance of payments difficulties. Shortages of foreign exchange both constrained the utilization of existing productive (and social) capital to levels well below potential, and at the same time limited the potential for necessary productive investment in expanded exports and efficient import replacements. These foreign exchange constraint problems – peculiar to the relatively rigid productive systems of the developing countries – could not be addressed simply by further demand restraint. Yet at this time this was the essence of most external advice.

At this time also, the IMF was publishing research studies (for example, Donovan, 1982) that purported to demonstrate the efficacy of its programmes in developing countries. The international financial community continued to be mesmerized by the traditional dichotomy between 'temporary' balance of payments shocks – to be handled by demand restraint and short-term credit – and 'permanent' ones – to be handled via appropriate 'development', and therefore not the business of the IMF. The need for balance of payments financing in the context of more supply-oriented adjustment programmes was recognized, in principle, both by the IMF (with its extended facility) and the World Bank (with its structural adjustment loans); but neither adequately addressed the emerging needs. The short-term demand restraint approaches of the IMF remained the dominant wisdom of the day. The special responsibilities of the international community in circumstances where balance of payments difficulties are the product of external shocks rather than domestic mismanagement, emphasized by Dell and Lawrence (1980), and recognized, in principle, in the IMF's 'compensatory financing facility', were explicitly rejected in favour of primary, if not quite exclusive, reliance on the temporary-versus-permanent dichotomy.

Experience teaches. The developing countries' financial crises continued. Demand restraint failed to achieve, or even contribute to, the required longer-term adjustment. Further analysis (and experience) of IMF programmes generated what were, at best, ambiguous results (see, for example, Killick, 1984; Loxley, 1984); and from the IMF finally came advice not to employ simplistic approaches, such as its own staff previously employed in its defence, to assess country programmes (Goldstein and Montiel, 1986).

Growth-oriented adjustment, such as this Group of Twenty-four study recommended, is now widely advocated by both the Fund and the Bank. But that which Secretary Baker, and, to a substantial degree, the World Bank, have frequently touted as 'structural adjustment' and 'growth orientation' is unfortunately still not *exactly* what this study recommended. The longer-term perspectives recommended in this chapter concern the need for investment, external resources and time in a process of restructuring toward increased export competitiveness and efficient import substitution. Current Washington approaches have that much in common with the Group of Twenty-four study's conclusions (although the required expansion in external resources has not yet materialized). They part company with the G-24 study, however, when they build in further specific, essentially ideologically-based, approaches to the promotion of more rapid growth. There is typically neither professional nor political agreement on the appropriate degree of reliance upon the market, the role of government, the degree of openness to external trade or capital, and the like, in any particular developing country. The market orientation of current US government approaches to developing countries' problems is understandable in the context of domestic US perceptions and politics. However, US biases are unlikely to be shared in all independent developing countries, each of which has perceptions and political processes of its own. As multilateral institutions, the World Bank and the IMF must be sensitive to *all* of their members' views as they develop their approaches to growth-oriented adjustment. By so doing they are much more likely to achieve the balance of payments adjustment with growth that all now purport to be seeking than if they seek to 'push' controversial further policies upon reluctant borrowers.

While there has recently been significant progress in international understanding of adjustment processes in developing countries, much thus remains to be done. Substantially expanded resource flows to foreign exchange-constrained developing countries must still be realized if the desired adjustment with growth (where possible, with a 'human face') is to be achieved in these countries. The developing countries and the international financial institutions that lend to them should not succumb to pressures for the adoption of politically and professionally controversial development strategies as they adopt longer-term approaches to balance of payments adjustment. Last, recognition of the importance of longer-term perspectives for adjustment and of the international community's responsibilities in respect of externally induced shocks must be translated into permanent workable international arrangements so that the unfortunate waste and suffering of the 1980s will not recur in the 1990s and beyond.

THE CONTEXT OF EXTERNAL SHOCKS

During the past 15 years the developing countries have been buffeted by a series of severe external shocks – oil price increases, global price inflation, recessions, high interest rates and exchange rate instability, and, most recently, interruption of supplies of accustomed external finance. From 1979 onwards they were hit by the longest and most severe recession since the Second World War and then by unprecedented increases in interest rates, appreciation of the US dollar (in which most of their external debt is denominated), low prices for their export commodities (other than petroleum) and, from mid-1982 on, sharp reductions in the inflow of commercial capital.

An IMF staff study placed the experience of the early 1980s in a longer-term context:

> During 1981–82, commodity prices declined further (25 per cent) and for a longer period (8 quarters) than they have in the last three decades. In 1981, real commodity prices reached a postwar low; and in 1982, they declined a further 11 per cent, to a level of 16 per cent below the trough reached in the 1975 recession ...The sharp decline in commodity prices during 1981–82 is ... a culmination of a trend toward more unstable prices that began in the early 1970s. The long-term downward trend in real commodity prices from 1972 to 1982 has been more than twice the trend from 1957 to 1971. In addition, primary commodity prices during 1972–82 were more than three times as unstable as they were during 1957–71, while fluctuations in world economic

> activity, exchange rates, and interest rates were significantly more pronounced in 1972–82 than in 1957–71. (Chu and Morrison, 1984:126–7).

As a consequence, the economic growth of most developing countries has been interrupted, and per capita income in many of them has declined.

The impact of the post-1978 events can be gauged from country-level macro-economic data for a broad sample of developing countries available in standard international sources. Table 6.1 shows that low-income, lower-middle income, and middle-income oil-importing countries (World Bank classifications) suffered declines in import volume while GDP increased in many cases at a rate barely sufficient to keep pace with population

Table 6.1 Macro-economic indicators, 79 developing countries 1978 to 1981–82*

	Average Annual Percentage Change in		
Medians for the following groups of countries	Constant Price GDP	Constant Price Gross Capital Formation	Import Volume
Low-income (29)	+2.8	+3.9	–4.2 (20)
Lower middle-income (34)	+3.2	+3.0	–1.9(28)
Upper middle-income (15)	+4.5	+6.6	+1.4 (13)
Middle-income oil importers (34)	+3.2	+3.6	–2.2 (28)
Middle-income oil exporters (16)	+5.7	+6.8	+6.4 (14)

Source: Calculated as simple averages of annual change from 1978 to the latest year for which data were available: 1981 or 1982 in the case of GDP, 1979 to 1982 in the cases of capital formation and import volume.
World Bank (1983). IMF, *International Financial Statistics*, Annual, 1983.
*Number of countries for which there are data is shown in brackets.

growth. Gross capital formation fared a little better in the low-income countries, implying relatively worse experience for consumers, but otherwise grew at roughly the same low rates as GDP. These median data obviously conceal experiences that vary from country to country and over time within the period. They also understate the extent of the decline in macro-economic performance since, for some countries, the most recent available data were those of 1979 or 1980, and the situation thereafter took a marked turn for the worse. Nevertheless, they indicate the breadth of recent prolonged experience with stagnation in investment and import decline, both of which, whatever happens in the next few years, are bound to affect medium-term growth. First-quarter 1984 data indicate a continuing decline in the imports of non-oil developing countries, particularly those of the Western hemisphere.

Massive arrears on external payments, necessitating partial or total suspension of debt servicing and a host of *ad hoc* official and private rescheduling arrangements, have characterized their international financial relationships since 1982. The former net flow of resources from the industrialized to the developing countries has now been reversed, as interest payments on accumulated external debt exceed net new inflows of foreign capital. Emergency financing for a few large debtors, including continuing 'involuntary' lending by commercial banks, has postponed the realization of the current account surpluses (but, because interest must still be paid, usually not the trade surpluses) that would otherwise be implicit for these developing countries in current global conditions; there is nontheless heavy pressure from creditors to restore 'normal' arrangements as quickly as possible.

It would be misleading to attribute all of today's domestic stagnation, inflation and external imbalance within the developing countries to global influences. The developing countries themselves are also responsible for some of their balance of payments and macro-economic difficulties. The relative importance of external and domestic influences upon the macro-economic experience of developing countries in recent years obviously varies greatly from country to country; and it is equally obviously a matter of intense controversy. Mutual interaction and cumulative processes frequently render it difficult clearly to disentangle the separate impacts of these influences. There is no disagreement however, with the proposition that severe external shocks have imparted heavy blows to the balance of payments and growth, and created difficult problems of macro-economic management for all of the non-oil developing countries.

An IMF staff study finds that the single most important variable 'explaining' recent experience with current account imbalances in 32 non-oil developing countries in the 1973–80 period is the terms of trade (Khan and Knight, 1983:835). Foreign real interest rates and the rate of growth of industrial countries are also found to be significant influences upon the current accounts of the developing countries concerned. (Presumably these results would be strengthened by the use of later data.) But the same study also finds that variables representing domestic policy – in particular the real effective exchange rate and the government's fiscal position (revenues minus expenditures) relative to GDP – are of significance. The authors conclude that 'at least some portion of the current account effects of adverse international developments could be offset by a combination of a more flexible exchange rate policy and tighter demand management policies' (Khan and Knight, 1983:836–9). The feasibility and efficacy of such policies in the particular contexts of individual countries obviously vary and must be a matter for much more careful investigation.

While recovery from the most recent recession is under way, particularly in the USA and Japan, projections of global growth remain cautious, real interest rates remain high, the terms of trade in most developing countries have not recouped recent losses, and protectionist pressures continue to restrain growth in export volume. Moreover, in the 1990s, the world economy looks like being far more unstable and its performance more uncertain than in the 1950s and 1960s.

The research summarized in this paper was undertaken to shed light upon the medium-term implications for the developing countries and for the international financial system as a whole of the massive shocks imparted to the balance of payments of the majority of developing countries during the 1979-83 period. It was obviously not possible in the time, and with the resources available, to undertake a comprehensive examination of these issues. What was attempted instead was the application of a uniform research methodology to a relatively small number of developing countries. The intention was to summarize the macro-economic experience of selected developing countries since the early 1970s, with particular emphasis upon the 1979–82 period; to document the importance of external shocks and adjustment needs; to assess recent efforts at balance of payments adjustment; and to evaluate these countries' medium-term growth prospects in the context of alternative national and international scenarios.

The paper reports only that portion of the study that relied upon internationally available data rather than in-depth country-level analysis. As is always the case in such 'library' investigations, country coverage was determined purely by the accessibility of data.

It is well known that the economic data for sub-Saharan African countries are particularly weak; and it has therefore unfortunately been impossible to incorporate as thorough an empirical analysis as this area's macro-economic problems, on grounds of humanitarian concern alone, undoubtedly deserve. Such data as there are suggest that the external shocks imposed upon the typical African country, overwhelmingly the product of terms-of-trade deterioration, have been severe and that total external finance has not expanded in response to the crises of the 1970s and

1980s. The structural adjustment capacities of these countries are almost certainly more limited than those of other developing countries.

Per capita income has been falling drastically in low-income Africa in recent years. Investment programmes have been savagely slashed and the high rates of depreciation of buildings and physical machinery and equipment in African climatic conditions imply that the usable capital stock is, in many areas, actually declining. The consequential deterioration of medical, health and educational facilities probably implies a further deterioration of human resources, in addition to the obvious decline of the quality of life.

Short- to medium-term prospects for Africa are exceptionally bleak.

> Even under relatively optimistic assumptions about the speed and magnitude of the economic recovery in the OECD area, the prices of relatively few of the export commodities of African countries are expected to show increases in real terms. Altogether, the average price level in the 1980s is expected to remain about 15-20 per cent below that prevailing in the 1960s or the level obtained in the second half of the 1970s. (World Bank, 1983:3)

Imperfections of data must not lead the international community to neglect the grave circumstances in Africa.

ALTERNATIVE APPROACHES TO THE ANALYSIS OF EXTERNAL SHOCKS AND RESPONSES TO THEM

External shocks of the kinds described above – terms-of-trade deterioration, reduced demand for exports, international interest rate increases – reduce national income directly by reducing demand and/or the purchasing power of existing output. Even if total national output were to be sustained, painful cuts in income would have to be borne, distributed in ways which are the product of the nature of the shock, the characteristics of the economy, and governmental policy responses. In terms of the conventional macro-economic accounting variables, either real national consumption or real national savings (or both) must fall. Other things being equal, a reduction in national savings will reduce real investment and thereby cut future output (and real income) as well. Real investment can only be sustained if the national savings rate (that is, savings as a proportion of national income) rises or if increased resources can be obtained from the rest of the world. Similarly, real consumption can only be sustained if the savings rate declines or increased external resources are available. Sufficient external resources thus make it possible to keep both consumption and investment at pre-shock levels. If the shock is expected to be a temporary one, there is a strong case, recognized in IMF practices, for making finance available for that purpose, so that policy-makers will not be tempted needlessly to resort to 'measures destructive of national or international prosperity' (IMF, Articles of Agreement, I(e)).

External shocks that *permanently* alter the terms on which individual countries interact with the international economy require that 'adjustments' be made if previous projections as to levels of consumption, investment and income are to be realized in the medium to longer term. There is no internationally recognized presumption in this case that finance will be made available to ease the effects of such shocks, since, in the absence of sufficient adjustment, the new finance would have to be provided on a permanent basis. There is widespread intellectual support, and even some precedent in multilateral lending, however, for the provision of credit to ease the costs of necessary adjustments (Williamson, 1983).

External finance can thus be an important, even a crucially important, determinant of the impact that external shocks have upon national macroeconomic performance. On the other hand, interruption of the 'normal' flow of external finance can itself be another source of external shock to the national economy.

These direct effects of external shocks are those that typically occupy most analytical attention; but they are not the only possible effects. Output may fall below the economy's capacity to produce, in consequence of a dearth of essential inputs that, at least in the short run, can only be obtained via imports. Foreign exchange is required for the purpose of imports. A decline in its availability or in its purchasing power constrains import volume to lower levels. In relatively good times some countries may have some 'slack' in their import bills that can quickly be reduced or eliminated. But recently these have been the exception. Output may consequently drop below already realized levels even though there has been no decline in the immediate availability of labour, capital or domestic resources. For instance, a shortage of oil may force industrial output or the transport system to operate well below capacity. Such a foreign exchange constraint may also impede investment and growth in future capacity if key capital goods, such as machinery and equipment, cannot be domestically acquired.

In highly flexible economies with a relatively diversified productive structure, when real foreign exchange earnings fall short of the economy's requirements, increased saving can reduce unnecessary imports and free output for diversion into exports. Thus the maintenance of investment and growth in the face of external shocks can, in many instances, quickly be achieved through an increased savings rate. Where, however, imports are already virtually all essential inputs to output or investment and export goods are not readily substitutable in domestic consumption or domestic consumption goods readily saleable on external markets, variations in savings cannot translate automatically into the desired effects upon import volume. In these latter cases – more typical of developing countries – a 'foreign exchange constraint' on output and growth, rather than a savings constraint, exists.

In the medium to long term, foreign exchange-constrained economies can restructure themselves by developing new import-substituting activities and new export industries. Even in the shorter run they may be able to alter the composition of overall demand somewhat so as to lower import requirements – for example, by increasing labour-intensive and local material using investment (such as construction) relative to others, and more generally substituting less import-intensive expenditures for more import-intensive ones. Typically, aggregate consumption expenditures are less import-intensive than aggregate investment activities; cutbacks in investment programmes are therefore particularly effective in reducing the import bill. However, a considerable degree of short- to medium-term rigidity characterizes the economy of most developing countries; and there are limits to what can quickly be achieved through restructuring of supply or demand. Inability to finance required imports then translates into reduced output, and particularly reduced investment. The resulting loss in current and future national income is *additional* to that which directly results from the external shock. It can result from the fact that the foreign exchange-constrained economy is forced to operate below its actual capacity to produce (as determined by its available factors of production – capital, skill, resources, labour, and the like.) In many instances, only the output of some sectors is constrained in this way. The distribution of the burden of these output (and income) cuts depends upon the precise means by which import volume is constrained – through reductions in public or private demand, direct import controls and allocations of foreign exchange, or by other means. Investment cutbacks obviously have implications for future growth, and, potentially, for future sectoral imbalance. Investment instability also disrupts planning processes and imposes further growth costs.

Required short-term national adjustments to external shocks for which there is inadequate offsetting financing available can therefore be seen in terms of:

1. increased savings (reduced consumption) and reduced investment; and
2. increased exports out of the existing output and reduced imports.

In the terminology of the empirical analysis which follows these two categories of national response are described, respectively, as changes (contraction) in 'domestic spending' and changes (improvements) in 'trade ratios'. In most developing countries, the latter, more fundamental, type of adjustment is likely to require increased, as well as restructured, investment.

Several empirical analyses of recent external shocks and policy responses to them in developing countries are now available. Their methodologies are broadly similar. All basically seek to decompose both shocks and policy responses into their principal constituent elements (Balassa, 1980; World Bank, 1981; Balassa and McCarthy, 1984; Mitra, 1983, 1984; Naya, Kim and James, 1984). The impact of external shocks is typically estimated by comparing actual events with what would have happened in the absence of the shocks. Thus the negative effect of the shocks upon the current account of the balance of payments and their adverse impact reflected in a worsening of the terms of trade, reduced export demand (volume), and higher interest rates can all be estimated by reference to a counterfactual world in which these blows are assumed not to have occurred. The estimated deterioration in the current account (relative to the assumed counterfactual world) is then usually expressed as a percentage of actual GNP or GDP.

This is, of course, a rather crude accounting procedure that gives little idea of the complexity of interrelationships within an economy. To begin to establish the full effects of particular external shocks one would need a complete model of the economy in which all the relevant interrelationships were taken more fully into account. Among the effects of any such shocks would, of course, be changes in GNP (or GDP) itself. Some recent empirical investigations have attempted to proceed in this manner (Mitra, 1983, 1984), and they have generated interesting preliminary results. For the purposes of our investigation, Edmar Bacha (1986) developed a relatively simple demand-driven macro-economic model.

Calculations of this type may be made either for short or longer periods. Table 6.2, for instance, shows the ratio of external shocks (defined in this

Table 6.2 *Size of external shocks and the ratio of external shocks to GNP (average of 1974–82)*

Country	External Shocks† (US$ million)	Ratio of External Shocks to GNP (%)
Newly industrializing	–2,833.7	–24.8
Province of Taiwan	–2,360.4	–12.7
Hong Kong	–2,800.1	–26.7
Korea, Republic of	–3,668.2	–13.3
Singapore	–2,506.1	–46.3
South-East Asia*	–2,462.9	–14.9
Indonesia	7,740.9	23.6
Malaysia	696.9	6.4
Philippines	–2,531.8	–14.5
Thailand	–2,394.0	–15.2
South Asia	–1,885.2	–14.2
Burma	–50.8	–1.8
India	–3,808.7	–4.6
Pakistan	–3,152.9	–26.8
Sri Lanka	–528.5	–23.5

Source: Naya, Kim and James (1984), p. 4.
* Average for the Philippines and Thailand only.
†'Shock' here means a worsening of terms of trade and decline in growth of export volume below trend (see text).

case as terms-of-trade deterioration relative to 1971–73 *plus* decline in export volume growth below the previous growth trend) to GNP for 12 Asian countries over the entire 1974-82 period. It can be seen that the oil-exporting countries of Indonesia and Malaysia enjoyed favourable shocks over the period, whereas Singapore, Hong Kong, Pakistan, Sri Lanka and the province of Taiwan experienced severely adverse ones. Analyses carried out within the World Bank (Mitra, 1983) have also covered the 1963–78 period for 13 oil-importing semi-industrialized countries and the 1974–81 experience of 34 developing countries (Mitra, 1984).

More frequently, calculations of these shocks have been undertaken with reference to shorter periods. The impact of an external shock is, after all, registered virtually immediately upon a national economy. Policy response, both at the national and international level, must take place in the short run. Among the crucial analytical questions are those concerning the length of time that appropriate adjustment requires, the adequacy of external finance permitting it to be made, and the medium- to long-term implications of inadequate or inappropriate short-term adjustment. These issues are being debated vigorously in the industrialized world as well as in the developing countries (Calmfors, 1983). It seems sensible, therefore, to conduct empirical investigations relating to shorter periods, such as those of the traditional business cycle and specifically, in the present context, the two recent periods of global recession following major oil price increases – 1973–75 and 1979–82/83. Of particular concern in this study has been the impact of the severe shocks of the 1979–82 period – principally a complex of export volume, terms-of-trade, and interest rate effects.

On the face of it, measurement of governmental response should be more difficult and problematic. The appropriate governmental response to an external shock is much easier to assess with the wisdom of hindsight than it is at the time when policies must be constructed. Information upon which policy is based is always imperfect. Expectations as to the temporariness of the shock and the availability of external finance are both particularly crucial and particularly difficult to get right. Neither rich countries nor poor are spared the difficulties of forecasting the future in circumstances of extreme uncertainty. Needless to say, governments also vary in their responsiveness to various domestic interests; their capacity to analyse and implement various alternative economic policies; their rates of time preference (or preference for current consumption versus investment in the interest of future generations); their degree of risk aversion; and their ideological preference with respect to the degree of external dependence, the role of the market, and so on. It would therefore be foolhardy to attempt to 'judge' governmental performance on the basis of some universal scale. What can be done, however, is to measure changes objectively in certain economic characteristics, analyse the role that governmental policies may have played in generating or offsetting such changes, and assess their implications for the (still uncertain) future. This emphasis upon changes implies the use of a 'norm' or 'counterfactual', just as in the 'shock accounting' described above, in which the economic characteristics in question remain the same. This procedure, adopted in this study as in others, does not imply that the unchanged counterfactual world is necessarily a desirable or even a sustainable one. And it remains a far cry from complete modelling of policy responses and adjustment processes.

Policy response to shocks to the current account may take a variety of forms. Durable structural adjustment, restoring external balance and normal rates of growth of economic activity, involves export promotion or import substitution which together may be described, in Bacha's terminology, as improved 'trade ratios'. Success may be measured, respectively, by increased shares of world markets and by reduced import coefficients in domestic spending. (To the degree that export 'success' is achieved through domestic deflation or that it engenders overseas protectionist response it may not be altogether so durable. There may also be medium- and longer-term problems associated with short-term reductions in import coefficients. These measures are nonetheless likely to be good indicators of the progress toward required structural adjustment.)

Alternatively, it may be necessary to restore external balance by reductions in aggregate demand – by reducing rates of investment and/or consumption (whether private or public) and thus both current and future GNP. In that such 'belt-tightening' lowers capacity utilization and growth, it is presumably only resorted to as a short- to medium-term measure pending more fundamental readjustments. As has been seen, a third option, for some, is resort to external finance, which is obviously not available in unlimited quantities or without a price. Like the measurement of external shocks, measurement (decompositon) of policy responses may be undertaken for long or short periods.

SUMMARY ANALYSIS OF EXTERNAL SHOCKS AND POLICY RESPONSES IN DEVELOPING COUNTRIES IN THE 1979-82 PERIOD

In our investigations of the impact and implications of external shocks, particular attention was directed at the implications for growth of the resulting scarcity of foreign exchange. There is a long tradition in the economics literature of devoting special attention, in the context of developing countries that are relatively rigid in their demand and production structures in the short to medium term, to the need to import certain essentials without which some economic activities cannot take place. Where imports cannot be obtained because external savings are insufficient to finance them and (saved) domestic output cannot be translated into foreign exchange, current output may fall below the potential implicit in the existing stock of factors of production and other inputs. Moreover, owing to constrained investment activity, future growth may also fall.

These traditional considerations have resurfaced during the recent years of near-universal blows to foreign exchange availability.

Bacha's methodology for decomposing the effects of changes in the current account deficit explicitly allows for the possibility of underutilization of capacity due to foreign exchange scarcity. In those countries in which the data permit the full calibration of his model to domestic circumstances, all of the 'effects' of external events or domestic policies are therefore expressed in terms of potential output (GDP rather than GNP because of data limitations). When one applies Bacha's projection model, the possibility of a foreign exchange constraint assumes major importance. Indeed, as will be seen below, it is the availability of foreign exchange, as determined by export demand and net foreign financial inflows that 'drives' his projection results. But neither in the analysis of the impact of recent shocks, nor in that of policy responses that follows, is the possibility of drawing a distinction between a savings constraint and a foreign exchange constraint in any way crucial to the analysis.

In the methodology employed in this study, external shocks are categorized as terms-of-trade deterioration, interest rate shocks, and retardation of world trade growth. All are measured as percentages of actual or potential GDP and in US dollars. A further determinant of the current account position is the burden of accumulated debt – that is, the impact on the current account of the increase in external borrowing since the last accounting period – which is also expressed as a percentage of GDP. Domestic policy responses are divided into changes in 'domestic spending' and changes in 'trade ratios'. The former are made up of the consequences of reductions in gross investment and in aggregate consumption. The latter comprise those in the 'export ratio' (national export shares in world markets) and those in the 'import ratio' (import coefficient of domestic spending). Each of these measures of domestic policy response is expressed as a percentage of actual or potential GNP or GDP. Allowing for interaction terms and errors, the sum of the measures of external shock, other external variables and domestic policy response should add up to the actual change in the ratio of the current account deficit to GDP.

It has not been possible as yet to piece together all the necessary data to permit a full Bacha-style analysis of the impact of the 1979–83 external shocks on developing countries and the range of their policy responses. However, Table 6.3 presents illustrative summary data on the main elements of such analysis of three important developing countries within our sample, each with its own specific adjustment experiences: Brazil, the

Table 6.3 *Sources of current account change between 1978 and 1983 as percentage of potential GDP*

		Domestic Spending†			Trade Ratios‡				
	External Shock*	Gross Investment	Consumption	Total	Export Ratios§	Import Ratio#	Total	Other¶	Observed Deficit Increase
Brazil	5.60	–0.40	–0.99	–1.39	–2.25	–2.65	–4.90	1.02	–1.20
Korea, Republic of	4.96	–0.98	–3.79	–4.77	0.12	–0.84	–0.72	1.14	0.61
Philippines (1982)	2.65	NA	NA	–0.44	1.01	0.48	1.49	–0.39	3.31

* A positive sign denotes an adverse external shock, such as a terms of trade deterioration, an interest rate increase, or a deceleration of world trade. A negative sign denotes a favourable external shock.

† A positive sign denotes an expansion of domestic spending, which increases the deficit. A negative sign denotes a contraction of domestic spending, which reduces the deficit.

‡ A positive sign denotes a movement of the trade ratios which increases the deficit. A negative sign denotes that the trade ratios moved to reduce the deficit.

§ A positive sign denotes a reduction of the exports to world trade ratio. A negative sign denotes an increase of the export ratio.

A positive sign denotes an increase of the import content of domestic spending. A negative sign denotes a reduction of the import ratio.

¶ The difference between the observed deficit increase and other recorded items. A positive sign denotes an unfavourable movement of other external variables, such as a net accumulation of foreign indebtedness between the beginning and the end of the period. A negative sign denotes a favourable movement of other external variables.

Republic of Korea and the Philippines. Each has incurred significant external debts, and each ranks among the top five debtor developing countries which are not members of OPEC (along with Argentina and Mexico). Brazil and the Republic of Korea are generally categorized as semi-industrialized economies and the Philippines, with a per capita income of $820 (1982 dollars), is the largest non-oil-exporting country among those classified by the World Bank as ‘lower middle-income’ developing countries. Access to credit and considerable supply adaptability have probably made the adjustment experiences of these three countries somewhat ‘easier’ than they have been in the majority of developing countries, and certainly than in the poorer and less diversified ones. These data are not intended to be, in any sense, representative of a ‘typical’ situation in developing countries but rather to be illustrative of a range of actual experiences.

Between 1979 and 1983 external shocks were severe enough to raise the ratio of the current account deficit to capacity output (potential GDP) by several percentage points in all three countries. In Brazil this shock amounted to 5.6 per cent of potential GDP, most of it attributable to terms-of-trade deterioration. In the Republic of Korea the initial shock, also primarily the product of terms-of-trade deterioration, was considerably greater than the 4.96 per cent shown for 1983 since by then some of the effects of the initial blow had already been reversed. Brazil and the Republic of Korea both restructured their activities in appropriate directions in response to these shocks, Brazil achieving both penetration of export markets and a further reduction of import coefficients in domestic spending beyond the significant reductions previously realized from 1975–78. The Republic of Korea's export success, which had been dramatic earlier in the 1970s, was limited during this period; but it achieved some success in reducing import coefficients. In neither case, however, were these adjustments sufficient fully to compensate for the effects of the external shocks plus the growing impact upon payments obligations of the rising external debt. Both were therefore forced to cut output and investment. In the Republic of Korea, the effect of the contraction in output upon imports was very nearly as large as that of the external shock itself, whereas, in Brazil, relatively much less of the adjustment burden was borne by domestic recession. The fact that Brazil adjusted primarily through restructuring its trade whereas the Republic of Korea did so primarily through domestic recession has not been widely recognized. In the Philippines, where the calculated external shock was smaller than in the other two countries, there was actually a deterioration in export performance and increasing import intensity in domestic demand; at the same time aggregate output did not contract significantly either. Major macro-economic contraction took place in 1984 and overdue structural adjustments was necessary later.

A slightly modified version of Bacha's methodology was employed for as many countries as possible on the basis of data available from international sources. It differs from the preferred methodology in that actual GNP rather than potential GDP is employed as the 'norm' for all measurements.

Table 6.4 summarizes the results of this analysis of external shocks and domestic policy responses in 25 developing countries (21 in the 1978–81/82 period) during the 1970s and early 1980s. The data indicate the *changes* between the first year and the last year shown, not averages over the period with reference to a prior base period as in Table 6.4.

External shocks have been very severe indeed, with the impact on the current account deficit averaging between 8.5 and 10 per cent of GNP (medians of between 4.6 and 7.5 per cent) in the countries that were

Table 6.4 *The impact of shocks and domestic policy responses upon current account deficits as a percentage of current GNP, 1973–75, 1975–78 and 1978–81/82*

	Countries Experiencing External Shocks			Domestic Policy Responses in Countries Experiencing Adverse Shocks*							
				Improved Export Ratio		Improved Import Ratio		Gross Investment Contraction		Consumption Contraction	
	Favourable No.	Adverse No.	Av. % (median)	No.	Av. % (median)	No.	Av. % (median)	No.	Av. % (median)	No.	Av. % (median)
1973–75	4	21	8.5 (7.5)	11	–0.7 (–0.6)	12	–0.8 (–0.3)	6	0.5 (0.2)	13	–0.6 (–0.2)
1975–78	7	18	7.3 (4.95)	11	–1.2 (–0.6)	8	–1.2 (+0.2)	5	0.1 (0.4)	13	–1.9 (–0.4)
1978–81/82	7	14	9.95 (4.65)	12	–3.0 (–2.9)	8	–4.5 (–0.65)	9	–0.5 (–0.35)	4	+0.0 (+1.5)

* Negative sign indicates deficit-decreasing policy change. Positive sign indicates deficit-increasing policy change.

negatively affected by them. The shocks of the post-1978 years arrived at a time when the negative impact of the 1973–75 shock had been only slightly eased. 'Shock accounting' for the entire 1973–81/82 period would obviously show considerably larger numbers than those that break it into two separate periods, as this analysis does.

Of those in our sample, the number of countries suffering adverse external shocks in the 1978–81/82 period was slightly smaller than the number experiencing them earlier in the 1970s, and the median adverse shock as a percentage of GNP also fell (although the mean rose). In this analysis, Sri Lanka is recorded as having experienced the largest adverse shock in the 1979–82 period; in the earlier (1973-75) period of shock, however, this dubious distinction rests with Zambia.

An important finding, on which other studies have not reported, is that there was a significant change in the nature of policy responses among those countries that experienced adverse external shocks in the later period. In the 1973–75 period, slightly over half of the countries experiencing current account shocks responded by means of improved export ratios (11 of 21) or import ratios (12 of 21); the average impact of these 'successes' was relatively modest, however, when expressed as a percentage of GNP (0.6 and 0.3 per cent respectively). By 1978 the impact of the earlier shocks had eased a little, reducing the total number of adversely affected countries and the average negative impact upon them. Previous import replacement was reversed among the majority of those still having experienced an adverse external impact since 1973; that is, the import intensity of domestic spending increased in 10 of 18 countries, with, on average, consequential adverse effects on the current account. Improved export competitiveness was, however, retained.

The 1973–75 external shocks also produced effects on aggregate spending in the adversely affected countries. In 13 of these 21 countries, current account improvements were realised by reductions in aggregate consumption; on average, the resulting impact upon the current account was smaller than either the export competitiveness or the import replacement effects, but it was favourable. Contraction in investment was not frequently undertaken during this period. Only six out of 21 adversely affected countries achieved current account improvements in this way, and four of them were of miniscule dimensions (0.1 per cent of GNP or less). On average, continued investment expansion contributed to a further deterioration in the current account in these countries. Between 1975 and 1978 these countries, on average, tightened consumption a little, whereas investment expenditures continued roughly as before (with one less country recorded as having reduced its current account by investment contraction since 1973).

In the 1978–81/82 period, of the 14 countries experiencing adverse external shocks, nearly all (12) offset them to some degree by increasing export competitiveness; and the impact upon their current accounts, expressed as a percentage of GNP, was a multiple of that achieved by such improved export deepening in the previous period. The median improvement in the current account achieved via export ratios (that is, increased export competitiveness), was nearly five times as large in the post-1978 period as it was in the previous 'shock' years; this may, in part, reflect lags in the response capacities of productive processes to new policies and incentives. Further improvements in the current account were realized by reduced import ratios during this period. While the number of countries achieving success in this respect was smaller in the post-1978 period than it had been between 1973–75, it was still more than half of the adversely affected countries, and the average improvement was much greater in the later than it had been in the earlier period. Again, the significantly larger average improvements in the current account recorded as resulting from reduced import ratios during the second period of shock may be the product, in part, of delayed responses to import replacement policies of earlier years.

So far as measured aggregate spending effects are concerned, the experience of the 1978–81/82 period was quite different from that of the 1973–78 period. Whereas in the earlier period a majority of adversely affected countries improved their current accounts by cutting consumption expenditures and only a small number of countries reduced investment, the pattern this time was reversed. Only four of 14 affected countries offset the shocks by contracting consumption (as against 13 of 18 in 1973–78 and of 21 in 1973–5); on average, consumption expansion tended to increase the current account deficit. On the other hand, nine out of 14 affected countries responded, this time, by investment expenditure contraction. On average, affected countries reduced their current account deficit in the 1978–81/82 period by means of investment cuts by roughly the same share of GNP as they had done by consumption cuts in the 1973–75 period. In both periods, the impact of expenditure cuts, as measured in this analysis, was dwarfed by adjustments in export and import competing performance. Of the nine countries resorting to investment contraction in the later period, five had resorted to consumption contraction but not investment contraction during the 1973–75 period, which suggests that while it may be possible to cut some 'slack' from consumption, a limit is reached beyond which it may be easier to 'borrow from the future' by reducing investment instead. (One other country that cut back investment in the 1978–82 period – Zambia – had previously reduced both investment and consumption, and now, while cutting investment, expanded consumption again.)

In the interpretation of these tables it is important to recognize the stringent underlying requirements for decreasing the proportion that the current account deficit makes up of GNP. Assuming an import coefficient for fixed investment of 0.33, the achievement of 1 per cent (of GNP) improvement in the current account via investment contraction implies a 3 per cent reduction in gross investment's prior share of GNP; in larger and more closed economies like those of Brazil and India, where the import coefficient of domestic expenditure is more like 0.10, the same improvement via investment cuts implies a 10 per cent reduction in the ratio of gross investment to GNP. Since the import coefficient of consumption expenditure is typically lower than that for investment, the achievement of similar current account improvements via reductions in consumption would imply even larger contractions in the ratio of consumption to GNP (increases in the savings rate). (In the 25-country analysis reported here data limitations did not permit differentiation between investment and consumption import coefficients.) In the simpler analyses that do not express investment (or consumption) as a percentage of some fixed output value (in Bacha's methodology 'potential output'), the required absolute reductions in domestic spending will be somewhat understated by even these large numbers since output is itself likely to be falling.

This analysis relates only to a limited sample of developing countries for which data are readily available, and employs a highly aggregative methodology. It nevertheless makes it possible to draw the following conclusions:

1. A large number of developing countries have suffered two successive periods of very severe externally originating shocks to their balance of payments.
2. On average, while there are important exceptions, these countries have achieved considerable structural adjustment by increasing export ratios (competitiveness) and to a lesser extent, decreasing import ratios (import replacement); and their accomplishments in these respects have grown with time.
3. While, during the first period of external shock, most of these countries were able to maintain investment programmes, the majority have been forced, during the second such period, to curtail them, with obvious negative implications for future growth and welfare.

SUMMARY AND CONCLUSIONS

The severe external shocks of recent years reduced incomes and output and gave rise to foreign exchange shortages in the majority of developing countries. In addition to a deterioration in their terms of trade, a decline in their export volume and an increase in real interest rates on external debt there was a sharp decline in the flow of capital to many of these countries. Import volumes virtually everywhere were forced to contract, in some instances by remarkable proportions. These import cutbacks were associated with declines in the utilization of existing productive capacity and even sharper declines in investment, with the consequence that prospects for further growth were gravely impaired.

The developing countries affected undertook major adjustments in response to these external events. Any remaining 'slack' in the import bill was quickly chopped away. Import substitution was encouraged and exports were expanded, both stimulated by extensive restructuring of incentives achieved through exchange rate devaluation and other devices.

These restructuring efforts take time and they are continuing. Where they were insufficient to balance external accounts – that is, where imports still were larger in value than the economies' capacity to pay for them – output, expenditures and income had to be cut as well. The less the short-term adjustment capacity of the productive structure, the greater was the need for cutbacks in overall demand, investment, output and income.

In the majority of developing countries output remains below the level that larger foreign exchange earnings would almost immediately permit. More important for the longer run, foreign exchange shortfalls also continue to constrain investment and limit the growth of future capacity; if vigorous and sustained recovery in global economic conditions were to be achieved in the next few years the capacity of many developing countries to respond would therefore be limited. If, however, there were a long-term worsening in the developing countries' prospects for foreign exchange availability, the implications for output, income, employment and growth in these countries over the medium and longer term would depend fundamentally upon what restructuring investment is undertaken at present. Either way, there will be serious medium- to long-run consequences for developing countries from the current foreign exchange-constrained levels of investment.

Moreoever, conventional macro-economic accounting may seriously understate the degree to which recent austerity (cutbacks in investment and GDP) reduces future output, welfare and growth. While it is quite evident that cutbacks in investment programmes are bound to have future implications, it is not always realized that many current expenditures also affect, for better or for worse, the welfare of future generations. In particular, expenditures upon child welfare, health, nutrition, education and other social goods significantly influence the productivity of future generations. Cutbacks in such 'productive' social expenditures may be far more socially costly than cutbacks in many types of investment as it is conventionally defined. The future costs of such cutbacks are likely to be highest where living standards, particularly those of children, are already very low and where nutrition, health and productivity are peculiarly vulnerable to further cuts in income. In a prescient section of its 1979 *World Development Report* the World Bank warned, with special reference to sub-Saharan Africa, of the

> ...serious danger that economic stringency in the next few years will lead to cutbacks in human development programs, despite the importance of their contribution – often exceeding that of additional physical investment – to ... long-term development potential. (World Bank, 1979:83)

UNICEF has documented some of the effects of the global recession upon the welfare of children (UNICEF, 1983; Jolly and Cornia, 1984). An increased incidence of malnutrition, reduced birthweight and height-for-age, and higher mortality rates have been recorded in particularly severely affected areas. The evidence also ominously suggests that there may be a considerable time lag between initial economic shocks and the full eventual effect upon children's health and welfare; presumably, there may then be an even longer lag between the shock and the effects upon overall growth and welfare.

The need to service debt, rebuild a depreciated capital stock, and restore foreign exchange reserves, in the face of the global prospect as most now see it, implies not only *very* modest progress in output, income and employment but also continuing underutilization of capacity attributable to import constraints.

Despite considerable efforts at restructuring and restraint, underlying rigidities cannot so rapidly be overcome. The application of sheer macro-economic restraint for the purpose of achieving medium-term external balance objectives implies very high longer-term costs. By implication, the provision of finance to permit a longer period of structural adjustment is, in every case, likely to be highly productive.

The lessons are straightforward ones. Most of the developing countries have undertaken significant restructuring in order to improve export performance and substitute for imports. Efforts in this direction are continuing, but they take some time to produce their full effects. Even in the better-off and the more diversified of these countries,the extent to which such structural adjustment can be achieved within a relatively short time-span is limited. Virtually all oil-importing developing countries have therefore also been forced to contract aggregate demand (particularly investment demand) and output in order to attain short- to medium-term external balance. The costs of this contraction in terms of forgone output and future growth are significant. They will not be fully evident for some time to come and they will be manifest not only in lower physical capacity to produce but also, and more tragically, in unnecessarily stunted human potential.

Some part of these costs may have been inevitable as shocks of unprecedented size and duration came upon a world that was unprepared to deal with them. Offsetting or modifying credits were not at first available in sufficient volume to prevent them. But, now that several years have elapsed, the evidence of the high costs of inadequate credit is at hand. So the evidence of what determined efforts at domestic restructuring can accomplish, as well as the evidence of the limits to what can be accomplished within a short space of time even in relatively advanced economies. Moreover, there is now something of a consensus as to what changes in global conditions are more or less irreversible in the medium term. The terms of trade for oil-importing developing countries are not expected to regain previous peaks for some time, real interest rates are now expected to remain high, and the aggregate growth of the industrial countries is expected to remain modest. It is also expected that primary commodity markets, interest rates and exchange rates will remain considerably more unstable for the rest of the century than they were in the 1950s and 1960s.

The need for more adjustment finance, both immediately for those now being forced to curb demand for the sake of short-term balance of payments objectives, and to ease future balance of payments shocks, could scarcely be clearer.

The mere provision of increased external finance will obviously not prove productive if the time that it buys is not well employed. This analysis suggests that levels of external finance higher than are now in prospect *can*, on reasonable assumptions as to domestic economic management, generate much improved economic performance – but not that they necessarily will. The evidence of recent years suggests, however, that in the majority of cases appropriate adjustment has been taking place and that it will continue to occur. It would be foolish to exaggerate the importance of the relatively few cases of failure to adjust as plans are made for appropriate levels of short- to medium-term official finance for developing countries.

Balance in external payments over some particular time period has never been an end in itself. Rather, the requirement of external balance should be seen as constraining the possibilities with respect to more important ultimate objectives – national income and welfare, employment, growth and so on. Where possible, such current account imbalances as can be financed should be phased so as not to impair the attainment of the latter objectives. External finance should itself be made available and phased to respond to broad systemic needs and agreed overall objectives. It is false economy for overcautious creditors to restrict their finance so as to force debtor nations unduly to deflate and/or restrict outward payments. Such restraint may have severe adverse implications not only for the directly affected developing countries but also for the entire world economy. The very high returns demonstrated above from the provision of increased foreign exchange in some developing countries, particularly in Brazil which has the largest external debt of all, implies higher feedback effects upon overall growth in the world economy than those that earlier global models not incorporating this fact have suggested.

So-called 'adjustment', that restores external balance by abandoning ultimate objectives, is not so much adjustment as retrenchment. Nor is adjustment assisted by 'forced' and 'involuntary' private lending a desirable or sustainable mode of adjustment. It is the function of governments and of the multilateral financial institutions, by timely and selective injections of international credit, to promote the achievement of the ultimate welfare objectives and, where possible, to restore the voluntary and efficient working of global financial markets. There are many ways in which short- and medium-term official international finance can be expanded as required. At present, the most straightforward ways are probably the restructuring of international debt and an expansion of the lending activities of the IMF and the World Bank. Improved compensatory financing arrangements – expanded to allow for changes in import prices and interest rates, permanent or long-term shifts, and increased volumes of credit when needed – are an obvious joint objective for IMF and World Bank credit expansion. Precisely how these objectives can best be pursued must be for others to elaborate. This study has focused on establishing the need rather than on the best means of satisfying it.

REFERENCES

Bacha, Edmar L. (1986), 'Terms of Reference for the Country Studies', *World Development*, vol. 14, no. 8.

Balassa, Bela (1980), 'The Newly Industrializing Developing Countries after the Oil Crisis', *World Bank Staff Working Paper*, No. 437, Washington, DC: The World Bank, October.

Balassa, Bela and Desmond McCarthy (1984), 'Adjustment Policies in Developing Countries, 1979–82', *World Bank Staff Working Paper*, no. 675 Washington, DC: The World Bank, April.

Calmfors, Lars (ed.) (1983), *Long-Run Effects of Short-Run Stabilization Policy*, London: Macmillan.

Chu, Ke-Young and Thomas K. Morrison (1984), 'The 1981–82 Recession and Non-Oil Primary Commodity Prices', *International Monetary Fund Staff Papers*, vol. 31, no. 1, March.

Dell, Sidney and Roger Lawrence (1980), *The Balance of Payments Adjustment Process in Developing Countries*, New York: Pergamon Press.

Donovan, Donal J. (1982), 'Macroeconomic Performance and Adjustment Under Fund Supported Programs: The Experience of the Seventies', *IMF Staff Papers*, vol. 29, no. 2, June.

Goldstein, Morris, and Peter Montiel (1986), 'Evaluating Fund Stabilization

Programs with Multicountry Data: Some Methodological Pitfalls', *IMF Staff Papers*, vol. 33, no. 2, June.

Jolly, Richard (1985), 'Adjustment with a Human Face', Barbara Ward Lecture, Rome: Society for International Development, July.

Jolly, Richard and Giovanni Andrea Cornia (1984), 'The Impact of World Recession on Children', *World Development*, special issue, vol. 12, no. 3, March.

Khan, Mohsin, S. and Malcolm D. Knight (1983), 'Determinants of Current Account Balances of Non-Oil Developing Countries in the 1970s: An Empirical Analysis', *International Monetary Fund Staff Papers*, vol. 30, no. 4, December.

Killick, Tony (1984), *The Quest for Economic Stabilization: The IMF and the Third World*, London: Heinemann.

Loxley, John (1984), *The IMF and the Poorest Countries*, Ottawa: North–South Institute.

Mitra, Pradeep K. (1983), 'Accounting for Adjustment in Selected Semi-Industrial Countries', mimeo, Washington DC: The World Bank.

Mitra, Pradeep K. (1984), 'A Description of Adjustment to External Shocks: Country Groups', *World Bank Discussion Paper*, June.

Naya, Seiji, D.H. Kim and W. James (1984), 'External Shocks and Policy Response: The Asian Experience', *Asian Development Review*, vol. 2, no. 1.

UNICEF, 1983, *The Impact of World Recession on Children*, New York: Pergamon Press.

Williamson, John F. (ed.) (1983), *IMF Conditionality*, New York: Institute for International Economics: MIT Press.

World Bank (1979), *World Development Report, 1979*, Washington, DC: The World Bank.

World Bank (1981), *World Development Report, 1981*, Washington, DC: The World Bank.

World Bank (1983), *Sub-Saharan Africa: Progress Report on Development Prospects and Programs*, Report no. 4630, July.

NOTE

1. The countries are Argentina, Brazil, Chile, Colombia, Costa Rica, Dominican Republic, Egypt, India, Indonesia, Ivory Coast, Korea (Republic of), Mexico, Morocco, Pakistan, Peru, Philippines, Sri Lanka, Sudan, Tanzania, Thailand, Turkey, Uruguay, Venezuela, Zaire and Zambia. Inadequate data at the time of the study required the omission of Costa Rica, Ivory Coast, Morocco and Zaire from the analysis of the 1978–82 period. Data for some of the other countries covered the period only through 1981. For a full account see the Special Issue of World Development devoted entirely to this study: vol.14, no.8, 1986.

7. Growth-oriented Adjustment Lending: A Critical Assessment

INTRODUCTION

The 1980s have seen an aggressive new approach to the application of policy leverage on the part of external sources of finance for developing countries. Over the broad sweep of history, policy conditionality has rarely been absent from relations between sources of finance and its recipients. Conditions have related to commercial considerations (the need for credit to be repaid), foreign policy, and aspects of domestic economic policy, particularly those deemed relevant to the international interest. Those typically imposing conditions of these various types in post-Second World War experience were, respectively, foreign investors and banks, bilateral aid donors, and the international financial institutions (IFIs – the IMF and the World Bank).

Conditionality is *not* now argued primarily on the basis of the need for ensured repayment. The lead institution in these debates today is frequently the World Bank which does not require its money back for some time; and grant-dispensing aid donors are as active in the clamour for conditions as are any lending institutions. The new international emphasis upon broad policy-based conditionality on development assistance in the 1980s evidently stems from the (external) view that domestic adjustment and development policies in the recipient countries have been seriously at fault and that governments require either external advice or pressure, or both, before they will set their own houses in order.

This 'new conditionality' is intended to move beyond the traditional IMF type by addressing the need for 'growth-oriented adjustment'. Previous IMF-based approaches to policy-based lending aimed merely at restoring short-term macro-economic balance, primarily via demand restriction because little else could be done in the short-term. The costs of pursuing too short-term an approach to adjustment in Latin America, sub-Saharan Africa, and elsewhere have been severe. The forced adjustment necessitated by short-term balance of payments arithmetic and the concomitant 'import strangulation' have not only rendered the investment required for recovery impossible but also damaged the limited and painfully accumulated existing capital stock. Worse still, it resulted in unnecessary output losses in consequence of underutilization of partially import-dependent productive capacity, and, of course, unnecessarily severe and extended human suffering.

The highest returns in import-strangled economies today are typically reaped from the provision of increased inputs for the rehabilitation and full utilization of existing capital stock rather than from the creation of new capital. Increased supplies of 'free' foreign exchange in situations of foreign exchange constraint can in fact yield extraordinarily high returns. (They could also, of course, in some circumstances, simply finance increased rents for those controlling mismanaged economies and/or increased capital outflow.) At the same time they can render many more potential investments remunerative. Growth-oriented adjustment requires investment for the restructuring of production towards tradable goods and services. There are obviously also continuing needs for the expansion of social infrastructure and the directly productive capital stock for steady longer-run development. There can be neither private nor public incentives for such investments in the absence of assurances of adequate provision of inputs for their effective operation.

Over-tight austerity programmes and continuing import strangulation thus have both reduced the efficiency of utilization of those limited public and private resources there are, and throttled incentives to invest. It is a matter of the highest priority therefore to take a broader and longer-term approach than the IMF has traditionally been able to do.

The extreme difficulties of so many developing countries in the 1980s have left them more desperate for external finance, and have emboldened the IFIs to tighten their demands of those to whom they lend. Spokesmen for the IFIs tend to attribute 'the new conditionality' to the *increased* need for policy reform in the developing countries. Those in the developing countries most directly responsible for development-oriented policies in a harsh international economic environment may be forgiven for seeing it as reflective, rather, of:

(a) an altered international development ideology in some of the major industrialized countries, notably the US and
(b) the opportunity, created by their own desperate conditions, for determined outsiders to extract concessions from unconvinced policy-makers who remained unpersuaded by mere rational argument.

Whatever the causes, there have been major changes in IMF and World Bank behaviour in recent years. During the 1970s, particularly after the first oil shock, the IMF provided substantial amounts of low-conditionality finance to developing countries. At this time, the bulk of the World Bank's finance was for development projects; its conditions typically related to the effective and remunerative functioning of the projects it financed. In the 1980s, virtually all of the IMF's finance has become highly conditional, and increasing proportions of World Bank lending are for 'adjustment' purposes – either via its 'structural adjustment' or its 'sector adjustment' loans – involving a far wider and deeper range of policy conditions (see Table 7.1).

The distinction between World Bank structural adjustment (SAL) and sector adjustment (SECAL) loans is not always clear. Both seek major reforms in policies and institutions, with the latter typically, but not always,

Table 7.1 World Bank adjustment lending, fiscal years (FY) 1979–87

	FY79	FY80	FY81	FY82	FY83	FY84	FY85	FY86	FY87	FY79–87
Structural Adjustment										
Number	–	3	6	6	7	6	3	7	13	51
US$ (Millions)	–	305	717	1071	1285	1082	163	610	665	5897
% Total lending	–	2.7	5.8	8.2	8.9	7.0	1.1	3.7	3.8	4.7
Sector adjustment										
Number	1	1	3	–	8	8	13	18	18	70
US$ (Millions)	31	65	137	–	641	1318	1475	2283	3452	9403
% Total lending	0.3	0.6	1.1	–	4.4	8.5	10.3	14.0	19.5	7.5
All adjustment										
Number	1	4	9	6	15	14	16	25	31	121
US$ (Millions)	31	370	854	107	1926	2400	1638	2893	4118	15300
% Total lending	0.3	3.2	6.9	8.2	13.3	15.5	11.4	17.7	23.3	12.2

Source: 'Lending for Adjustment: An Update' *World Bank News*, Special Report, April 1988

more narrowly focused upon specific sectors. Issue coverage in sector adjustment lending has been extremely broad in some instances – for example, reconstruction in Ghana and Guinea-Bissau, or trade policy in Colombia and Morocco – but it is usually related to more narrowly defined areas, such as export development, agriculture, industry, energy, fertilizer or public enterprises. Policy reforms required under the conditions of sector loans typically relate to liberalization, rationalized pricing and other purportedly efficiency-raising measures.

Sector adjustment loans are generally seen as both less complex and less intrusive than structural adjustment loans. A comprehensive structural adjustment loan may simply be too complicated to negotiate in a country like Brazil whereas it is quite feasible for Ghana and Niger. It is also possible that the degree of intrusion in domestic policies implied by a structural adjustment loan is today politically intolerable for larger and more powerful countries, particularly those with major debt 'leverage'. It is noteworthy that, whereas there have been few structural adjustment loans in major Latin American countries, there have been large sector adjustment loans to Brazil, Colombia, and Mexico, among others. The Bank has thus been quite pragmatic and flexible in its utilization of these alternative lending instruments in its various member countries.

Other, even larger, 'sector operations' have included 'sector investment and maintenance' loans, and loans to local financial intermediaries. Non-project loans also are available for technical assistance and for emergency reconstruction after disasters. Non-project and programme finance has thus constituted a major and rising proportion of overall World Bank lending activity.

Table 7.2 *World Bank adjustment loan recipients (classified by number of adjustment loans received, 1979–1987)*

One Loan	Two Loans	Three Loans	Four+ Loans
Bangladesh	Argentina	Bolivia	Ghana (6)
Burundi	Chile	Brazil	Jamaica (8)
Burkina	Colombia	Cote d'Ivoire	Malawi (4)
C.A.R.	Costa Rica	Kenya	Morocco (5)
Dominica	Guinea Bissau	Korea	Pakistan (4)
Ecuador	Mexico	Madagascar	Philippines (4)
Gambia	Niger	Mauritania	Turkey (8)
Guinea	Nigeria	Mauritius	Zambia (4)
Guyana	Panama	Senegal	
Hungary	Sudan		
Indonesia	Tanzania		
Nepal	Thailand		
Sao Tome	Tunisia		
Sierre Leone	Togo		
Somalia	Uruguay		
Uganda	Yugoslavia		
Zimbabwe	Zaire		

Source: 'Lending for Adjustment: An Update, *World Bank News*, Special Report, April 1988

In the post-Baker Plan period (after October 1985), with ever-increasing IFI emphasis upon 'growth-oriented adjustment' and its own growing use of policy-based lending, the World Bank acquired much greater prominence in IFI overall policy leverage in developing countries. It offered adjustment loans to over 50 countries in the 1980s (see Table 7.2). While the IMF still exercises its traditional demand-side and monetary responsibilities in respect of short-term macro-economic management in its member countries, even IMF activities are increasingly directed at increasing growth – not least via increased cooperation with the World Bank – in developing more growth-oriented policy frameworks and conditioning.

Growth-oriented conditionality involves a much greater degree of intrusion into matters of domestic economic policy and development strategy than traditional IMF-style demand-side conditions ever did. Thus, the focus for developing country concern about external policy leverage has perceptibly shifted from the IMF (with which there are still struggles) to the World Bank. Where the IMF and World Bank jointly develop policy framework papers for recipients of the IMF's SAF or ESAF (structural adjustment facility and 'enhanced' SAF for low-income countries) loans, one cannot easily distinguish World Bank from IMF influences; nor should one bother to try. The essential point is that the institution with prime responsibilities for development policy guidance has always been, and remains, the World Bank.

The World Bank's views as to desirable development objectives and policies have varied over time – for instance, as between the McNamara and the Clausen Bank. The Bank has always carried significant influence in policy-making circles, not only from the power of its research and rhetoric but also from the character of the projects it financed. In recent years it has sought even greater influence in overall policy matters, but has unfortunately often exerted this influence in politically and technically controversial directions. Yet, by no means all of the Bank's new policy pressure is equally controversial. What it has to say about short-term macro-economic management is generally consistent with the IMF's approach and, while debatable in many of its particulars, is at least familiar and geared toward the achievement of external balance via demand restriction and, eventually, supply-side restructuring towards tradable goods production. When it comes to overall growth- and development-oriented policies of a longer-term nature, however, the debate becomes much more intense and difficult.

POLICIES FOR MEDIUM-TERM ADJUSTMENT AND DEVELOPMENT: HOW MUCH IS TECHNICALLY AGREED?

What are the key elements of a sound macro-economic framework for structural adjustment and development? There can be general agreement on the desirability of achieving and maintaining an appropriate real exchange rate, appropriate incentive structures more generally, adequate rates of domestic savings and productive investment, and responsible fiscal and monetary policies. It is not typically as easy, however, to achieve agreement as to how one can best move from disequilibrium situations to those of greater internal and external balance and, therefore, on the precise meaning at any one time of 'appropriate', 'adequate' and 'responsible' policies.

The economics profession is much more comfortable with the analysis of alternative equilibrium or steady states than it is with that of transitions between them. The dynamics of change, within which market imbalances and alterations of behaviour are of the essence, are extremely difficult to model. There is, in fact, no agreed methodological framework for the analysis of the medium-term macro-economic adjustment process which is now the prime object of policy (Yagci *et al.* 1985). Nor is there an agreed approach or even much understanding of the complex interactions between financial and real variables in different kinds of countries – particularly not in the current confused circumstances of rampant inflation, debt crisis and capital flight. In short, while they know, and agree on, the sort of macro-economic conditions at which they would like to arrive – sustainable external balance with reasonably stable prices and growth – macro- and development economists have no agreed route for getting there.

At least as important to the longer-run restoration of external (and internal) balance is the ongoing process of economic growth and development. Those countries that have pursued less-than-perfect development policies (and presumably all have some room for improvement) may be able to 'tighten up' under the current pressure. Improvements in allocative efficiency and x-efficiency, utilization of previously underutilized resources, and encouragements to longer-run savings and productive investment may all increase medium- and longer-term growth. Many governments have acted forcefully in these areas in recent years. Unless there are reasons for believing that previous political and other constraints on policy have been eased, however, there may not be room for much manoeuvre in these respects.

Beyond these generalities concerning the requirements for structural adjustment and more rapid growth, matters become considerably more controversial. While there can still be widespread agreement on the need for greater selectivity and care in public investment, and greater efficiency and consistency in economic management in general, there are major debates about strategy and tactics in particular country cases. More fundamentally, there is both political and professional disagreement regarding such matters as the appropriate overall role of the state, the scope for private enterprise, the degree of 'outward orientation' and the distribution of income, both in general and in particular countries. The heart of the problem lies in the fact that the quasi-technical (but still difficult enough) issues relating to medium-term balance of payments adjustment frequently, and perhaps inevitably, overlap, in the Bank's policy-based programme lending, with much more controversial and highly political issues of development strategy.

The analytical framework for IMF analysis of short-term balance of payments analysis may not be beyond dispute, but it is clear and it is understood by all. Similarly, the analytical underpinnings of World Bank (and others') approaches to project analysis are straightforward. The appropriate analytical framework for structural adjustment lending, whether at the economy-wide or the sectoral level, however, remains unclear. World Bank and other approaches to structural adjustment therefore have both the advantages and the uncertainties of flexibility. On the one hand, this flexibility eases the desirable practice of intercountry differentiation of approach (a matter with which the IMF has had some difficulty) but, on the other hand, it leaves borrowers vulnerable to passing fashions and/or subjective interpretations of what development is all about, matters with which the World Bank management and staff continue to wrestle.

Despite these complexities, the World Bank possesses a fairly consistent approach to policy-based lending. Like the IMF it stresses monetary and fiscal orthodoxy, appropriate real exchange rates, positive real interest rates and liberal approaches on external account. So far as longer-term development strategy is concerned, the Bank urges: export expansion and overall outward orientation as against import-substitution; the liberalization of import barriers and an approach toward unified import incentives; and maximum reliance upon markets rather than government ownership or direction in the domestic economy. Its prime emphasis is on price incentives and 'getting the prices right', and its obvious presumption is that, even in a world of pervasive imperfections, markets can normally be trusted to achieve that objective better than governments. Even in the world of the second-best, its approach is consistently to liberalize that which can be liberalized.

The Bank has stated its own view of its primary emphasis much more generally, as follows:

1. mobilization of domestic resources through fiscal, monetary and credit policies (particularly on interest rates);
2. improving efficiency of allocation and resource use in the public sector (including rationalization and divestiture of public enterprises);
3. trade regime reforms;
4. other pricing reforms;
5. 'institutional reforms supportive of adjustment with growth' (Michalopolous, 1987: 39)

Table 7.3 indicates the prevalence of some of the most frequent conditions on Bank SALs in the first half of the 1980s.

Just as the IMF has been criticized for the oversimplicity and inflexibility of its short-term models and approaches, the Bank now attracts criticism for the generalized character of its recommended development policies. Certainly, its general approaches can only be defended if they are flexibly applied; as universal rules they are neither economically defensible nor politically acceptable.

In the circumstances of the contemporary debt-distressed Third World, disagreements over longer-run strategy should, and frequently can, be at least partially set aside in the interest of agreed needs for medium-term rehabilitation and recovery. For the present, there is widespread agreement on the need for restructuring production toward efficient exporting and import-substituting activities, and, in the most difficult cases, the restoration of credible and effective government. There is also sometimes widespread agreement on the typical main elements of previous supply-side policy error, for example, in Africa – on the relative neglect of agriculture, over-ambitious aspirations for the role of the state in the productive sector, inappropriate or ineffective pricing policies, the neglect of maintenance and recurrent costs relative to the further expansion of capital stock, and inappropriate technology in all sectors. (Stanley Please has accurately noted that the common elements in ECA and World Bank approaches to Africa's economic future far outweigh differences,(1984: 91–3).

The degree and timing of required and/or politically possible policy changes are much more controversial than their appropriate directions. Not

Table 7.3 Types of policy measure requested in return for SAL finance, 1980–October 1986

Measure	Percentage of SALs Subject to Conditions in This Area
Trade policy:	
Remove import quotas	57
Cut tariffs	24
Improve export incentives and institutional support	76
Resource mobilization:	
Reform budget or taxes	70
Reform interest rate policy	49
Strengthen management of external borrowing	49
Improve financial performance by public enterprise	73
Efficient use of resources:	
Revise priorities of public investment programme	59
Revise agricultural prices	73
Dissolve or reduce powers of state marketing boards	14
Reduce or eliminate some agricultural input subsidies	27
Revise energy prices	49
Introduce energy conservation measures	35
Develop indigenous energy sources	24
Revise industry incentive system	68
Institutional reforms:	
Strengthen capacity to formulate and implement public investment programme	86
Increase efficiency of public enterprises	57
Improve support for agriculture (marketing etc.)	57
Improve support for industry and subsectors (including price controls)	49

Source: Paul Moseley, 'Conditionality as Bargaining Process: Structural-Adjustment Lending, 1980–86', *Essays in International Finance, Princeton University*, no. 168, October, 1987, p. 5.

only is there frequent political disagreement as to where exactly one wants an economy to end up in terms of economic and political structure; but there is also professional disagreement as to the efficacy of different speeds of adjustment and the deployment of particular policy instruments. It is misleading to depict, as some do, conflict over the character of stabilization and adjustment programmes in terms purely of divergent interests. In any particular country the precise dimensions and sequencing of required policy changes and external resource infusions are unlikely to be matters of total agreement even among professionals who agree as to the broad direction of required change.

Donor-recipient debates over the details of adjustment programmes that, whatever their detail, can clearly move countries toward agreed medium-term objectives will unnecessarily slow progress and sow pointless resentment. Confusion between the needs for medium-term balance of payments adjustment, on which there can be relatively easy agreement, and appropriate longer-run development strategy, on which debate will rage, risks aborting recovery. Particularly controversial and subject to debate are the efficacy of such policies as the following:

1. massive devaluation and/or floating of the exchange rate;
2. sharp increasing of nominal interest rates, and domestic financial liberalization;
3. import liberalization;
4. generalized expansion of exports;
5. openness to external private capital;
6. policies relating to income distribution, and/or the poorest and most vulnerable;
7. increasing the role of markets and prices relative to that of government.

KEY CONTROVERSIAL ISSUES

Exchange Rates

Real exchange rate devaluation has obviously been necessary in the typical problem country. But a sustained change in the real effective exchange rate is not so easy to attain. Nor is it sufficient for this purpose simply to preach concomitant fiscal and monetary restraint. A serious approach can only be based upon a sophisticated appreciation of the functioning of local labour, financial and product markets, the nature of the fiscal system, and the relative importance of various political and economic interests. A massive once-for-all nominal devaluation – typically preferred both by the IMF and the World Bank – may not always be the most cost-effective means of reaching a desired and sustainable level for the real exchange rate, even assuming that such a level was agreed. Nor are floating rates or auction systems necessarily the optimal means of sustaining appropriate real exchange rates. An eclectic, flexible and, to a degree, even experimental approach to exchange rate management seems more appropriate than overly rigid adherence to norms that are themselves unproven in their cost-effectiveness.

Financial Liberalization and Interest Rates

The role of interest rates in developing countries remains somewhat uncertain. Increased (preferably positive) real rates may improve the allocative efficiency of investment, reduce capital flight, and even attract savings from abroad in economies with relatively developed financial markets. The IMF's own research department concludes, however, that "Despite the amount of research expended on the interest responsiveness of savings in general, and in developing countries in particular, it is still uncertain whether an increase in interest rates will, on balance, raise the savings rate" (Khan and Knight, 1985:14).

Differences in behavioural responses in this sphere appear to be linked in a predictable fashion to the stage of (financial) development of different areas or countries. Because of capital market imperfections (severe constraints on liquidity and borrowing by private firms and individuals), private consumption and savings do not respond as much to real interest rate changes in low-income countries as in higher-income ones. A recent IMF study's results imply that 'the effective mobilization of domestic savings through changes in savings incentives is likely to require changes in the real interest rates, which, given the existing constraints, may prove unfeasible, especially in low-income developing countries' (Rossi, 1988:126).

There also remains some uncertainty as to the implications of segmented and imperfect capital markets. Conventional analysis has often assumed away the extensive network of informal (or curb) credit markets. Yet, in careful modelling of real/financial interactions in Korea, allowing for the distinction between 'curb' and regulated financial markets there, there are 'unconventional' results from orthodox monetary and interest rate policies: higher (regulated) interest rates and monetary restraint lead, in combination, to a serious slowdown in investment and growth, the effects of which exceed any positive effects for household savings (Van Wijnbergen, 1983).

Nor are the advantages of financial liberalization for overcoming 'financial repression' unambiguously favourable. Painful experience with over-enthusiastic financial liberalization in the Southern Cone has bred a new respect for governmental supervision and control of the domestic financial system, and caution in respect of external capital market 'opening'. (Diaz-Alejandro, 1985)

Import Liberalization

Trade policy reforms have been the most frequently supported of Bank structural adjustment policies. Few economists would quarrel with the aspiration to remove or reduce import controls wherever possible. Although often performing an important role in short-term balance of payments management, they tend to introduce inefficiency and corrupt practices when they are long maintained. The timing of their removal and/or rationalization must be determined, however, in the overall context of the economy's circumstances. With foreign exchange constraints today so crippling, it may be more productive in many countries to assist in streamlining and increasing the efficiency of foreign exchange management systems (however faulty they may remain) than simply to promote decontrol. Until reliable and sustained sources of foreign exchange become more readily available, it is often unrealistic to expect severely foreign exchange-constrained countries significantly to ease their import restraints. Import liberalization measures are likely to be both easier to sell and more productive at later stages of a medium-term adjustment and recovery programme. At such stages, legitimate debate about the longer-run ('normal') role of administrative as against market-oriented policy instruments can, of course, be expected; and its outcome will vary from country to country. To advocate liberalization during periods of foreign exchange crisis is to risk the imposition of even greater economic costs upon an economy already operating under stress and below capacity. Premature and ill-timed liberalization episodes may set back the prospect for greater efficiency and improved overall economic performance in the longer run.

The debate over the appropriate nature, degree and timing of trade liberalization thus remains active. The Bank's missions typically recommend the earliest and fullest possible import liberalization, beginning with the replacement of quantitative import restrictions by tariffs, thereby creating both government revenue and greater transparency of incentives. Following the phasing-out of controls, reduction in the levels and dispersion of tariffs is urged. Gradualist approaches have generally been favoured by pragmatists in the liberal camp. Balassa, for instance, used to recommend a desirable sequence for semi-industrial economies running from:

> First, a partially compensated devaluation, involving the imposition of optimal export taxes, together with a reduction of differences in incentives between manufacturing and primary activities and between sales in domestic and foreign markets. This would be followed by the replacement of quantitative restrictions by import tariffs, reductions in the level and the dispersion of tariffs, and eventually the equalization of tariff and subsidy rates. (Balassa, 1982:77)

The timing of these moves and the duration of the entire sequence remains unspecified in his formulation.

Many have noted the importance of favourable macro-economic conditions (capital inflow, terms of trade, weather, and so forth) in the timing of successful major policy changes such as import liberalization and currency devaluation. The World Bank itself has argued:

> The more ambitious and long-lasting liberalizations – in Portugal, Greece, Spain, Israel, Chile and Turkey – all started with macro-economic stabilization. The countries which have tried to liberalize trade in the midst of macroeconomic crisis have failed ... . The evidence also stresses the importance of balance of payments equilibrium once trade liberalization is under way. A large deficit involving a substantial loss of foreign exchange reserves is almost sure to undermine trade reform ... what seems to matter most to successful liberalization is export performance. (World Bank, 1987:109)

The link between export expansion and import liberalization, however, is one that remains controversial – even within the Bank. Some of the protagonists in this debate have altered their views over time. Advocates of 'shock' treatment for the trade regime – as well as other reforms – are at present in the ascendancy. In the words of one current representative Bank economist:

> Experience ... suggests that future reforms ensure that export expansion programs be accompanied by import liberalization ... Experience ... does *not* in our view suggest that import liberalization should be undertaken only after export reforms have increased the supply of foreign exchange. This kind of sequencing is likely to be self-defeating, since it is extremely difficult to reorient producers toward export markets as long as heavily sheltered domestic markets offer them assured profits. (Michalopoulos, 1987: 45)

There appears to be agreement, in principle, at least within World Bank headquarters, that stabilization needs to *precede* such structural adjustment if the latter is to succeed. In practice, however, Bank missions have typically pressed for maximum policy reform packages at the earliest possible time. Despite much research and rhetoric regarding the appropriate phasing of policy changes, the Bank has sought short-cuts through normal stabilization and development experience. 'There is presently a dangerous myth that governments can work their economies out of any difficulties, no matter how severe, if only the correct policies are followed' (Sachs, 1987: 305). The 'lessons' from East Asian experience in respect of the transition from stabilization to liberalization, if they are transferable at all, are the following:

1. There is likely to be a long time interval between stabilization and successful exporting or liberalization effort.
2. Substantial external financial assistance is likely to be an essential element in successful transition.
3. Overall import liberalization (as distinct from that for the export sector only) is likely to follow successful exporting with a fairly long time lag, and is *not* an essential or typical part of successful export promotion efforts.
4. The public sector is likely to play an important role in the shift into successful industrial exporting (Sachs, 1987:303–10).

Beyond 'tariffication' of quantitative restrictions and import liberalization for exporters, on which most can agree, further efforts toward 'liberalization' and *laissez-faire* are considerably more controversial. There exist respectable arguments for non-uniform incentive structures as second-best policies for a second-best world. Modern trade theory has knocked the struts from under the conventional arguments for the uniformity of treatment that free trade achieves.

Krugman has recently put a new and more theoretically sophisticated case for liberal (free) trade. Abandoning the traditional comparative advantage arguments based upon the assumption of efficient markets, he posits instead a world in which the sophisticated trade (and other) interventions for which 'the new trade theories' call are likely to be difficult to implement, low in their returns, and subject to hijacking by special interests. Simple policy rules are best 'in a world whose politics are as imperfect as its markets' (Krugman, 1987:143). This stands previously conventional approaches on their head. Whereas political influences used to be blamed for the inability of governments to pursue rational free trade policies, now political factors are deployed to defend free trade policies against the rational economic arguments for sophisticated intervention. But his advocacy of simple policy rules would also seem to permit, say, 30 per cent cross-the-board industrial tariff protection.

Export Expansion

No one quarrels with the aspiration of expanding exports from foreign exchange-constrained economies. The prospect of all of the developing countries simultaneously expanding export volume in similar products, whether primary or manufactured, however, is one that must be analysed in detail. Primary product prices are likely to suffer and protectionist barriers to manufactures are likely to increase in consequence of concerted efforts at export growth. Even Bhagwati, among the most enthusiastic and influential of trade liberalizers, acknowledges that the international economic environment may be an important determinant of the efficacy of outward-oriented policies (1987: 260 and 269–83) although he believes modern 'export pessimism' to be unjustified. (A little inconsistently, he also argues that export subsidies cannot be employed by developing countries because of the ubiquity of anti-dumping and countervailing duties in the industrialized countries.) Export strategy must therefore be quite carefully constructed; and information about market prospects coordinated and made more widely available.

It is not good enough to argue, as some do, that only a relatively few countries will actually act on the advice to expand exports, and that the adding-up problem can therefore be ignored. Nor is it sufficient to argue, as do others, that since world prices are 'given' to small countries they can do nothing about them and should respond to current ones as best they can.

The keys to successful expansion of exports are realistic exchange rates and sustained governmental support, not import liberalization and *laissez-faire*. It is noteworthy that the export promotion policies of Korea were successfully undertaken by a thoroughly *dirigiste* government simultaneously employing tight import controls and a tightly regulated capital market. 'The Asian experience ... suggest(s) ... that successful development might be helped as much by raising the quality of public sector management as by privatizing public enterprises or liberalizing markets' (Sachs, 1987: 294).

The efficacy of export subsidies as a significant weapon of trade policy also emerges as an important area for debate. Granting the greater administrative ease of currency devaluation for the purpose of rectifying anti-export bias, there may nonetheless be an important case for targeted/selective export subsidy for infant industry export promotion. Such selective export promotion was an important element in Korean penetration of overseas markets for its manufactured exports (Westphal, 1981). WIDER research on alternative stabilization programmes has also noted the efficacy of targeted export subsidies as an important short-term stabilization policy instrument (Taylor, 1988).

Openness to External Private Capital

Controls over external private portfolio capital flows – whether inward or outward – are now fairly universally seen as desirable in low-income countries. Experimentation with financial openness in the Southern Cone of Latin America had generally unhappy consequences. Policies toward direct foreign investment remain, however, a matter of some controversy. Increased incentives and receptivity to foreign investors (including the much-touted 'debt-equity swaps') may simply generate quasi-rent for them if, as much of the recent evidence suggests, their investment decisions are based primarily on more fundamental and long-run factors (Moran, 1986). In recent years, direct investment in developing countries, which was always highly concentrated in the same countries that attracted commercial bank lending, dropped just as far and as fast as that lending; and it is unlikely to resume until the overall economic outlook in these countries improves. Quite apart from the sensitivities of many countries regarding foreign ownership and control of domestic industries, and however desirable increased equity or equity-like finance might be, the elasticity of response by direct foreign investors to improved investment incentives in developing countries is, for the present, likely to be low.

Distribution, Poverty and the Vulnerable

Too often neglected in stabilization and adjustment programmes are policies relating to the alleviation of bottom-end poverty and the welfare of the poorest and most vulnerable groups. In the restructuring and expansion of economic activity there may be (perhaps inadvertently) devastating implications for the weakest and poorest. The provision of staple foods, basic health services and incomes for the poorest during stabilization and adjustment periods are matters of international interest, even when, or perhaps particularly when, their domestic political strength is not such as significantly to affect locally constructed programmes. The high social costs of global recession and the availability of alternative policies for overcoming some of them have been demonstrated (Cornia *et al.*, 1987). At a minimum, the distributional implications of agreed programmes should be understood; at least the inadvertent effects upon poverty can then be minimized.

In its new emphasis on improved policies for overall efficiency in the early 1980s the Bank noticably downgraded its previous concern for equity and the alleviation of poverty. Only recently has more than lip service been paid to the social impact of adjustment programmes and, even now, serious policy attention to these issues is limited to a relatively few countries. Difficulties in agreeing upon appropriate approaches and finding reliable data can explain some of the failures in this area; but, if there had been more will, more progress would undoubtedly have been made. It has even been persuasively argued that at least one of the reasons why Korea, Taiwan and Japan could be so effective in the efficiency-oriented restructuring that led them into their successful industrial export experience was that they had *previously* achieved reasonable equity in income distribution through major land reforms and other measures. (Sachs, 1987: 299–302 and 321–2).

Prices, Markets and Government

The relative roles of prices, markets and governments in development are particularly controversial and politically sensitive. To acknowledge the importance of prices and incentive structures is certainly not the same as to advocate the universal use of markets. In a second-best world there can be no theoretical presumption that even 'well functioning' markets will render signals conducive to the achievement of static efficiency, let alone ones that promote development efficiently.

Improved incentive systems, in any case, only generate the desired responses in an appropriate overall context. Non-price impediments may severely constrain performance whatever the incentive structure. In African agriculture, for instance, short-run improvements in agricultural performance are limited by inadequate marketing systems, inability to obtain key inputs or sufficient credit, absence of consumer-goods on which to spend earnings, and deficient transport and storage arrangements, while inadequate land and technology set bounds to longer-run prospects (Please, 1984: 297–8). Where, as is frequently the case, total agricultural supply response is small, the main impact of food price increases may simply be to increase poverty (Mellor, 1985: 3). Moreover, targeted and selective governmental incentives and interventions – anathema to some orthodox economists – may be far more cost-effective than the application of fairly blunt policy instruments across the board.

Nor is it always easy to engineer or sustain real price changes through changes in nominal variables. As has been seen, price inflation can be expected substantially to offset nominal exchange rate devaluation; and the most cost-effective route to a sustainable new real exchange rate may not be to seek to reach it in one fell swoop.

The World Bank and IMF are committed by their articles of agreement to liberal, market-oriented approaches to international economic affairs. Direct controls over foreign exchange earnings and expenditures are explicitly forbidden by the IMF except in stipulated circumstances (which include authorization for capital controls), and the World Bank is mandated to encourage and rely upon private capital flows to the maximum degree possible. Appropriate pricing – particularly in respect of the exchange rate –and incentives for individual and corporate enterprise are important elements in development policy. But there are other important elements as well. Both the IMF and the Bank were created to overcome 'market failures' and their very existence is testimony to the postwar founding states' recognition of the important role to be played by government in pursuit of universally agreed social goals. It is therefore somewhat surprising to find these institutions emphasizing the universal virtues of the market in the developing countries to the degree to which they have recently done. The role of the state in development processes *has* at times been oversold and governments have frequently been over-ambitious and/or incompetent. But the 'market fundamentalism' of much of the World Bank's recent advice cannot have been based upon a sophisticated understanding of political and economic requirements for development, or experience in varieties of 'successful' countries.

There can certainly be wide agreement that governments should be selective in their activities and, where possible, more efficient in their own enterprises. Divestment is undoubtedly appropriate in many cases; as a universal prescription, however, it is of dubious merit. Market imperfections and failures, distributional and 'non-economic' objectives, and political pressures of various kinds are likely to continue to generate significant government interventions in developing countries' economies. The political and economic efficacy of markets and governments varies across countries and in individual countries over time. The complexities in this realm are dramatically illustrated by the fact that two articles were recently published within months of one another in leading US journals presenting econometric findings that were diametrically opposed: one showed that the size of government in GNP was associated with more rapid growth (Ram, 1986), the other that it was associated with slower growth (Landau, 1986). Policy generalizations based on ideologically or experientially rooted 'priors' can only be viewed with scepticism.

Far and away the most pervasive and consistent result in the increasingly sophisticated economic analyses of adjustment policy alternatives is the impossibility of offering generalized prescriptions to fit all country circumstances.

Liberalization may frequently be appropriate, but it is not always so. The very meaning of the term 'liberalization' can also be ambiguous. 'Liberalization' may refer either to 'getting prices right' or to reduction in the degree of governmental intervention; the two are not synonymous, as the former may be achieved, as it is to some degree in Korea, with an activist state no less than via *laissez-faire*. 'Liberalization' of either kind is possible, and may be conducted in many different spheres. Cooper (1987: 518–9) specifically lists six:

1. domestic goods and services;
2. external goods and services – within which exports may be distinguished from imports;
3. the domestic financial system;
4. the link with the international financial system;
5. the domestic labour market;
6. the link of labour with the rest of the world.

There is now much more agreement, he notes, on the need for getting export prices right than on liberalizing imports. There is also now a consensus that premature external financial 'opening' may be counterproductive, and that there remains an important prime prudential and regulatory role for government in domestic financial systems. It is also widely agreed, as seen above, that import liberalization is best undertaken with comfortable levels of external support or foreign exchange reserves. These emerging consensus views illustrate the need for humility and learning in an environment of frequently altering lurches in 'conventional' policy advice.

How much improved economic performance – measured in terms of growth or broader measures of development – can one, in any case, reasonably expect from such liberalizing policy reforms alone, assuming they are in the 'right' direction? Much of the international rhetoric and recent World Bank writing (World Bank, 1983; Agarwala, 1983) suggests that it would be quite considerable. In fact, there is very little evidence to support such a presumption. One recent study of 31 developing countries found that growth experience in the recent past can be significantly related to only two major categories of price 'distortion' – exchange rates and real wages – with some limited further relationship to the degree of protection of manufacturing (Aghazadeh and Evans, 1986). No association was found between growth and the degree of taxation (or protection) of agriculture, the pricing of capital (interest rates), the rate of price inflation or energy pricing (see also Fishlow, 1985:140–1). Evidently not all pricing policy changes are likely to be equally productive. Wages are self-evidently among the most 'political' of prices, and policies relating to them are likely to be part of a broader politico-economic strategy. In short, 'the correctness of the prices must be decided by reference to a comprehensive development strategy, and not independently of it ... Getting policies right is more than a matter of getting prices right' (Fishlow, 1985:141). In any case, the adequacy of external resources interacts with domestic policy, and typically today is still the binding constraint on overall performance.

John P. Lewis' survey of the state of development economics in the mid-1980s noted that there exists a 'new orthodoxy' composed of what is probably a minority of 'mainstream' development economists 'headquartered at the World Bank'

> Their orthodoxy is, as to economics, neoclassical. It carries forward with redoubled vigor the liberalizing pro-market strains of the thinking of the 1960s and 1970s. It is very mindful of the limits of governments. It is emphatic in advocating export-oriented growth to virtually all comers. And it places heavier-than-ever reliance on policy-dialoguing, especially between aid donors and recipients (Lewis, 1986: 9).

Members of the more eclectic and more modest majority are typically much more concerned to differentiate approaches as between different countries and circumstances; many retain interest in distributional equity and the alleviation of poverty as important conscious policy objectives; most are also more interested in and concerned with political processes and constraints on policy action (Lewis, 1986:10).

A 'pragmatic neo-structuralism' (the phrase is Albert Fishlow's, 1985) seems to be gaining ascendancy among economists and policy-makers not only in Latin America (about which he was writing) but also in the rest of the developing world. Recognition of the inadequacy of overly aggregative approaches to macro-economic analysis is coupled with that of the need to differentiate carefully among countries with different structural characteristics. The important role of markets and incentives is accepted; and there is a new scepticism of the capacities and interests of governments. At the same time, however, the potential for a productive, if more carefully selective, role for the state is recognized. Simplistic recommendations for reliance upon the 'magic of the marketplace' are, properly, seen as ideology rather than the outcome of careful analysis.

INSTITUTIONAL AND POLITICAL ASPECTS OF POLICY-BASED LENDING

Development-oriented conditions are not only more complex and more intrusive than IMF-style demand management ones, they are also much more time-consuming to develop, achieve agreement on, and eventually monitor. It is in their nature that funds requested in the form of programme loans from the Bank cannot be disbursed as quickly as can IMF funds. Nor can performance be as effectively and quickly monitored. The data required for reliable assessment of real development performance typically take much longer to assemble than do the Fund's financial variables, if they are available at all; and trade-offs among the various elements of developmental performance must somehow be considered in an agreed manner. Bank-style (structural and sector adjustment loan) conditionality has thus often engendered more delay and controversy, both at the outset of a Bank-backed adjustment programme and subsequently, than IMF conditionality. The 'tranching' of structural adjustment and sector adjustment lending would normally be more efficient if based upon relatively few indicators related, above all, to balance of payments management and/or limited sector-specific objectives rather than upon broad and controversial matters like the size of government and the degree of market liberalization.

Whereas developing countries have long argued for longer-term and more supply-oriented approaches to current adjustment problems, and hence, implicitly, for a greater role for the World Bank relative to the IMF, many have been having second thoughts. Concern over the World Bank's inappropriate mixing together of medium-term adjustment issues with more controversial matters of long-term development strategy have led to nervousness about an expanded Bank role in programme lending. IMF conditionality, however imperfect and inappropriate, is seen as less intrusive and, conceivably, despite its limited time horizon, less potentially damaging to national development aspirations than that of a World Bank with idiosyncratic convictions as to the universal recipe for growth. It also tends to be more consistent and predictable in its country-level application.

The one point on which virtually all those with experience in the attempt to impose policy conditions in IMF and Bank lending agree is that the required policies do not hold if there is not a serious commitment to them on the part of the borrower. If the relevant policies are not fully understood and supported by the government – or if they cannot carry domestic political support (or opposition cannot be repressed) – agreement will only be transitory and the adjustment programmes ineffectual. While there can be a certain amount of external education and persuasion concerning appropriate policies, there cannot be effective external imposition. When all is said and done, borrowing governments must, above all, pursue their own interests.

Much more likely than the successful imposition of external conditions upon unenthusiastic borrowers is the lender's rationing of its assistance to only those governments that are already behaving appropriately. Policy conditionality thereby functions as a device for rewarding good behaviour (or, implicitly, punishing bad). It can thereby provide a technical rationale for shifting the overall distribution of lending to those whose behaviour is considered appropriate in dimensions well beyond those associated merely with the finer points of adjustment programmes.

Whatever may be the lenders' illusions about the efficacy of conditionality, policy-based programme lending is therefore most constructively seen as a potential device for encouraging overall *genuine* 'policy dialogue'. Genuine policy dialogue on matters of mutual interest among parties interacting on a basis of parity and mutual respect is a worthy objective. The manner in which World Bank and IMF terms are frequently dictated to member countries, particularly the smaller and weaker ones, however, is a poor substitute for such aspirations. While there may be room for some modest tinkering about the edges of an IMF–Bank suggested policy framework paper in the low-income countries – seemingly creating an element of dialogue – the 'bottom line' is an overall policy package which is typically available only on a 'take it or leave it' basis. Developing country governments with views of their own (and, unfortunately, many have had great difficulty constructing feasible alternative policy packages) face protracted delays and even rejection in their pursuit of urgently needed IFI finance. Overwhelmingly, 'dialogue' concerns subjects of the creditors' choosing and takes place on their terms. Efforts of debtors to open a dialogue, say, on debt reduction, have been labelled 'confrontational' and 'counterproductive' by aid donors and creditors. 'Policy dialogue' has too frequently actually been a euphemism for the nailing down of the details of lender conditionality.

Those who have dominated recent decision-making in the Bank argue that the credibility, and therefore the sustainability, of policy reform is enhanced by strong action at the outset. Smaller, more gradual, changes are likely, in this view, to be easily rolled back and indicate a lack of governmental commitment. It can equally be argued, however, that targets and policy changes that are modest, but firm and realistic, are likely to be more credible and sustainable than large changes that are, to a degree, 'leaps into the unknown'. Attempts at 'forced marches' toward large-scale policy change strain governmental capacity and strengthen the impression (dangerous in local politics) that the policy programme is externally imposed rather than internally generated.

The ambitions of the Bank in respect of the *breadth* of coverage of their recommended policy package are no less controversial. It is difficult to disagree with the assessment by Feinberg (1986), quoted with approval by Mahmadou Touré of Senegal: 'A long list of requirements either holds an entire program hostage to a secondary issue or is open to highly subjective assessment' (Touré, 1987: 505; see also Avramovic, 1988 on this and related issues). Moreover, when one Bank mission after another descends with detailed piecemeal recommendations upon a country (Ghana has been receiving over 40 such missions per year recently), there is bound to be a certain amount of confusion, inconsistency, and, of course, recipient annoyance. Since career advancement depends in part on the 'success' with which their advice is translated into policy change (one hopes on the success of the policies as well), the pressures exerted by these external advisors may be considerable. The borrowing governments' absorptive capacity for external advice is limited, maintenance of a domestic consensus on policy change is difficult, and it is counterproductive to 'overload the political circuits' (Sachs, 1987: 294). It is therefore almost certainly best to concentrate on a few key areas of policy rather than to dissipate external advice over too wide a range of issues.

Within the Bank, just as outside it, there is probably a majority who advocate support for step-by-step changes in the appropriate direction, avoidance of unproductive confrontation over less important issues, and attempts to influence only a few major policies at a time, rather than more dramatic reforms. Even some of those who might be expected most vigorously to support orthodox Bank policies advocate lower expectations and longer time horizons (Berg and Batchelder, 1985).

Many also recognize the enormous importance of appropriate timing of difficult policy reforms. Other things being equal, major policy changes involving restructuring of incentives (and therefore losses for some) should be both politically easier to introduce and sustain, and more effective of themselves, when the economy is experiencing relatively good times. The elimination of consumer subsidies or exchange rate devaluations are likely to generate less inflation in years of good harvests than in bad years. The problem in recent years has been an unusually protracted sequence of *very* bad years, leaving little room for any such 'catching of policy breath'. On the other hand, there may be the converse dilemma – that when external circumstances ease up a little, policy-makers are tempted to relax rather than seize the chance.

Knowledge of the details of country-level practices and experiences, and sensitivity to them, are critically important in the elaboration of appropriate and credible policy packages. The qualities of the individual Bank personnel most directly involved in the negotiation and monitoring of policy-based loans are thus frequently more important than generalized prescriptive proclamations emanating from the Bank.

External proponents of major policy change in developing countries have often been quick to point to the role of vested interests in domestic opposition to what they see as desirable reforms. But the interests of the external advisors are not themselves beyond suspicion. Political and economic interests and ideological considerations may well influence the decisions of donor governments or the international institutions in which they have dominant influence. Nor can local policy-makers always have full confidence in the professional 'neutrality' or in the relevant knowledge and experience of outside advisors. In recent years, developing country policy-makers have complained bitterly about the professional rigidity and ignorance of the detail of local circumstances of some IFI missions.

There can never be total agreement on policy questions. Counsels of policy 'perfection', even if they could be agreed, would only in exceptional (and typically rather unattractive) circumstances be politically translatable into action. As John Sheahan has suggested 'The ideal is not maximum possible efficiency but an optimum degree consistent with the particular country's economic structure and capacity for change' (1980:29). Improved data, more careful analysis, increased public discussion of the options and, ultimately, a stronger base of indigenous and locally based economists will do more for the quality of national decision-making (always within domestic political constraints) than any amount of pressure from ostensibly high-minded external institutions.

In the meantime, tensions between the Bank and debtor governments may be eased by expanding the practice of involving 'neutrals' in bilateral dialogue. Outside experts have occasionally been involved in controversial cases in the past – for example, India in the 1960s and Tanzania in the 1980s (Please, 1984: 78, 93–4); and they have been liberally drawn upon in Bank research and other consultancies. The Bank's traditions in this respect have involved far greater openness to independent assessments and utilization of external research and opinion than has been typical of the Fund. These traditions should now be drawn on, both for overall assessment of Bank policies and, in individual country cases, for the assessment of adjustment programmes and external resource requirements. An outside review panel has been suggested for an examination of the appropriateness of the conditionality attached to structural adjustment loans (Bacha and Feinberg, 1985); such a panel could be even more useful if it addressed the broader issue of policy-based programme lending of all kinds, and did so in conjunction with a review of Bank–Fund relations. At the country level, the use of knowledgeable authorities not in the employ of the Fund or Bank in the production of 'neutral' background papers for consultative groups and debtor-creditor mediation efforts could be highly productive (Ranis, 1985; Helleiner, 1986).

CONCLUSIONS

The principal questions at issue between the IFIs and their borrowers in the realm of policy-based lending are thus the following:

1. the substance of development strategy in terms of the efficiency of alternative approaches in securing overall growth and development;
2. the basic objectives of overall development including such 'ideological' matters as the role of the state and income distribution;
3. the appropriate pace and sequencing of suggested policy reforms, and, in particular, their technical and political sustainability;
4. the degree of external intrusion into matters of national policy and the appropriate *modus operandi* of 'policy dialogue'.

On each, there is room for considerable anxiety concerning the World Bank and IMF's performance. Greater humility, longer time horizons, more realistic expectations, and increased recognition of the specific circumstances of individual borrowers would both raise their effectiveness and improve their public relations.

REFERENCES

Agarwala, R. (1983), 'Price Distortions and Growth in Developing Countries', *World Bank Staff Working Paper*, no. 575.

Aghazadeh, Esmail and David Evans (1986), 'Price Distortions, Efficiency and Growth', mimeo, Sussex: IDS.

Avramovic, Dragoslav (1988), 'Conditionality: Facts, Theory and Policy – Contribution to the Reconstruction of the International Financial System', *WIDER Working Paper*, 37, Helsinki, February.

Bacha, Edmar L. and Richard Feinberg (1985), 'The World Bank and Structural Adjustment in Latin America', mimeo.

Balassa, Bela (1982), *Development Strategies in Semi-Industrialized Economies*, New York: Johns Hopkins for the World Bank.

Berg, Elliott and Alan Batchelder (1985), 'Structural Adjustment Lending, A Critical View', mimeo.

Bhagwati, Jagdish (1987), 'Outward Orientations: Trade Issues', in Vittorio Corbo, Morris Goldstein and Mohsin Khan (eds), *Growth-Oriented, Adjustment Programs*, Washington DC: International Monetary Fund and World Bank, pp.257–90.

Cooper, Richard N. (1987), 'Round Table Discussion', in Vittorio Corbo, Morris Goldstein and Mohsin Khan (eds), *Growth-Oriented Adjustment Programs*, Washington, DC: International Monetary Fund and the World Bank, pp. 516–23.

Cornia, G.A., Richard Jolly and Frances Stewart (eds) (1987), *Adjustment With a Human Face*, Oxford: Clarendon Press.

Diaz-Alejandro, Carlos F. (1985), 'Goodbye Financial Repression, Hello Financial Crash', *Journal of Development Economics*, vol. 19 (1/2).

Feinberg, Richard *et al.* (1986), *Between Two Worlds: The World Bank's Next Decade* Washington DC: Overseas Development Council.

Fishlow, Albert (1985), 'The State of Latin American Economics' in *Annual Report, IDB*, Washington, DC: Inter-American Development Bank.

Helleiner, G.K. (1986), 'The Question of Conditionality' in Carol Lancaster and John Williamson (eds), *African Debt and Financing*, Washington DC: Institute for International Economics.

Khan, Mohsin S. and Malcolm D. Knight (1985), 'Fund-Supported Adjustment Programs and Economic Growth', *IMF Occasional Paper*, no. 41, November.

Krugman, Paul (1987), 'Is Free Trade Passé?', *Journal of Economic Perspectives*, American Economic Association, vol. 1, no. 2, Fall.

Landau, Daniel (1986), 'Government and Economic Growth in the Less Developed Countries: An Empirical Study for 1960–1980', *Economic Development and Cultural Change*, vol. 35, no. 11, October, pp. 35–75.

Lewis, John P. (1986), 'Development Promotion: A Time for Regrouping' in John P. Lewis and Valeriana Kallab (eds), *Development Strategies Reconsidered*, Washington DC: Overseas Development Council.

Mellor, John W. (1985), 'Agricultural Change and Rural Poverty', International Food Policy Research Institute, *Food Policy Statement*, no. 3, October.

Michalopoulos, Constantine (1987), 'World Bank Programs for Adjustment and

Growth' in Vittorio Corbo, Morris Goldstein and Mohsin Khan (eds), *Growth-Oriented Adjustment Programs*, Washington DC: International Monetary Fund and the World Bank, pp. 15–62.

Moran, Theodore H. (1986), 'Overview: The Future of Foreign Direct Investment in the Third World' in T.H. Moran *et al.*, *Investing in Development: New Roles for Private Capital?*, Washington DC: Overseas Development Council.

Please, Stanley (1984), *The Hobbled Giant, Essays on the World Bank*, Boulder, Col. and London: Westview Press.

Ram, Rati (1986), 'Government Size and Economic Growth: A New Framework and Some Evidence From Cross-Section and Time-Series Data', *American Economic Review*, vol. 76, no. 1, March.

Ranis, Gustav (1985), 'Debt, Adjustment, and Development: The Lingering Crisis' in Khadija Haq (ed.), *The Lingering Debt Crisis*, Islamabad, Pakistan: North South Roundtable, pp. 207–16.

Rossi, Nicola (1988), 'Government Spending, the Real Interest Rate, and the Behavior of Liquidity-Constrained Consumers in Developing Countries', *IMF Staff Papers*, vol. 35, no. 1, March, pp. 104–40.

Sachs, Jeffrey D. (1987), 'Trade and Exchange Rate Policies in Growth-Oriented Adjustment Programs' in Vittorio Corbo, Morris Goldstein and Mohsin Khan, eds., *Growth-Oriented Adjustment Programs*, Washington DC: International Monetary Fund and the World Bank, pp. 291–325.

Sheahan, John (1980), 'Market-Oriented Economic Policies and Political Repression in Latin America', *Economic Development and Cultural Change*, vol. 28, no. 2, January, pp. 267–91.

Taylor, Lance (1988), *Varieties of Stabilization Experience: Towards Sensible Macroeconomics in the Third World*, Oxford: Clarendon Press.

Touré, Mahmadou (1987), 'Roundtable Discussion', in Vittorio Corbo, Morris Goldstein and Mohsin Khan (eds), *Growth-Oriented Adjustment Programs*, Washington DC: International Monetary Fund and the World Bank, 1987, pp. 502–5.

Van Wijnbergen, S. (1983), 'Interest Rate Management in Developing Countries: Theory and Simulation Results for Korea', *World Bank Staff Working Paper*, no. 593, May.

Westphal, L. (1981), 'Empirical Justification for Infant Industry Protection', *World Bank Staff Working Paper*, no. 445, March.

World Bank (1983), *World Development Report*, Washington, DC.

World Bank (1987), *World Development Report*, Washington, DC.

Yagci, Fahrettin et al. (1985), 'Structural Adjustment Lending, An Evaluation of Program Design', *World Bank Staff Working Paper*, no. 735.

8. Stabilization, Adjustment and Poverty*

INTRODUCTION

The impact of stabilization and adjustment programmes upon income distribution and the poor is a matter upon which argument rages. 'Usually,' Lance Taylor has said, 'income [re]distribution against labour and the poor is implicit in stabilization attempts' (Taylor, 1983: 200). Particularly controversial in this context is the appropriate role of the international financial institutions, particularly the International Monetary Fund (IMF), in the construction and support of such programmes. On the other hand, the Managing Director of the IMF declares:

> It is often said that Fund programs attack the most disadvantaged segments of the population, but people forget that how the required effort is distributed among the various social groups and among the various public expenditure categories (arms spending or social outlays, productive investment or current operations, direct or indirect taxes) is a question decided by the governments. A question that may be raised in this connection is whether the Fund should exert pressure in the determination of government priorities and even make the granting of its assistance contingent on measures that would better protect the most disadvantaged population groups. An international institution such as the Fund cannot take upon itself the role of dictating social and political objectives to sovereign governments. (de Larosiere, 1984)

On the other hand,

> ...by remaining aloof from such questions [of income distribution] the Fund tacitly accepts the distributional policies of the government in power, whether it likes them or not. This, more often than not, implies a *de facto* alignment with forces opposed to reduced inequalities...the politics are inescapable. (Killick, 1984: 198)

* I am grateful to the following for comments on an earlier draft: Sidney Dell, Joan Nelson, Vito Tanzi, Rolph van der Hoeven, Frances Stewart and Steve Triantis. None bears any responsibility for the contents of the current version.

UNICEF has also offered a view quite different from that of the IMF:

> The tendency for governments faced with recession to cut back on child-focused social expenditures (and measures which support poorer families) arises from many sources, domestic as well as international. But international influence is often critical, especially when linked to the negotiation of an IMF agreement or an international loan...as a clear condition of an agreement, as the technical advice of international experts or as the orthodox wisdom promoted in courses or less formal contacts. (UNICEF, 1984: 169)

Considerable professional attention is now directed at the effects of macro-economic experiences and policies upon distribution and/or poverty. Even within the IMF, distributional objectives are at last widely regarded as important components of overall macro-economic performance. They also have obvious political implications, although there is no easy link between poverty and political stability (Nelson, 1984). Whether they are consciously intended (or professionally analysed) or not, all adjustment programmes, indeed all policy packages, imply certain distributional effects. There can therefore be no *analytical* escape from consideration of the questions of income distribution in assessments of global or national economic experience and policy alternatives.

CONCEPTUAL APPROACHES AND PROBLEMS

Until recently, most theorizing about income distributional effects of macro-economic change has primarily addressed the question of functional distribution and has done so in terms of comparative statics rather than via analyses of adjustment paths (Knight, 1976; Ahluwalia and Lysy, 1981). The existence of a large informal sector and the importance of a smallholder farm sector, within both of which incomes are an amalgam of returns to labour, capital and land, greatly complicate such traditional theoretical analyses of the distributional impact of policy changes in the African context. Analyses based upon changes in factor earnings, while theoretically tractable, therefore prove hopelessly unusable here. While there is always some policy interest in issues of functional, regional, sectoral, and public–private distributions, the prime policy focus is typically upon size distribution (by household or individual) or distribution by socioeconomic group. Of particular interest is the impact of adjustment experience and policies upon bottom-end poverty (Addison and Demery, 1985; Cornia, Jolly and Stewart, 1987).

Immediate (short-run) distributional or poverty effects of macro-economic imbalances or stabilization and adjustment programmes may be quite different from longer-run effects. Short-run cutbacks in the consumption levels of the poor may be outweighed by future gains for them that current austerity helps to make possible; then again, future social benefits may not accrue to them at all. Where, in addition to the usual distributional issues, there are also intertemporal reallocations of consumption, the appropriate methodology for assessing distributional effects is presumably the calculation of changes in the present value of future income streams, consequent upon the introduction of alternative stabilization programmes. Apart from the inherent difficulty of undertaking plausible calculations of this type with respect to an uncertain future, there is the usual analytical *imbroglio* over the choice of an appropriate discount rate. Wishful thinking on the part of policy-makers is likely to generate considerably smaller calculated effects upon the 'permanent income' of the poor than upon their immediate income levels. Moreover, the poorest can be assumed to employ a significantly higher rate for the discounting of the future than others do. And the question as to whether there may have been other ways in which to assign the burden of short-run cutbacks always remains. For these reasons, while longer-run effects upon poverty and income distribution should also where possible be addressed, the *prime* issue should normally be the degree to which the *immediate* burden of adjustment falls upon the poor.

Analytical problems and statistical deficiencies have long blocked satisfactory analysis – either at the level of specific countries or more generally – of the question of exactly 'who are the poor'? The most convenient procedure has typically involved the identification of certain socioeconomic categories as 'target groups' – for example, small farmers, landless workers, unskilled labourers, informal sector workers, members of particular ethnic groups or castes, women, children, and so on.

Virtually all of the available general equilibrium analyses of the distributional effects of policy changes (summarized in Dervis *et al.*, 1982: 406), which in their nature are comparative static and long-run in character, conclude that size distribution of income is remarkably stable, and thus difficult to alter via policy intervention. The composition of 'the poor', however, is highly susceptible, in these studies, to macro-economic and policy changes. Urban unskilled workers may replace rural smallholders at the bottom end of the income distribution, or conversely, even if there is no recorded difference in the proportion living at absolute poverty levels. Despite overall stability of size distribution, the welfare of the poorest and subgroups thereof can still be altered to a degree that is highly significant *for them* by macroeconomic experience and policy.

In recent analysis, poverty concerns are said to relate to three broad categories of poor people:

1. those who are 'structurally' poor, and unlikely to achieve improvements in levels of living except via the longer-run development of the economy;
2. those who are 'newly' poor, the direct 'shock' victims of recent recession and austerity programmes (for example, newly unemployed workers); and
3. those vulnerable groups who have been pushed over the borderline into real poverty by the overall problems and policies (for example, cutbacks in social programmes, higher food prices, and the like) of the economy (Zuckerman, 1989; World Bank, 1988: 29–30, 47–9).

The problems of the structurally poor must be addressed in the design of longer-run development; growth may not impact favourably upon them unless it is consciously designed to do so, via the provision of rural infrastructure, education and so forth. Those in this category may nonetheless be cushioned against further deterioration by conscious governmental policy to that end. Short- to medium-term adjustment programmes more typically have addressed the problems of the 'newly' poor and the 'borderline' poor, via targeted compensatory programmes including severance payments, public works, food-for-work, targeted feeding, subsidies, and other interventions. This adjustment-related poverty is easier to tackle and is probably politically more significant, at least in the short-term; but these features do not make it inherently any more *important* to address than more deeply-rooted structural poverty. Ideally, an adjustment programme should incorporate distributional (specifically, anti-poverty) objectives within its overall design, rather than 'adding on' a compensatory programme *after* the 'orthodox' growth-oriented one has been initiated. Thus far, poverty concerns have typically been addressed in IMF/Bank programmes much too little and much too late.

ELEMENTS OF ADJUSTMENT POLICY

Introduction

Adverse external shocks of a long-run or permanent nature require restructuring towards tradables but, if this cannot quickly be achieved, and if there is inadequate offsetting expansion in external finance, external balance requires that overall spending contract. The degree to which such macro-economic restraint is required depends both upon internal restructuring success and external circumstances over which a country has very little influence. While restructuring can itself, as will be seen, have either positive or negative effects upon the welfare of labour and the poorest (two categories which are not synonymous) contraction of overall spending is almost certain to lower the well-being of both. The pursuit of poverty-related objectives therefore requires minimizing the need for such deflationary measures. This, in turn, calls for special attention to supply-side policies, above all, targeted investment in bottleneck-breaking and restructuring activities. The obvious requisites for minimizing the need for, and the impact of, deflation are thus:

1. an appropriate incentive structure, particularly an appropriate real effective exchange rate;
2. targeted domestic investment spending, via governmental and parastatal budgets, targeted credit, and tax-cum-subsidy arrangements; and
3. the necessary input of external finance.

The faster is domestic structural readjustment or the greater is the provision of external finance to ease the adjustment process, then the less will consumption and income have to be cut. Econometric models that allow for production and consumption elasticities and reallocations – and, implicitly, longer time horizons – will therefore simulate less devastating results from external adverse shocks for the welfare of the poor.

Conceptually, it is important to distinguish between the effects upon distribution and poverty of:

1. macro-economic contraction or reduction in absorption, of various kinds;
2. efforts at restructuring the economy towards the production of relatively more (and the consumption of relatively less) tradable goods

and services (exportables and import substitutes), principally via the rejigging of relative product and factor prices – for example, through (real) exchange rate devaluation, and necessary investments; and
3. broader changes in overall strategy that are designed to increase efficiency and stimulate growth – for example, deregulation, financial or trade liberalization, reduction in the size of the public sector and so on.

Macroeconomic Restraint

There must be a strong presumption that, all else being equal, macro-economic contraction will worsen poverty. While the relationship is not tight, and there is room for offsetting policies, there must also be a presumption that the greater is the reduction in overall absorption the greater is the adverse impact upon poverty.

In recent years, despite significant restructuring success, inherent rigidities together with inadequate external finance have forced the non-oil developing countries to respond to major external shocks via severe cutbacks in overall spending, and thus in both consumption and, relatively even more, in investment. Disproportionate cutbacks in investment, made necessary by the political limits to further reduction in consumption, have themselves slowed the restructuring process and thereby created a need for continuing resort to restraint policies.

The root of macro-economic imbalance often also lies in domestic 'overheating', sometimes itself induced by adverse exogenous shock. Macro-economic contraction in response to such domestic overabsorption may be thought normally to follow a course that simply reverses previous inappropriate expansion or overabsorption, and thus to reverse any associated income redistribution. But there should be no such presumption with respect to the incidence of contractionary monetary and fiscal policies. If, for example, previous overexpansion of demand was associated with attempts to improve the welfare of the poorest, it may be appropriate or even politically necessary to allow for a 'ratchet' that limits any reversal in their gains and imposes the required cutbacks somewhere else.

Fiscal contraction

While there may be some exceptions, and detailed empirical analysis is rare, the usual presumption is that overall non-interest government expenditures are more equitably distributed than private ones, and that public sector non-interest expenditure cutbacks are more likely to harm the poor than are private expenditure cutbacks of equal size. Such social expenditures as dispensary health care, primary schooling, school feeding programmes, community water supplies, childcare facilities for working women, key public health interventions (for example, immunizations against the major childhood diseases) are likely to be of particular importance to the poor. Employment-intensive public works or construction activities may also be very important to preserve or even expand. (In fact, cutbacks in public expenditure may also engender further reductions in private expenditure.) There is also evidence, however, that the poorest may not always be major beneficiaries of social expenditures; if this is the case, they will obviously not lose from cutbacks. Data on changes in aggregate expenditure on 'social' spending categories such as 'education' or 'health' may be quite misleading in terms of their presumed social and distributional implications. In many countries budget stringency has brought with it major poverty-worsening *compositional* shifts within such categories of government expenditure – for example, from rural dispensaries to urban hospitals, from primary education to universities, from key inputs to salaries, and so on. In principle, again, at least at the technical level, it should be *possible* to target expenditure cutbacks (and increased taxes) so as to minimize the effects upon the poorest.

In this context, the issue with respect to food or other consumer subsidies (such as medicine, water, education, shelter and transport) is not so much whether they *always* raise the welfare of the poorest or how they might be constructed so as to achieve that result as the likely effects of their removal, on fiscal policy grounds, in specific country cases. Raising agricultural prices *may* severely worsen poverty problems. In the absence of simultaneous targeted efforts to break production and marketing bottlenecks, such price increases may not even generate the desired supply responses (or generate them only via inordinate price changes and long lags). While the principal beneficiaries of such subsidies are typically urban dwellers, and these are not always the poorest, a number of careful analyses of specific country cases demonstrates that appropriately targeted food subsidies *can* have significant poverty-alleviating effects (Pinstrup-Andersen, 1988). Existing subsidy schemes can often be improved; ostensibly poverty-oriented market interventions often fail to achieve their objectives. Targeted subsidies on key consumption items of the urban poor, although always vulnerable to some leakage, may have significant anti-poverty effects; the more so in the context of increased privatization of public services and emphasis on 'cost recovery'.

Major cuts in government real non-interest recurrent expenditures can have profound social implications. Allowing for some rationalization, some employment attrition and the prospect of some real wage reductions one must typically think in terms of significant lay-offs of government employees. Rationalizations in publicly owned corporations are likely to add to their number. These cuts will have the most obvious and immediate social impact:

a) since many real services previously provided by government will no longer be available, particularly to those without the capacity to pay for them; and
b) because of the direct income losses suffered by those who have lost their accustomed employment and their families.

To ameliorate the poverty impact of these and other related financial measures, there are three kinds of policy responses:

1. minimization of the cost to the economy and society, particularly its most vulnerable members, via prior careful analysis of the human costs of cutting government expenditures and employment in different ways. Across-the-board equi-proportionate cuts are unlikely to be socially or economically efficient. Among the issues to be explored are:
   - the identification of priority programmes in maternal and child health care, early childhood nutrition and education, community health inputs (water, sewerage, immunization programmes and so on), that must at all costs be preserved or even expanded in the light of recent deteriorations;
   - the identification, where possible, of expenditures and activities with very little evident impact on human welfare, particularly of low-income women and young children, either in terms of entire divisions, offices, Ministries, programmes, or job classifications, functions, and the like;
   - the appropriate geographic incidence of cuts (special attention to the most disadvantaged areas);
   - the appropriate balance in the treatment of employees between age/experience/seniority/pension rights etc., on the one hand, and the problems of untried, insecure youth on the other; and between females and males, taking into account in each case differing non-governmental income and employment prospects.

2. directed assistance to those who lose their employment, particularly those on the lower end of the wage scale. This might include modest severance payments, provision of information regarding future employment prospects, credit to encourage the start-up of small enterprises and self-employment, and so forth.
3. accelerated efforts to offer *targeted* assistance to all those in greatest need of employment, income, nutrition, education and health care. Among the measures generally worth exploring are the following:
   a) re: employment and income:
      - labour-intensive public capital expenditures (particularly on maintenance, repairs, rehabilitation of roads, buildings, urban and agricultural infrastructure, and so on);
      - the payment of lower 'emergency special programme' wages and/or food in some of the above programmes, either in locally organized community self-help schemes (with external NGO support) or in 'top-down' government quasi-relief projects;
      - increased encouragement (and removal of disincentives or obstacles) to small-scale enterprises and self-employment, especially for women, including the possibility of credit and inputs, and conceivably with external NGO (or local foreign embassy) support;
      - in some countries, increased effort to expand unskilled labour-intensive manufacturing activities for export.

   b) re: nutrition, education and health:
      - targeted school feeding programmes in nursery schools and early primary education, incorporating requirements for weekends and vacations for the most needy;
      - programmes for the provision of appropriate food (such as local milk, protein supplements) for low-income infants, preschool children, and pregnant and lactating women in local health clinics;
      - provision of free maternal and infant health care, essential drugs, infant growth monitoring and so forth for low-income women and children and the indigent via health clinics, mobile facilities, and paramedical personnel;
      - access to the WHO/UNICEF essential drugs (low-cost) procurement facility for the above programme;
      - schemes to encourage primary school attendance by the poor – for example, targeted book subsidies, abolition of school uniforms.

If adequately prepared and 'packaged', programmes in these areas may attract ready external support. In the current ODA environment, bilateral donors (with NGOs and UN agencies) may respond more quickly to requests for such socially-oriented project or programme support than to any others. Support for human resource protection and development is generally receiving a fresh burst of international support.

Spending upon child health, nutrition and education can be regarded as long-gestation investment that will eventually yield high returns. The World Bank, which actively encouraged a basic-needs-oriented strategy in the 1970s, as did many other aid donors, specifically warned, as seen in Chapter 6, of the 'serious danger' of cutbacks in human development programmes, despite the importance of their contribution – often exceeding that of additional physical investment – to 'long-term development potential' (World Bank, 1979: 86). This is, in fact, precisely what has happened both in Africa and elsewhere and is at last being widely recognized. It is now widely seen to be critically important to protect the condition of children, both on humanitarian grounds and in terms of long-term economic development prospects.

Monetary and credit policies

The analysis of the effects of generalized monetary contraction and/or credit ceilings upon poverty or income distribution is difficult because these effects are mediated through a complex system of credit rationing and financial markets. In all economies, credit restraint and interest rate increases hit some groups with much greater impact than others. Those who can finance themselves are least affected, and those who are most dependent upon credit, least flexible and least influential in financial institutions are hit the hardest; but the identity of these groups obviously varies from place to place. Generalized monetary restraint is never neutral in its impact.

Financial liberalization and associated interest rate reform may also influence income distribution and poverty. Increasing interest rates is unambiguously likely to draw savings into the formal financial intermediation sector, including parts owned or controlled by the state, and thus to reduce 'financial repression' where it exists. (The evidence that interest rates are significantly correlated with aggregate domestic savings rates is by no means unambiguous, and orthodox argument has eased away from firm pronouncements in this regard (Giannini, 1983; Khan and Knight, 1985: 14). In some instances it may also reduce capital flight abroad or even engender inflows of both previously expatriated domestic capital and fresh foreign capital.) Whether redirecting savings into organized financial markets improves allocation, or stability, or equity, remains a matter of some dispute. It may reduce the role of efficient curb markets and even lower the total supply of loanable funds. It may also reduce the credit rationing role of the state. In both of these instances, the welfare of lower-income groups may suffer from the change in allocation mechanisms. Particularly deserving of analysis in financial restraint and liberalization packages is their impact on governmental attempts explicitly to influence the distribution and cost of credit to identifiable lower-income groups, such as small enterprises and marginal farmers.

Restructuring

Efforts to restructure incentives in order to increase the production of tradables may take many forms, including various administrative devices, but typically involve attempts to alter the real exchange rate by nominal devaluation. Devaluation must have immediate distributional consequences. An IMF staff member has put the point well:

> An exchange rate action becomes a highly charged political decision precisely because it produces change in the distribution of income between producers (or potential producers) of foreign exchange and consumers of foreign exchange. (Mohammed, 1984: 188)

In cases of severe initial imbalance, it may also 'validate' price changes that have already occurred in local markets, thereby reducing economic rents enjoyed by those previously enjoying favoured access to underpriced foreign exchange.

The short-run effects of nominal exchange rate devaluation will frequently be both deflationary for demand and inflationary for prices. Such demand deflation may reduce employment in the short run, beyond the reductions already created by reduced absorption as discussed above. (If there is excess capacity in the tradable goods sector, however, employment may soon rise again.) Even if this further unemployment is likely to be temporary, its political implications may, on the margin, be severe. As has been seen, whether these employment effects translate directly into conclusions as to bottom-end poverty effects depends on the nature of the economy. In many cases, the urban unemployed are *not* the poorest.

The effects of the changing structure of prices cannot be understood without knowledge of domestic market structures, effective price control systems and the like, and the typical budgets at different income levels or in different socioeconomic groups. (Strictly speaking, one also needs information as to the substitutability of various items in consumption as relative prices alter.) In the first instance, those who consume tradables will be hardest hit by increased prices. If more generalized inflation results, the consequences become even harder to unravel.

The distributional implications of price inflation and financial disorder are not as simple as they are sometimes portrayed. One simply cannot generalize from the evidence of higher-income countries – to the effect that the poor are hit the hardest because 'lower-income groups tend to have the least access to assets whose values rise *pari passu* with inflation' (Johnson and Salop, 1980: 3). In sub-Saharan Africa those engaged primarily in subsistence activities, typically among the poorest, have often been very little affected by raging inflation in the monetized sector. It has also been plausibly argued that the casual (and very poor) workers found in many of the developing countries' labour markets, through the frequency of their recontracting, have built-in resistance to the real wage deterioration that typically follows from unexpectedly high rates of price inflation in more 'formal' labour markets (Nugent and Glezakos, 1982). On the other hand, there are both theoretical reasons and some evidence to suggest that rapid price inflation often generates faster increases in food prices than in the general price level; and this will impact disproportionately upon major poverty groups – landless rural workers, urban labour and the urban unemployed (Killick, 1984: 47). 'Price shocks' can have major and rapid impacts upon the real incomes of those with 'sticky' nominal incomes and/or those whose consumption of the 'shocked' items makes up a large share of their total expenditures.

The restructuring which it is the object of altered incentive structures to accomplish will, of course, also carry distributional implications. Apart from the possibility of expanded employment via the use of previously underutilized capacity, what other overall effects upon employment, poverty and distribution would one expect from shifts out of some productive activities (notably non-tradables) into others (tradables)? This depends, above all, upon the labour-intensity of the expanding sectors relative to that of the declining ones. The presumption must be that most non-tradables are highly labour-intensive – for example, construction, government, and other services. Indeed, switching from nontradables to tradables may sometimes be seen as little more than a euphemism for reducing wages and employment in government and the organized service sector, relative to other sectors. Clearly, much also depends on the intersectoral mobility of labour (and other resources and factors). The overall impact of restructuring upon total factor *demand* may thus generate redistribution at the expense of labour, particularly that in the formal sectors, even when resources are shifted primarily in the direction of export activity that appears to be labour-intensive relative to most import-competing activity.

How such changes affect income distribution and poverty depends very much upon the specifics of each case. Where resources are shifted from urban services to smallholder farmers to permit them to grow either more import-substituting food or export crops, as is likely to be the case in most adjustment programmes in sub-Saharan Africa today, equity is likely to increase and poverty decline. This is even more likely if displaced urban workers still have the option of returning to their villages. On the other hand, similar resource shifts toward estate agriculture (or mining activity) may, in other cases, widen income disparities and worsen the problems of urban marginal groups.

Development Strategy

Changes in overall strategy may be initiated at the same time as a stabilization and adjustment programme. Pressure from international financial institutions today directs borrowing governments toward increased reliance upon market forces, trade and financial liberalization, and a reduced role for the state and state-owned enterprises. In the 1970s the World Bank also exerted pressure upon prospective borrowers to pursue strategies, policies and projects that would improve the welfare of the poorest; this thrust was largely abandoned in discussions of structural adjustment in the 1980s, at least in part because of diminished confidence that ostensibly poverty-oriented programmes were actually helping the poor. Under pressure from UNICEF and aid donors, it now seems to be returning.

Issues of development strategy relating to such matters as the role of the public sector, the degree of 'openness', and the appropriate degree of attention to be devoted to income distribution remain matters of political and professional disagreement, in which ideology and politics are at least as important as economic analysis (see Chapter 7).

In the context of the renewed non-ideological concern with the welfare of the poorest, however, it is possible to be a little more specific about one strategic issue. The encouragement of smallholder agriculture, rather than estates (whether public or private), is likely to be relatively beneficial to the poor. The appropriate orientation as between large and small farms in *all* dimensions of agricultural policy is likely to be of far greater distributional significance than the food-versus-export orientation (or commercialization) issue, about which there has been so much discussion. Studies of the latter issue in a wide variety of environments suggest that most countries either manage a *combination* of growth in food production and export cash-cropping or they fail to manage either (von Braun, 1989). Smallholder farmers think in terms of farm systems in which returns and risks are jointly optimized and in which both food and cash crops figure. Appropriate policies on the supply of inputs and credit, rural infrastructure, and output marketing will benefit poor smallholders whatever they choose to do (as well as, in many instances, some better-off farmers). It is nevertheless true that the choices of crop (or crop mix) and technology by farmers, and government policies influencing these choices, have major implications for the generation and distribution of income and employment, both on and off-farm (for instance, in processing, local goods and services supply, marketing). Not least important is the potential impact of alternative cropping patterns upon the gender distribution of labour inputs, income, nutrition, and decision-making power; and this may also influence child welfare.

FURTHER CONSIDERATIONS IN PUTTING TOGETHER AN ALTERNATIVE PROGRAMME

One cannot simply develop an adjustment programme that is 'easier' on poverty by *assuming* that there will be more resources, particularly external resources, than are in fact likely to be there. Obviously, governments in difficulty will seek further net external resource flows from abroad. Equally obviously, reasonable people of goodwill may occasionally disagree on forecasts of various elements of a nation's economic future. But one cannot carry on discussions about the detailed make-up of a programme if there are different underlying assumptions about the resource constraints. Alternative domestic programmes should therefore be built *both* on very conservative assumptions *and* on the basis of alternative more optimistic, and perhaps realistic, forecasts. One can then logically begin to separate the debate about the internal consistency of the programme (with common assumptions about resource availability) from that about resource availability.

Among the issues on which a government must reach a measure of internal agreement, only some of which are distribution or poverty-related, are the following:

- priority investments, particularly of the bottleneck-breaking kind – minimum acceptable expenditures upon them, their precise composition, and likely gestation periods;
- other key objectives that are virtually 'non-negotiable' and what they are likely to cost – for example, food security, defence, protection of vulnerable or other key groups and so on;
- the overall distribution of the required burden of adjustment over time, at least in broad terms – as among income groups, socioeconomic classes, geographic areas and so on;
- the proposed deployment and phasing of major policy changes, particularly in the realms of government-controlled prices and wages, government budget, credit expansion, the nominal exchange rate and the like;
- contingency plans for unexpected changes in variables beyond the authorities' controls, particularly unfavourable changes;
- proposed targets over a time horizon of its own choosing for the balance of payments, and other key macro-economic indicators. (See also Taylor, 1988.)

Governments which are themselves very weak in manpower and planning capacity are entitled to ask for the presentation of *alternative* programmes from the IMF and World Bank, programmes that reflect domestic aspirations, including those relating to income distribution – achieving different kinds of trade-offs among conflicting objectives while still 'adding up'. It is the responsibility of the Fund/Bank staff, as well as local governments, to consider the relative merits of a range of possible programmes, rather than simply considering one basic programme on a 'yes or no', 'take it or leave it' basis. The 1988 Annual Report of the IMF states:

> The Board also discussed the implications of Fund-supported adjustment programs for poverty. While it is agreed that questions of income distribution, as such, should not form part of Fund conditionality, considerable importance is attached to improving program design so as to protect the poorest segments of the population during the period in which adjustment policies are being implemented. There was a broad consensus to mitigate, without sacrificing the goals of macro-economic adjustment, the impact of adjustment programs on poverty, as well as for the Fund to strengthen its capacity to respond more effectively to members' requests for advice in this field. (IMF, 1988: 48)

This should now be taken at face value. Technical assistance in the design of poverty-sensitive adjustment programmes should, if necessary, be requested; and the seriousness and capacity of the Fund and Bank to offer it should be tested. In the meantime many governments will also find it useful to draw on such other 'external' sources of information and advice as UNICEF, ILO, IFAD, aid agencies, and universities.

REFERENCES

Addison, Tony and Lionel Demery (1985), *Macro-Economic Stabilization, Income Distribution and Poverty: A Preliminary Survey*, Overseas Development Institute, Working Paper no. 15.

Ahluwalia, S. Montek and Frank J. Lysy, (1981), 'Employment, Income Distribution, and Programs to Remedy Balance-of-Payments Difficulties' in William R. Cline and Sidney Weintraub (eds), *Economic Stabilization in Developing Countries*, Washington DC: The Brookings Institutions, pp. 149–89.

Cornia, Giovanni Andrea; Richard Jolly and Frances Stewart (1987), (eds), *Adjustment With A Human Face, Protecting the Vulnerable and Promoting Growth (A Study by UNICEF)*, 2 vols, Oxford: Clarendon Press.

Dervis, Kemal, Jaime de Melo, and Sherman Robinson (1982), *General Equilibrium Models for Development Policy*, A World Bank Research Publication, Cambridge: Cambridge University Press.

Giannini, A. (1983), 'The Interest Elasticity of Savings in Developing Countries', *World Development*, vol. 11, no. 7, July.

International Monetary Fund, (1988), *Annual Report*, Washington, DC: IMF.

Johnson, Omotunde and Joanne Salop (1980), 'Distributional Aspects of Stabilization Programs in Developing Countries', *IMF Staff Papers*, vol. 27, no. 1, March.

Khan, Mohsin and Malcolm D. Knight (1985), *Fund-Supported Adjustment Programs and Economic Growth*, IMF Occasional Paper no. 41, November.

Killick, Tony *et al.* (1984), *The Quest for Economic Stabilisation, the IMF and the Third World*, London: Heinemann.

Knight, J.B. (1976), 'Devaluation and Income Distribution in Less Developed Economies', *Oxford Economic Papers*, vol. 28, no. 12, July.

Larosiere, J. de (1984), 'Does the Fund Impose Austerity?', Washington, DC: International Monetary Fund.

Mohammed, Azizali F. (1984), 'Fund Conditionality: A View from Inside' in Khadija Haq and Carlos Massad (eds), *Adjustment with Growth, A Search for an Equitable Solution*, Islamabad: North-South Roundtable, pp. 180–97.

Nelson, Joan (1984), 'The Political Economy of Stabilization: Commitment, Capacity, and Public Response', *World Development*, vol. 12, no. 10, October.

Nugent, Jeffrey B. and Constantine Glezakos (1982), 'Phillips Curves in Developing Countries: The Latin American Case', *Economic Development and Cultural Change*, vol. 30, no. 2, January.

Pinstrup-Andersen, Per (ed.) (1988), *Food Subsidies in Developing Countries:*

Costs, Benefits and Policy Options, Baltimore and London: International Food Policy Research Institute, Johns Hopkins University Press.

Taylor, Lance, (1983), *Structuralist Macroeconomics, Applicable Models for the Third World*, New York: Basic Books.

Taylor, Lance (1988), *Varieties of Stabilization Experience, Towards Sensible Macroeconomics in the Third World*, Oxford: Clarendon Press.

UNICEF (1984), *The State of the World's Children*, Oxford and New York: Oxford University Press.

Von Braun, Joachim (1989), 'Commercialization of Smallholder Agriculture: Policy Requirements for Capturing Gains for the Poor', Washington DC: IFPRI mimeo.

World Bank (1979), *World Development Report*, Washington DC: The World Bank.

World Bank (1988), *Adjustment Lending: An Evaluation of Ten Years of Experience*. Washington, DC: The World Bank.

Zuckerman, Elaine (1989), 'Adjustment Programs and Social Welfare', World Bank, mimeo.

9. Direct Foreign Investment and Alternative Forms of External Non-concessional Finance for Developing Countries

INTRODUCTION

Whereas domestic savings rates did not alter much, on average, in the oil-importing developing countries (other than China and India) over the 1960–80 period, increased external finance made possible significant increases in gross domestic investment as a percentage of GDP (see Table 9.1). The particular mix of foreign governmental, transnational corporate and world financial market contributions to development finance in the Third World changed markedly over these years. The 1970s saw a remarkable relative increase in the role of bank finance. The debt crisis of the 1980s reversed this shift. The 1990s seem likely to witness a push towards relative resurgence of direct foreign investment. Within the OECD there is agreement 'on the desirability of diversifying the developing countries' sources of external finance, and in particular fuller use of the potential for direct investment' (1982). To the extent that portfolio finance is made available, it seems likely increasingly to be tied to trade flows and specific projects in the middle-income countries.

Direct foreign investment in developing countries grew in value during the 1970s at rates greater than those of the 1950s and 1960s, but its relative importance declined as new sources of commercial finance expanded even faster. While the developing countries' share of total world direct foreign investment actually increased in the 1970s, direct foreign investment made up a declining share of their total investment, capital imports and GNP. According to the OECD, direct foreign investment made up 17 per cent of total financial flows to the developing countries in 1970–72 but only 14 per cent in 1979–81 (OECD/DAC, 1982: 51). Table 9.2 shows the dramatic change in the make-up of developing countries' debt and investment obligations between 1971 and 1981. Direct investment's role fell from 32 per cent to 20 per cent (and its importance in servicing costs fell even more). Bank loans climbed from 8 per cent of the total in 1971 to 27 per cent in 1981.

Direct investment is concentrated in the better-off developing countries, as is commercial bank lending. Table 9.3 shows that low-income oil-importing countries (LICs) experienced stagnation in their already very low flows of direct investment in the 1970s while middle-income countries' direct investment receipts continued to grow. As is well known, the LICs received only a small proportion of the great expansion of commercial bank lending, but their experience in this respect is considerably better than that in direct investment. Also noteworthy is the fact that official development assistance (ODA) grew more rapidly in middle-income countries than in low-income ones.

Table 9.1 *Savings and investment ratios in developing countries, 1960 and 1980*

	Gross Domestic Savings as % of GDP		Gross Domestic Investment as % of GDP		Resource Balance as % of GDP	
	1960	1980	1960	1980	1960	1980
Low-income economies excluding China and India	9	7	11	15	–2	–8
Middle-income oil-importing economies	19	21	21	27	–2	–6

Source: World Bank, *World Development Report*, 1982, p. 118.

Declared nominal rates of return on direct foreign investment in developing countries have typically exceeded nominal rates of interest paid on commercial bank borrowing by creditworthy developing countries (see Table 9.4). (The real costs of external borrowing are also influenced, of course, by the currency denomination of repayment obligations and the rate of global inflation.) In the 1972–81 period, US direct foreign investment in developing countries earned a rate of return averaging 13.1 per cent in manufacturing and 15.8 per cent in other non-petroleum areas (plus about another 2 per cent on average from fees and royalties). These rates have been reasonably stable, varying in manufacturing between 11 and 16

Table 9.2 Debt outstanding and direct foreign investment in developing countries, 1971 and 1981 (US$ billion)

	Year-end 1971		Year-end 1981	
	(US$ billion)	%	(US$ billion)	%
Disbursed debt	*90*	*68*	*530*	*80*
of which concessional	33	25	116	18
of which non-concessional	57	43	414	63
of which bank loans	11	8	180	27
of which export credits	27	20	128	19
Foreign direct investment stock	*43*	*32*	*130*	*20*
Total debt plus foreign direct investments	*133*	*100*	*660*	*100*

Sources: UN Centre on Transnational Corporations, *Transnational Corporations in World Development: A Re-examination*, New York, 1978, p. 254; DAC, OECD, *Development Cooperation, Efforts and Policies of Members of the Development Assistance Committee, 1982 Review*, Paris, p. 57, OECD, *External Debt of Developing Countries, 1982*, Paris; UN Centre on Transnational Corporations, unpublished.

Table 9.3 Capital flows to low-income and middle-income developing countries by category, 1970–80 (US$ billion at 1978 prices)

	1970	1975	1980
Low-income oil-importing countries			
Direct foreign investment	0.3	0.4	0.2
Commercial loans	0.5	0.8	0.7
Official development assistance	3.4	6.6	5.7
Middle-income oil-importing countries			
Direct foreign investment	3.4	3.8	4.5
Commercial loans	8.9	21.0	27.1
Official development assistance	3.3	5.3	7.9

Source: World Bank, *World Development Report*, 1981, p. 49.

per cent (13 and 19 per cent including fees and royalties) over the decade. Eurodollar borrowing rates over the same period varied between 5 per cent and 17 per cent (plus spreads for developing countries which themselves varied between 0.6 per cent and 1.6 per cent on average). More important, interest rates have often been negatively correlated with developing country capacity to pay, as indicated by such measures as the terms of trade. During the terms of trade collapse (of over 30 per cent) in the 1977–82 period, Eurodollar interest rates rose from 6 per cent in 1977 to an average of 16.8 per cent in 1981 (exclusive of spreads), and even higher levels in 1982. At the same time, rates of return on US direct foreign investment rose in 1980 but then fell back to mid-1970s levels by 1981, continuing their fall in 1982.

Table 9.4 *Cost of external finance in developing countries, and terms of trade, 1972–81*

	Rate of Return on US Direct Foreign Investment in LDCs				Euro dollar Interest Rate† (%)	Non-oil LDC Terms of Trade (1975=100)
	Manufacturing		Other Non-petroleum			
	Only on Investment (%)	Including Fees and Royalties* (%)	Only on Investment	Including Fees and Royalties* (%)		
1972	12.4	14.7	10.2	13.4	5.46	106
1973	13.3	15.8	14.4	16.9	9.24	109
1974	13.9	16.2	20.9	23.8	11.01	109
1975	13.9	16.1	18.7	21.6	7.02	100
1976	11.5	13.2	19.8	20.9	5.58	99
1977	11.6	13.0	18.2	20.1	6.03	107
1978	15.2	16.8	18.4	20.8	8.74	100
1979	14.3	16.6	21.2	22.8	11.96	91
1980	16.3	18.8	20.8	23.0	14.36	81
1981	12.5	15.2	18.0	20.6	16.79	72

* Calculated by the author from data in cited source.
† Exclusive of spreads and fees.

Sources: US Department of Commerce, *Survey of Current Business*, various issues; *US Federal Reserve Bulletin*, various issues; UNCTAD, *Handbook of International Trade and Development Statistics*, and data supplied by UNCTAD.

DIRECT FOREIGN INVESTMENT VERSUS COMMERCIAL BANK FINANCING

Both borrowers and lenders have reasons for preferring different forms of finance at different times and places. As borrowers see it, commercial bank credit is available on a relatively competitive market. The room for bargaining is therefore fairly limited in respect of either price or other conditions. It has the advantages of being fast-disbursing and untied. Its use requires the addition of management of a debt portfolio to the other responsibilities of national monetary authorities. Direct foreign investment, on the other hand, as an oligopoly phenomenon, is much more susceptible to variation in its terms and conditions; effective bargaining can improve the conditions under which it is made available, and the dimensions of bargaining and monitoring of performance are multiple and complex. Contracting (transactions) costs are likely to be higher and tie-in provisions may limit borrowers' flexibility. Financing through this device, however, may enable the borrower to acquire better or cheaper access to technology, information and markets. The traditional direct investment package became relatively less attractive to individual developing countries in the 1970s as they developed their own managerial, technological and marketing capacity, and obtained access to arm's-length sources of foreign finance on Euro-currency markets. On the other hand, increased competition among TNCs from a greater variety of home countries probably improved the terms on which traditional packages of direct investment were available, at least in some sectors, in the 1970s.

Creditors, notably TNCs, also calculate the advantages of alternative financing forms in developing countries for themselves. Firm-specific advantages relating to technology, markets or managerial skills may be best realized by TNCs through internalized transactions with subsidiaries in the traditional direct investment form. On the other hand, the growth of governmental regulations (on the extent of foreign equity participation in particular types of domestic enterprise, among other matters); performance requirements; the continuing risk of expropriation; and the frequent prospect of their own continued control without ownership, have generated increased TNC interest, in many sectors, in non-equity forms of overseas involvement. A much-quoted Brookings Institution study argued that:

> American policy . . . should abandon entirely the idea of direct ownership . . . and encourage the provision of production and marketing skills through service or management contracts . . . such contracts, because they offer a highly leveraged return on corporate assets, can be extraordinarily lucrative (Bergsten *et al.*, 1978: 160).

Services are the most rapidly rising segment of US exports. These 'new forms' of investment by transnationals were of increasing overall relative importance in their activities in developing countries in the 1970s. (For a good review of these issues, see Dunning, 1982.)

The form of external financial involvement in domestic enterprises may be a matter for bargaining between host governments and foreign firms (together with their local allies) where preferences diverge. But in the 1970s there was frequently a degree of mutual interest in the increased use of bank finance and non-equity arrangements. There may now be a mutual interest in more flexible alternative forms of finance.

The 1970s witnessed a burst of commercial financing of development beyond most prior expectations. This external finance was primarily, though far from exclusively, employed for productive purposes, permitting the increase or maintenance of investment rates that could not otherwise have been easily achieved. This commercial financing of productive investment nevertheless generated subsequent debt difficulties because of the particular forms it took (and, of course, because of the difficulties of the world economy).

Commercial bank financing is characterized both by more rigid servicing obligations than equity finance, and by shorter terms to maturity than bond finance. The introduction of floating interest rate bank lending – which by the early 1980s accounted for the bulk of commercial bank lending to developing countries, and over 85 per cent of these countries' outstanding commercial debt – created even greater servicing problems for debtors by introducing still further uncertainties to the already rigid servicing obligations. (It is important to recognize that it made *real* interest payment obligations more unpredictable, not just nominal ones.) It also substantially increased the degree to which the middle-income developing countries' macro-economic performance is dependent upon events in the main industrialized centres.

The pressures upon debtors, and indeed upon the entire financial system, created by inappropriate forms of development financing have been eased by *ad hoc* flexibility on the part of creditors, backed (and sometimes pushed) by national and international monetary authorities in respect of debt servicing schedules. By rescheduling and/or refinancing existing debt and arranging new emergency credits for debtor countries experiencing 'crises', the commercial banks and monetary authorities staved off defaults and moratoria which might otherwise have created havoc in the international financial system reminiscent of the 1930s.

In retrospect, one can see that the development financing system became seriously unbalanced by the events of the 1970s, notably by the fortuitous explosion of international commercial bank lending which followed the first 'oil shock'. Overly liquid commercial banks were only too happy to lend to middle-income developing countries determined to maintain their development efforts in the face of external adversity, at least some of which was reasonably perceived as being temporary. The development of offshore banking during the previous decade had created the perfect vehicle for mutually advantageous intermediation between oil surplus countries' depositors and developing countries' borrowers. Indeed, there was a certain amount of self-congratulation in the commercial banking community in respect of the ease and efficiency with which they 'recycled' the first round of oil surpluses.

By now the inequities and risks of assigning so heavy a role in international monetary management to commercial institutions are widely recognized. The search is on for better means of providing short- to medium-term balance of payments finance to countries experiencing temporary difficulties, particularly those that are not of their own making; at the same time, there is considerable rethinking about the optimal set of policies and paths for adjustments to permanent (fundamental) changes, and the best ways of ensuring that adjustment accompanies the provision of finance. These efforts centre on strengthening and reforming the activities of the IMF and the World Bank in the context of a greater effort to coordinate or even multilateralize macro-economic management at the global level.

While the size and longer duration of external 'shocks' during the past 15 years have muddied the traditional distinction between IMF-type balance of payments financing and development financing (a muddiness visible in the greater overlap between IMF and World Bank activities), it is still possible to consider the issue of development finance *per se*. How are external savings best channelled towards the ongoing investment programmes in the poorer parts of the world – programmes which ought to continue to carry overall global priority both on efficiency and distributional grounds? More particularly, how are commercially motivated savers and investors, whether private or public, best mobilized in the development financing effort? For better or worse, commercially motivated flows seem likely to dominate development finance in all but the poorest developing countries in the 1990s.

LONGER-TERM (BOND) FINANCING

One possibility is to seek to lengthen maturities in current lending and, in particular, to restore bond finance to the pre-eminent position which it held in nineteenth-century development finance. Bond finance has traditionally possessed the virtues of long maturities and widespread dispersion of ownership. While finance is always fungible, long-term finance is clearly preferable to short-term finance if the investments which are to be financed have long gestation periods. Certainly, overall 'development' is a long-run proposition. Short-term finance can be continually rolled over to generate the same eventual effect as long-term finance in normal circumstances; the only difference has been the variation in interest rates which accompanies the rolled-over finance. Now that bonds also frequently carry variable interest rates, this distinction has lost importance, but that relating to the certainty of actually having the finance on a long-term basis remains. Should the confidence of the creditors be shaken, by however irrational a process or however short-term a set of events, the short-term financing system can bring 'development' finance to a halt in a way in which long-term finance is not similarly vulnerable. That is what has caused the greatest difficulty in the 1980s. Had monetary authorities not twisted their arms, commercial banks would have cut their new lending by even more than they did. New or rolled-over or rescheduled loans were, for a long time, made available only at higher spreads over LIBOR, with higher fees and with even shorter maturities.

Once a 'steady state' of external borrowing is reached, there is a maturity structure of debt which involves a constant proportion of the debt maturing every year; the shorter the term of the average debt, the higher is the proportion maturing every year, and therefore the more unreliable is finance in any given year. During a period of debt expansion, such as typifies countries seeking to accelerate development efforts, uncertainty as to the *net increase* in development finance which is to be made available may be as damaging to the management of a sound investment programme as uncertainty as to the prospects of rolling over existing debt. (In the well known Domar formulation, positive balance of payments effects from external financing depend upon the growth rate in the stock of external debt exceeding the rate of interest being paid on it.) In such circumstances, short-term debt is particularly ill-suited to the borrowers' requirements.

Commercial bank financing is far more concentrated among the lending institutions than bond financing has traditionally been. While many smaller banks have been brought into syndicated lending activities, and European and Japanese banks have expanded their loans to developing countries, very high proportions of total developing country debt are still concentrated in a relatively few major banks. Moreover, these banks are sufficiently important in the total financial system that their health must remain beyond question. Not only can they not be permitted to fail but confidence in their strength must not be permitted to flag. Defaults upon major parts of their lending are therefore less likely to be tolerated by governmental authorities than have been defaults on bonds – ownership of which has typically been much more widely spread – or expropriation of foreign equity. Since the major banks are aware of their importance in the system, this creates a potential 'moral hazard' in which they may take greater risks than they would if they were not confident that they would be backed. (On the other hand, some say that their knowledge of their role could also lead them to especially prudent and responsible behaviour.) All things considered, commercial bank credit has severe disadvantages as a source of Third World development finance.

MORE FLEXIBLE CREDIT INSTRUMENTS

There has always been a strong case for gearing servicing obligations to the borrower's capacity to pay. Provided that lenders receive their expected rate of return over the entire period of investment there is no obvious reason for them to care about the precise schedule for servicing of the debt. The stability of the lender's income may demand some limits upon flexibility of payment, but there is no objective reason for the borrower to carry the entire burden of the risk of fluctuating fortunes.

All else being equal, the importance of flexible repayment provisions on external debt varies with the degree of instability and uncertainty of balance of payments experience. Countries that are particularly vulnerable to external shocks because of the high relative importance of the external sector, the commodity composition and degree of concentration of their exports, the absence of 'slack' in their import bills, and the rigidity of their productive structure will run particularly high risks when they take on rigid obligations. Table 9.5 indicates that the least developed (though not the poorest) countries tended to suffer the greatest instability of terms of trade, export purchasing power and import volume in the 1960s and 1970s. These countries are also usually quite rigid in their production structure, and most of the slack has long since gone from their imports. In the absence of offsetting credit, the import volume fluctuations necessitated by external fluctuations in such cases are generally only attainable by GNP fluctuations.

This table also demonstrates the significant increase in external instability experienced by developing countries of all types in the 1970s. The better off and manufactures-exporting developing countries managed

*Table 9.5 External instability in developing countries, by type, 1960–69, 1970–79**

	Commodity Terms of Trade (%)		Purchasing Power of Exports (%)		Import Volume (%)	
	1960–69	1970–79	1960–69	1970–79	1960–69	1970–79
Fast-growing exporters of manufactures	0.0052	0.0112	0.0137	0.0191	0.0284	0.0140
Least developed countries	0.0125	0.0180	0.0065	0.0226	0.0114	0.0237
Other non-oil developing countries	0.0080	0.0100	0.0091	0.0108	0.0067	0.0125
Developed market economies	0.0025	0.0073	0.0054	0.0105	0.0049	0.0103
Developing countries by income level (1977)						
Over $1000 per capita	0.0077	0.0497	0.0085	0.0347	0.0176	0.0154
$500–$1000 per capita	0.0077	0.0227	0.0130	0.0213	0.0055	0.0189
Under $500 per capita	0.0091	0.0128	0.0086	0.0133	1.0096	0.0160

* Coefficients of variation (standard error as a percentage of the mean) around a linear time trend calculated on the relevant indices based on 1975.

Source: Calculated from UNCTAD, Handbook of International Trade and Development Statistics, 1980 (and later data supplied by UNCTAD).

nevertheless to stabilize their import volume with increased access to external credit.

In the 1960s and 1970s most developing countries expanded the degree of their integration with the world economy, a development which was generally welcomed as in their own, as well as in the global, economic interest. In consequence the links between macro-economic performance in the industrialized countries and developing countries' exports strengthened; at the same time the link between developing countries' growth and their export performance seems also to have strengthened. These developments are attributable to the increasing relative importance of manufactures in Southern exports: manufactures are characterized by higher income elasticity of demand than those of traditional primary product exports, and they also generate more growth spin-offs (Goldstein and Khan, 1982). There is also some evidence, however, that commodity prices became more elastic in response to world industrial production during the 1970s (Bank of England, 1981:47).

Increasing integration with an increasingly unstable world economy in circumstances which also involve increasing correlation between overall macro-economic and export experience suggests the need for increasing attention to the problems which instability generates. It is commonly argued that

> ... a relatively high degree of integration with the world economy carries both benefits and costs. Relatively high sensitivity of domestic growth with respect to industrial country growth is beneficial when industrial countries grow rapidly and costly when they grow slowly. Turning inward as a response to projected slow industrial country growth rates might reduce the short-run fluctuation in non-oil developing country growth rates but would also be likely to reduce the medium-term level of their growth. (Bank of England, 1981:37)

The incentives for turning inwards could be reduced by reducing the risks attached to integration into the international economy. The provision of more flexible credit instruments (together with the provision of adequate compensatory finance) should therefore be seen as profoundly liberalizing innovations, designed to make the entire global system work more effectively.

'Bisque' clauses in financial contracts, in which the borrower is permitted to defer servicing obligations in times of difficulty, have a long history. More automatic mechanisms for 'triggering' reductions and increases in debt servicing obligations, or what has been termed 'bisque both ways' (Harvey, 1981:7), seem even better devices for increasing servicing flexibility.

There are precedents in some official arrangements, such as those of the IMF and the Lomé Conventions's STABEX scheme. Borrowers may be prepared to pay some premium over the normal rate of interest in return for increased flexibility in respect of payments obligations, but this may not be necessary since flexibility may increase the orderliness and predictability of debt servicing for all. So far as bank lending is concerned, recent events have shown that 'creditors can only get their money back if they are willing to provide, *after* the event, the flexibility in repayment terms that should perhaps have been written into the original loan terms, but was not' (Harvey, 1981:4). Whereas borrowers' creditworthiness suffers in these rescheduling exercises (and not merely that of the borrowers directly involved) lenders lose in terms of the time spent in negotiations, nervousness and ill will. More flexible repayment obligations involving a greater degree of risk-sharing on the part of lenders may be attractive to creditors as well as debtors.

Overly rigid payments obligations in an increasingly unstable world, or even in a world which is subject to only occasional but severe disruptions, can generate major problems not only for the debtors but also for the international trading and financial system as a whole. Payments can only be made by adjustments in international trade, contraction of imports and expansion of exports. In times of overall global recession, the cumulative effect of a number of such individual national trade adjustments may seriously strengthen contractionary forces and place new stress upon the maintenance of liberal trading arrangements. Financial over-rigidity can thus spill over into beggar-my-neighbour trade policies and protectionism in the trade regime. On the other hand, if rigidly specified payments are not made, confidence in the financial system is impaired, with potentially equally devastating systemic effects. Systemic interests would therefore be served by more appropriately flexible debt instruments at the international level.

Efforts should be made to develop flexible debt instruments, both in private markets and in official lending schemes, which incorporate increased risk-sharing. They should be employed for medium- to long-term balance of payments loans to sovereign governments, as well as for the purposes of particular projects or export sales.

New financial instruments may emerge spontaneously from the market in response to new demands. But 'the magic of the marketplace' tends to be biased in the direction of tricks that have an established record of success. The inertia and conservatism of the financial community may be somewhat reduced by demonstrations of the viability of other options. The obvious place to which developing countries should be able to look for innovative approaches to their financing problems is the World Bank. Its 1:1 gearing ratio, well diversified portfolio, no-default record, and continuing triple-A credit rating leaves it room to engage in rather more innovative approaches to development finance than it has so far shown much sign of considering. In 1982 it followed, sheep-like, the commercial banking community down the convenient (for lenders) road of floating interest rate debt at a time when it might have exerted its influence in more innovative and stabilizing directions. Borrower pressures did achieve a reform in currency denomination practices in World Bank lending in mid-1980; exchange risk has been reduced, especially for smaller borrowers, by the new practice of offering the same currency mix to all Bank borrowers (see Chapter 5). Perhaps borrower pressures might now be mobilized in favour of more appropriate risk-sharing financial instruments in World Bank lending. This seems a more important area for Bank initiative than that of co-financing using traditional instruments which, despite the limited evidence of any consequent additionality of financial flows, has received so much attention. Innovation could occur not only in the nature of the Bank's lending contracts but also in the instruments it offers to the investors from which it draws its resources. The former might well precede the latter, with the Bank intermediation consciously taking on some extra risks in the meantime.

EQUITY FINANCE AND DIRECT FOREIGN INVESTMENT

Until such new instruments are developed, the principal existing mechanism for the creditor's assumption of greater risk is equity finance. Equity financing at the project level does not, however, ensure that national foreign payments obligations are correlated with national servicing capacity, since project success may be uncorrelated with aggregate national performance.

Equity finance has been associated with direct foreign investment and transnational corporate control in the developing countries, but this association can mislead. Direct investment may involve greater rigidities in some dimensions of external relationships than other non-equity financing arrangements; and not all expansion of direct investment is in equity form.

Direct investment usually brings intrafirm international trade along with it. Intrafirm trade, whether in goods or in services, is likely to be more stable and predictable than arm's-length trade. There is some empirical support for this proposition in disaggregated estimates of US import functions, in which intrafirm import price elasticities are significantly lower than those on arm's-length imports – although there was no difference in income elasticities (Goldsbrough, 1981). Both volume and unit values of US related-party imports were found to be more stable than those for non-related party imports in a sample of products from LDCs (Jarrett 1981). Where direct investments involve exporting, they may therefore stabilize national export earnings; but, otherwise, they can impart extra rigidity to the import bill (which may also be higher in direct investment projects than elsewhere). Management and marketing fees, royalties and so on, within direct investment packages, may be contractually specified in different ways, but are typically less directly and positively related to firm performance than are dividends. Intrafirm loans generate interest obligations which may be just as rigid or inappropriately flexible as any other external loans – as do arm's length international bank loans employed for the purchase of domestic equity by foreign firms. Moreover, parent control over transfer prices on intrafirm transactions may engender actual external remittances which vary a good deal less over time than do recorded dividend payments (although this must be purely a matter of conjecture). Direct investment *per se* may not therefore be characterized by appropriately flexible international payments obligations. It appears most likely to be helpful, relative to alternative arrangements, in exporting activities.

There exist spheres in which the role of direct foreign investment is likely to continue to play an important role, regardless of the arguments concerning the relative merits of other financing forms. Direct foreign investment is likely still to be demanded and achieved by foreign firms in circumstances where technology rents may be dissipated in arm's-length contracts, and in which their bargaining strength is particularly great. 'High' technology manufacturing activities are much less likely to be financed through non-equity forms and licensing agreements than are other activities. For many developing countries, however, the potential structural change engendered by the introduction of 'highest' if not 'high' technology activities is not currently of primary developmental significance.

Of wider structural significance – particularly in the current period of severe balance of payments difficulty in the non-oil developing countries and protectionism in the industrialized countries – is the potential role of direct foreign investment in attaining access to export markets. Developing country penetration of industrialized countries' markets for manufactures has been achieved primarily *without* transnational corporate ownership of the overseas producing enterprises. Direct investment is clearly not necessary for export-oriented policies, but it *can* matter to future market access, and the relative costs of alternative product mixes in export efforts.

OWNERSHIP TIES AND EXPORTING

There are obvious advantages to the importing country from direct ownership ties between its own firms and the sources of competitive imports. Willingness to adjust rather than seek protection is bound to be greater on the part of private firms which are themselves involved in the overseas production. Even if they nevertheless seek to 'manage' imports from their foreign subsidiaries and affiliates in order to slow the pace of change, there are unlikely to be unexpected 'surges' generating painful dislocations. Governments, too, are less likely to be receptive to protectionist pressures when the imports which they are invited to restrict originate from firms owned by, or affiliated to, corporations owned by their own nationals. In this instance, the intrafirm character of the trade does not constitute the essence of politicians' concern; rather it is national ownership of the producing firm that matters to their calculations as to which imports to encourage and which to discourage.

Growing proportions of developing countries' manufactured exports to the USA originate with US majority owned firms in these countries. Between 1966 and 1977, such developing country exports rose from 7.6 to 15.4 per cent of total US imports from these countries. The developing countries' US trade thereby became more US firm-related than that of any other area except Canada (for which the share was 27.2 per cent excluding the Auto Pact, down from 30.2 per cent in 1966; and 54.7 per cent including it, up from 43.4 per cent) (Lavergne and Helleiner, 1981). Table 9.6 shows the very low share of US imports originating in US majority-owned foreign affiliates (MOFAs) in the principal current areas of US trade policy 'crisis'.

Table 9.6 Imports from MOFAs as a percentage of total US imports in 'crisis' sectors, 1977

Sectors	%
Textiles	0.6
Apparel	0.9
Primary metal products, ferrous	1.8
Leather footwear	2.5
Motor vehicles	
Canada	93.3
Other DCs	13.0
LDCs	60.5
Japan	0
Colour televisions	
Canada	22.4
Other DCs	10.6
LDCs	38.2
Japan	0

Source: Lavergne and Helleiner (1981)

Japanese imports are subject to similar influences, extending well beyond the usual considerations of governmental tariffs and other trade restrictions into marketing and business practices. It has been reported, for instance, that

> ...exports of clothing to Japan (from Korea) are greatly facilitated if either the firms doing the exporting or those supplying the fabric are at least partially Japanese-owned. This may be for no reason other than to assure the precise style or quality desired by Japanese consumers, but it may also follow from the problems faced by non-Japanese in penetrating the domestic Japanese marketing network. Exports of textiles and apparel to other destinations have typically been unrelated to DFI. (Westphal *et al.*, 1979: 381–2)

Also relevant are the tariff provisions in the USA, the EEC and Japan favouring 'outward processing' or 'offshore assembly'. These encourage overseas production which is directly linked, although not necessarily via ownership, with productive enterprises in the importing country. In the cases of the EEC and Japan, in order to benefit from these tariff provisions the importing firm must be based in the importing country. In the USA, where the data are most readily available, trade under items 806.30 and 807.00 of the tariff schedule – those authorizing freedom from duty for the value of inputs originating in the USA – continues to expand at rapid rates. (Such imports from developing countries grew at a rate of 26.3 per cent a year in the 1975–81 period, when total US imports from developing countries grew at a 20 per cent rate.)

Authorization is found in the international MFA for similar special treatment to be accorded 'outward processed' textile and clothing trade. The EEC's bilateral arrangements under the umbrella of the MFA typically include a reserved portion of negotiated quotas for such trade. The Lomé Convention and the Caribbean Basin Initiative of the USA also encourage links with home firms in their rules of origin, governing access to preferential tariff treatment for developing country exports.

Also indicative of the role which ownership ties play in the evolution of manufactured goods trade is the growth of Japanese direct investment in the sectors and countries in which their export sales are restrained and the growth of joint production arrangements between US and European firms and their Japanese counterparts in Japan in the same sectors. If recent Japanese experience is any guide, one can anticipate that successful external penetration of other industrialized countries' markets for manufactures will generate political pressure for the location of minimum proportions of internationalized investments in the importing countries.

Domestic content legislation or more discreet political pressure may be brought to bear on both local and foreign corporations to reduce the employment impact of international industrial redeployment. The effect seems likely to be a reliberalized trading environment, and increased Northern importing from foreign affiliates, whether on an intrafirm basis or not.

So far as the exporting countries are concerned, the advantage of eased market access through the intermediation of foreign direct investors must be weighed against the danger of unusual dependence upon external decisions, notably those as to whether to relocate production away from any particular exporting country. The relative steadiness of such exports as there are may be offset by periodic 'shocks' as new production and sourcing decisions are made abroad; and such shocks may arrive at times of overall balance of payments distress. Whether developing country locations are disproportionately disadvantaged in times of overall production cutbacks is an empirical question on which there is, as yet, little systematic evidence. However, a study of Ireland found foreign investors no less stable than domestic firms in their employment over the cycle (McAleese and Counahan, 1979).

CONCLUSIONS

High technology and exporting apart, it is the risk-sharing characteristic of equity arrangements that is most important. In principle, equity finance could be made available directly to Third World firms, whether private or public, without the entire 'package' of direct investment attributes. Investors in industrialized countries could, and would, add Third World equity to their portfolios, provided that the yields and risks were sufficiently attractive and regulatory authorities, both in the investing and borrowing countries, permitted such investments. Pension funds, trust funds, life insurance companies and merchant banks might be encouraged more than they have been in the past not only to invest more in developing country bonds, as has often been suggested, but also to participate directly in minority equity holdings of Third World firms. One could envisage , alternatively, their provision of equity finance to new international intermediaries which might also supply equity-type finance to developing countries' governments in the form of commodity price-linked bonds or other innovative financial instruments. A little more institutional imagination seems to be called for in this area.

Greater use of financing arrangements that involve flexible repayment obligations in which short-term risks are borne by the creditor, as well as by the debtor, seems a reasonable objective for international financiers in the 1990s. Such arrangements should be applied to projects as well as to nations. In normal times, mechanisms for the financing of individual projects cancel out in their overall balance of payments effects at the national level; except in small countries, where a large project or two may dominate overall performance, there will always be offsets as between the more successful and the less successful projects so that, in the aggregate, the choice of financing mechanisms may not have great balance of payments significance. In unstable times, however, when entire economies are subjected to severe shock and all projects are likely to turn bad (or improve) simultaneously, methods of project financing are no longer a matter of indifference; and equity or equity-like arrangements reduce the overall risks for the debtor country.

Without minimizing the potential importance of an appropriate international framework for direct foreign investment or denigrating the efforts of those who continue to strive for improved legislative and regulatory mechanisms, international codes, improved insurance mechanisms and so on, one may nevertheless wonder whether efforts to bolster traditional direct foreign investment are not, today, being relatively overemphasized. Reactions to experience with commercial bank lending may combine with the predilections of key current Northern administrations to promote more direct investment than are in the developing countries' or systemic interests. There are clearly areas in which this form of external financing is either advantageous or inevitable. There are others in which equally good or better choices exist. Better balance in the flow of development finance to the Third World – an objective on which most can agree – is a matter of increasing the equity and equity-like component of the total rather than necessarily of raising the direct investment share. Means of achieving this objective deserve more attention than they have received.

REFERENCES

Bank of England (1981), 'Commodity Prices in the 1970s', *Quarterly Bulletin*, vol. 21, no. 1, March.

Bergsten, Fred C., Thomas Horst and Theodore H. Moran (1978), *American Multinationals and American Interests*, Washington DC: Brookings Institution.

Dunning, John H. (1982), 'International Business in a Changing World

Environment', *Banca Nazionale del Lavoro Quarterly Review*, no. 143, December.

Goldsborough, David J. (1981), 'International Trade of Multinational Corporations and its Responsiveness to Changes in Aggregate Demand and Relative Prices', *IMF Staff Papers*, vol. 28, no. 3, September.

Goldstein, Morris and Mohsin, S. Khan (1982), 'Effects of Slowdown in Industrial Countries on Growth in Non-oil Developing Countries', *IMF Occasional Paper*, no. 12, August.

Harvey, Charles (1981), 'On Reducing the Risk in Foreign Finance – for Both Parties', *Discussion Paper*, no. 167, Brighton: University of Sussex, Institute of Development Studies.

Jarrett, Peter J. (1981), 'Recent US Imports: Does Relatedness Make any Difference?', study prepared for the UN Center on Transnational Corporations, mimeo.

Lavergne, Réal P. and G.K. Helleiner (1981), 'US Transnational Corporations and the Structure of US Trade Barriers: An Empirical Investigation', study prepared for the UN Center on Transnational Corporations, mimeo.

McAleese, D. and M. Counahan (1979), '"Stickers" or "Snatchers"? Employment in Multinational Corporations during the Recession', *Oxford Bulletin of Economics and Statistics*, vol. 41, no. 4, November.

OECD/DAC (1982), *Development Co-operation , Efforts and Policies of Members of the Development Assistance Committee*, 1982 Review, Paris: OECD.

Westphal, L.E., Y.W. Rhee and G. Pursell (1979), 'Foreign Influences on Korean Industrial Development', *Oxford Bulletin of Economics and Statistics*, vol. 41, no. 4, November.

PART III
Developing Countries in the Global Trading and Investment System

10. Primary Commodity Markets: Recent Trends and Research Requirements

INTRODUCTION

Although primary commodity trade is seen as pre-eminently the poor countries' problem, industrial countries continue to dominate many world primary product markets, on both the selling and the buying sides. Oil apart, in 1979–81, 'industrial countries dominated both exports and imports of food, agricultural raw materials and metals, accounting for about 70 per cent of imports; for beverages, developing countries accounted for the bulk (79 per cent) of exports, whereas industrial countries accounted for the bulk of imports (88 per cent)' (Chu and Morrison 1986). The current collapse of international commodity prices is therefore of no less concern to many industrialized countries and significant sectors of all of them than it is to the developing countries.

Primary products nevertheless are of far greater relative importance on the export and income sides in developing countries than in industrial economies. (They are of roughly equivalent relative importance in import bills; see Table 10.1.) In low-income sub-Saharan Africa, primary commodities account for over 90 per cent of exports. In primary products, as in external debt, the size of the low-income countries' involvement in the world economy is small, but the importance of the issue of primary product market functioning for them is very great; indeed much greater than for better-off developing countries that are quantitatively more significant in the relevant markets. For these reasons, much of what follows is couched in terms of developing countries' concerns.

The relative importance of primary products in overall world trade has remained roughly the same over the past decade, but that of non-oil primary products has declined sharply, from 23 per cent in 1968–70 to 16 per cent in 1979–81 (Chu and Morrison 1986). Virtually all groups of developing countries have reduced their dependence on non-oil primary

Table 10.1 Primary products as a percentage of total exports and imports, 1982

	Exports			Imports			
	Fuels, Minerals and Metals	Other Primary Commod-ities	Total Primary Commod-ities	Food	Fuels	Other Primary Commod-ities	Total Primary Commod-ities
Low-income	20	30	50	17	18	11	46
China and India	21	23	44	17	15	15	47
Other low-income	15	55	70	16	24	4	44
Sub-Saharan Africa	22	69	91	15	23	3	41
Middle-income	37	21	58	12	21	6	39
Oil exporters	79	12	91	15	10	4	29
Oil importers	13	27	40	10	26	6	42
Lower middle income	47	34	81	20	19	5	44
Upper middle income	34	17	51	11	22	6	39
High-income oil exporters	96	—	96	13	2	2	17
Industrial market economies	12	14	26	11	26	8	45

Source: World Bank, *World Development Report*, 1985.

exports in recent decades. Even low-income sub-Saharan Africa reduced the primary product share of exports from 95 per cent to 91 per cent between 1965 and 1982.

The main focus of the developing countries' efforts to promote international economic reform during the second half of the 1970s was the functioning of world non-oil primary commodity markets. After years of diplomatic activity they succeeded, in principle, in having a (weak) new international institution established – the Common Fund – whose principal function would be to support price stabilization activities in international commodity agreements. But the relevant agreement was only recently ratified by enough signatories for it to come into effect, and in the meantime, international commodity agreements (ICAs) encountered increasing difficulties. In the 1980s, other major issues – notably financial and debt crises, and protectionism – have tended to push discussions of non-fuel primary commodity problems on to the back burner. Nevertheless, primary commodity markets are in crisis. The policy problems surrounding investments, production and trade have certainly not disappeared and, until addressed more satisfactorily in both rich and poor countries, will continue to generate dispute and uncertainty.

HIGHLIGHTS OF RECENT COMMODITY MARKET EXPERIENCE

It may be useful to offer a list of significant elements in recent primary commodity market experience as context for consideration of current issues and research needs.

First, the recent downward movement of non-oil real commodity prices, particularly those exported by developing countries, is now seen as unlikely to unwind itself within the next few years. Whatever the merits of the Prebisch–Singer thesis, actual longer-run historical trends (Spraos

Table 10.2 Indices of real non-fuel primary commodity prices (1980=100)

Year	Commodities Exported by Developing Countries	Commodities Exported by Industrial Countries	All Commodities
1970	107.9	109.8	108.9
1971	95.8	105.2	100.9
1972	92.7	105.7	99.8
1973	121.0	152.4	137.9
1974	131.3	148.0	140.4
1975	95.1	108.9	102.7
1976	109.7	111.6	110.8
1977	124.2	102.2	112.2
1978	101.5	95.4	98.2
1979	104.4	103.9	104.1
1980	100.0	100.0	100.0
1981	90.4	96.9	94.0
1982	83.4	88.5	86.2
1983	92.5	97.3	95.1
1984	99.4	100.8	100.1
1985	86.8	87.8	87.4

Note: Weights are based on 1979–81 average world export earnings. Nominal price indices are deflated by the UN index of the unit value of manufactures exported by industrial countries.

Source: IMF, *World Economic Outlook*, April 1986, p. 140.

1980), or 'long-cycles' (Rostow 1984), the fact is that since 1960 (and even earlier) there *has* been a downward trend in the real prices of commodities other than petroleum exported by less developed countries – faster in the post-1973 period than in the 1960–72 one (see also Chu and Morrison 1984). Table 10.2 shows IMF data on 1970–85 real price trends for commodities exported by both developing and industrial countries. (It would be helpful if the IMF, World Bank, UN Conference on Trade and Development [UNCTAD], and other sources could standardize their commodity price series, or at least report them in such a way as to make their differences, and the reasons for them, more evident.) Evidently both have fared badly. Small gains in real commodity prices realized in 1983–84 were offset by reductions again in 1985 (and further reductions thereafter, not shown in the table). From 1979 to 1985 the terms of trade of non-fuel-exporting developing countries deteriorated by nearly 13 per cent and subsequently fell further, despite petroleum import price declines.

The causes of this observed trend lie on both the demand and supply sides, varying in their specifics from market to market. Broadly, slow growth in the major markets, particularly Western Europe (which accounts for half of total world primary product imports and only a slightly lower share of total apparent consumption), technical changes (including synthetic development), structural change away from commodities-using activities and sectors and, in some instances, low income elasticities have held back demand. At the same time foreign exchange pressures in developing countries and technical changes have contributed to expansion of supplies and, in some cases, reduced price elasticity of supplies as well.

Second, short-term instability of real and nominal commodity prices and of national-level earnings from commodity exports have been sharply higher in recent years and periods of recession have been longer. According to an IMF study, already cited in Chapter 6:

> During 1981–82, commodity prices declined further (25 per cent) and for a longer period (8 quarters) than they have in the last 3 decades . . . primary commodity prices during 1972–82 were more than 3 times as unstable as they were during 1957–71. (Chu and Morrison,1984:94)

Generally, primary product prices continue to be more volatile than manufactured goods prices, and those exported by less developed countries especially so. In the 1960–82 period, primary product prices also experienced shorter upswing periods and longer downswing periods than manufactured goods prices (Thirlwall and Bergevin 1985).

The causes lie primarily in the increased instability of global economic conditions. Severe recessions in 1973–75 and 1980–83, rapid global inflation, which stimulated speculative activity in commodities markets as well as elsewhere, and unusually wide interest rate fluctuations all contributed. Unstable oligopolistic arrangements in the oil market also obviously played a role.

Third, difficulties in negotiating and implementing international commodity agreements over the post-Second World War period culminated in the dramatic collapse of the International Tin Agreement in October 1985 as the buffer stock ran out of funds and major sovereign governments (including industrial countries whose governments and bankers have spoken bravely of the need for poorer countries to honour their debts) reneged on their obligations. The Tin Agreement, one of the earliest of the postwar agreements (1953), had often been considered the most effective of the ICAs although its stockpile had long been dwarfed by that of the US General Services Administration. Whatever its causes and some were quite unnecessary (notably an inappropriate support price and dubious management), its collapse cast a pall over the future prospects for both other ICAs in various stages of disrepair – cocoa, coffee, rubber, and sugar – and new such arrangements in other commodity markets. The Common Fund for commodities, already so emasculated as to be scarcely recognizable as a relative of the original proposal, now looks more like an academic enterprise than ever.

The positions of the major industrialized nations on the desirability of governmental interventions in international commodity markets are much 'harder' today than they once were. Contemporary economic analysts, typically not very knowledgeable of history, seem unaware that at the Havana Conference it was agreed *by all* that international commodity agreements were appropriate in *unusually severe* circumstances such that market forces threatened to result in 'burdensome surplus' and/or 'widespread unemployment or under employment' in commodity-exporting countries (Article 62, International Trade Organization Charter). There was disagreement only on the desirability and feasibility of market interventions for the purpose of price or income stabilization in *normal* circumstances. By any reasonable standard, the 1980s have more than met the requirements for unusual action. In specific instances, the US government has in fact implicitly recognized this by using its strategic stockpile purchases to support the commodity exports (for example, Jamaican bauxite) of selected developing countries experiencing 'burdensome surpluses' and domestic economic difficulties. However, like so much else undertaken by recent US administrations, these measures were developed and undertaken on a unilateral or bilateral, rather than a multilateral, basis.

Fourth, the problems created by instability and decline of real export earnings, and the imperfections of existing international compensatory (or supplementary) financing mechanisms, have also been dramatically evident in the 1970s and 1980s. Particularly in the lower-income countries, where instability has been greatest, financing possibilities most lacking and structural adjustment most difficult, the impact of commodity price and earnings fluctuations has been severe. Fluctuations in import volume have been statistically related to growth in sub-Saharan Africa in the 1960s and 1970s (Helleiner,1986). Forced reductions in imports in the 1980s have brought severe current underutilization of capital and labour and reduced prospects for growth for the rest of the decade in most of Latin America and sub-Saharan Africa.

Compensatory or supplementary finance has been woefully inadequate. Even with strict limitations on eligibility (in respect of the circumstances and the amounts in which such finance is made available), those who benefited from the IMF's compensatory financing facility and the Lomé Convention's Stabex programme received only 62 per cent and 59 per cent, respectively, of calculated eligible shortfalls in the 1977–82 period (World Bank, 1986). Needless to say, the eligibility criterion itself generates flows that, if met, fall far short of needs; IMF quotas have always been a particularly unsuitable guide for the measurement, and prime determinant, of compensatory financing requirements. The IMF' s compensatory facility is also now more conditional than it used to be (Dell,1985). Nor have other IMF or World Bank loans made up the gap. The inadequacy of short- and medium-term finance for balance of payments adjustment in primary exporting low-income countries has created unnecessary suffering and economic waste, and contributed to international financial disorder. The sustained Northern advocacy of compensatory finance as a substitute for commodity market stabilization during the period when Third World pressure for ICAs was at its height now looks rather hollow. Developing countries have, in fact, had little of either.

Fifth, short- and medium-term exchange rate fluctuations and misalignments among the major currencies have added new complexities and uncertainties to international commodity markets. Currency risk has always been part of any trader's world, but the post-1973 exchange rate 'non-system' has necessitated fresh attention to the availability of adequate cover against volatile fluctuations that are frequently unrelated to the conventional 'basics' of balance of payments adjustment and unpredictable even as to general direction. In commodity markets, dollar or sterling price indices are no longer the sole, or even the primary, barometers of price change. In a world of truly unified and perfect markets, exchange rate fluctuations should have no effect upon real prices. 'Stickiness' of prices denominated in particular currencies and lags in their adjustment to such fluctuations, varying from commodity to commodity, however, are typical of real-world markets. Generally, primary commodity markets are probably faster to adjust to currency fluctuations than manufactured goods markets (McKinnon 1979). The degree and timing of 'pass-through' of exchange rate fluctuations into key-currency commodity and other prices and the currency composition of imports have thus become important elements in the short-term determination of traders' and countries' terms of trade. It is now an accepted stylized fact that, other things being equal (evidently in 1985–6 they were not), primary commodity exporters' experience worsened or improved terms of trade in line with the appreciation (or depreciation) of the US dollar. The resulting increase in exporter uncertainty is *in addition* to that deriving from traditional concerns over commodity market instability. The relative significance of this new source of terms of trade instability and uncertainty as against the traditional sources deserves more research exploration than it has received. (See, for instance, Fleisig and van Wijnbergen (1985), who argue that dollar appreciation worsens primary commodity exporters' terms of trade more when the US share of the world market for the commodity is smaller, US demand elasticity for the goods is smaller, the demand elasticity of other importers is lower, and the US share of exporters' imports is higher.) The adequacy of means of overcoming terms of trade instability via altered terms of contracts (currency of invoicing, forward markets and so on) would also be of research interest.

Sixth, agricultural export price wars, in which rich countries vie with one another and with innocent weaker competitors for third-country markets, have emerged as a major threat to international trading harmony. Direct export subsidies, subsidized export credit, and 'food aid' combine with extravagant domestic agricultural protection policies to produce major distortions and instability in particular commodity markets, like those for beef, sugar, dairy products, and grains. (For a recent summary, see World Bank, 1986.)

Finally, the previous trend toward the 'unpackaging' and 'decentralization' of world primary commodity markets seems now to have come to a halt. Nationalization and other devices for driving governmental 'wedges' into the internalized production and marketing systems of international firms, in particular minerals and other primary commodity markets, peaked in the 1960s. There may now be something of a movement back to more integrated systems.

Still, the implications of the 'new order' in primary commodities – the product of inexorable economic and political forces rather than of international diplomatic effort – are only very imperfectly understood. In this new order the management of investment, production, processing, transport, trade and marketing of primary products is no longer principally the prerogative of traditional transnational corporations but is also undertaken by independent governments, parastatal bodies and private firms based in the developing countries. Instead of the relatively stable, internalized decision-making systems of the large private international firms, primary product arrangements are determined in a complex and rapidly changing set of decision-making loci and new international networks. Governments, marketing boards, producers' associations, international banks, independent consulting firms, and various United Nations institutions are all involved in a number of ways, varying with the product, the location and the time period. The principal elements in forthcoming disputes under the emerging international primary commodity order are likely to be much less associated with the much discussed price stabilization schemes than with the location, ownership and control of processing, marketing and distribution systems for primary and processed primary products.

To a much greater degree than in the case of price stabilization schemes – where it has proven difficult enough to achieve intergovernmental agreement – there is potential for international conflict in the development of new arrangements for the management of primary commodity systems. Decision-making regarding investment, production, processing, and marketing is inevitably influenced by who is ultimately in control. Ownership, control and power relationships are therefore of the essence in the emerging primary commodity order. At issue is much more than the smoothing and tidying of more or less commonly agreed market mechanisms.

ISSUES FOR FURTHER RESEARCH

Issues in particular need of further research include national and global economic instability, and income enhancement for developing-country primary commodity exporters. In addition, it could prove fruitful to apply industrial organization approaches to primary commodity issues.

Issues in Instability: National and Global

The last decade or so of experience with more or less freely floating exchange rates has produced a majority professional consensus on the desirability of reducing erratic short- and medium-term fluctuations. Few believe that 'market intervention' can successfully withstand the 'fundamentals' of market price determination for very long. Most emphasize the need for mutually consistent monetary and fiscal policies in efforts to achieve mutually acceptable exchange rates. International capital flows and the asset market character of foreign exchange markets nevertheless generate fluctuations large enough to cause concern. There is little consensus as to the economic costs of exchange rate volatility and misalignment, but few today would argue that they are non-existent. Central banks, in any case, had long been smoothing out some of the pointless volatility in currency markets. Curiously, however, volatility and misalignment in international commodity markets are seen by a majority of Northern (though typically not Southern) professionals as part of the natural order of the international economy, either impossible or costly (or both) to attempt to correct.

The industrialized countries' expressed dislike of quotas and management of trade in primary commodities of interest to developing countries does not square well with international policies on dairy products and grains, not to speak of textiles, clothing, footwear, steel, and automobiles and a host of domestic interventions. While two economic 'wrongs' do not make an economic 'right', hypocrisy is still hypocrisy. US domestic price support programmes for sugar, cotton, rice, wheat and peanuts, and European support for milk, beef, sugar and grains, together tie up far more resources than all of the Third World's non-oil primary product schemes, real or imagined. Perceived national political and economic interests and domestic pressure group politics typically determine policy outcomes, not the finer points of the theory of markets; and international economists would do well to understand these matters of political economy better.

Primary commodity markets have served as a major 'legitimate' device for pouring resources into or out of the developing countries at fairly short notice. Fluctuations in North–South official or private capital flows of similar dimensions would be considered outlandishly disruptive and intolerable. Yet offsetting or modifying resource flows – even on commercial lending terms – are not available in anywhere near sufficient amounts to prevent unnecessary economic costs. The short- and medium-term recycling of resources is not, in principle, a very difficult matter to arrange.

Why has there been such resistance to the provision of compensatory finance sufficient to offset greater proportions of externally caused changes in import purchasing power and thus to prevent much unnecessary disruption and suffering, particularly for the poorest countries who face the greatest difficulties both in making short-term adjustments and in acquiring finance (or holding reserves)? In part, it may be the product of today's dominant development/adjustment ideology. The current Washington obsession with conditionality on resource flows to the developing countries has stood the old 'trade not aid' slogans on their heads. Officials in both the US government and the international financial institutions can be heard complaining when, for example, the increased price of coffee allows some countries to evade 'sound' economic policies. Automatic resource flows and entitlements are 'out'. Targeted and conditional flows are 'in'. Needless to say, the developing countries do not see it this way. These differences and changes of approach are matters of ideology rather than economic analysis.

Much of the debate over commodity price stabilization is analogous to that over exchange rate policies – confusion between 'fixing' prices and smoothing their change; between short-term volatility and medium-term misalignment; debate over the feasibility and costs of alternative partial stabilizing mechanisms, and so on. The long and intellectually intriguing discussion in the journals over interrelationships between instability and earnings, seems at last, mercifully, to have spent itself. We now know that the welfare results depend upon such factors as the character of national and world supply and demand functions, the sources and nature of shocks, and the degree of individual or group risk aversion. And we know that most individual developing-country commodity exporters can, for all intents and purposes, be considered 'small countries' with very limited market power; the exceptions are few (Brazilian coffee, Bangladesh's jute, Ghanaian cocoa). Shocks come in the form of uncompensated domestic supply changes or world price changes(caused either by global demand or the rest of the world's supply changes). Partial price stabilization typically does *not* destabilize income at the *national* level; the theoretical possibility that it could received vastly more attention from economists concerned with stabilization in developing countries than it ever deserved. The important interactions between price and earnings instability relate to aggregate (worldwide) effects, not to national-level ones. And the aggregate (global) impact of commodity price (and earnings) fluctuations, oil apart, remains understudied. Why?

As the most important 'flexprice' sector of the global economy, world primary commodity markets have played an important role in the propagation of global shocks and in global stabilization programmes. Sharp increases in oil prices twice showed the importance of global 'demand-shift' inflation during the 1970s. Later, the global fight against inflation was, to a significant degree, 'won' via the holding down of oil and other commodity prices in the 1980s (Sachs,1985; UNCTAD,1986; Beckerman and Jenkinson,1986; see also Kaldor,1976).

It has been suggested that primary commodity price increases typically generate cost–push inflation, real wage resistance by labour in industrialized countries, and further inflation in the North; this engenders macro-economic restraint policies that drive primary commodity prices down again. Commodity price declines, on the other hand, create deflationary effects through their effects upon earnings and purchasing power in the exporting sectors and countries; not only may these effects not be rapidly offset by countercyclical expansionary policies in foreign exchange-constrained countries, but, worse, they may generate further cumulative effects. On the other hand, Peter Drucker (1986) has argued that 'the raw material economy has come uncoupled from the industrial economy' and interactions between the two are now minimal. The impact of commodity price instability upon global macro-economic performance, and most notably upon performance in the industrial countries, is still only imperfectly understood. The Comlink portion of the LINK project (at the University of Pennsylvania) seeks to join country and commodity models, but the most appropriate means of capturing the key interrelationships requires further investigation (Kanbur and Vines, 1984; Adams, 1985).

Interactions between individual global commodity markets and their aggregate implications for global demand deserve more exploration. How correlated or uncorrelated are demand or supply shocks in international primary commodity markets, and what difference does it make to global macro-economic performance? Earlier brave attempts to estimate the foregone output from demand restraint designed to offset commodity-price-induced inflation for industrialized countries were undoubtedly crude (for example, Behrman 1979), but they were better than nothing. It was an editorial in *The Economist,* rather than a serious research undertaking, that first estimated the impact of Northern anti-inflationary policies upon the developing countries in the 1980s! Better models and improved understanding of the functioning of the global economy, allowing in particular for a flexprice commodity sector and a fixprice industrial one, will have to be developed. Many have by now explicitly or implicitly made the point that the commodity market stabilization issue is much less a matter of income effects and little triangles than one of global macroeconomic management.

That is not in any way to play down the significance of the stabilization issue for the developing countries themselves. The interaction of global commodity market experience with individual exporting countries' performance has not always been adequately understood either. Who ultimately bears the burden of commodity price and earnings fluctuations within individual national economies with differing institutional and structural characteristics? What are the welfare and growth implications of different domestic stabilization mechanisms? These issues used to receive more analytical attention than they now do. The University of Pennsylvania project (Adams and Priovolos,1981; Lasaga,1981; Obidegwu and Nziramasanga,1981; Priovolos,1981; Adams and Behrman,1982) provided valuable new insights into how these matters might more effectively be approached and econometrically modelled. But it offered far from the last word on the subject, and it is somewhat distressing that there has been little subsequent parallel or related research elsewhere.

Much of the traditional developing-country concern with commodity price instability boils down to the question of risk management. What insurance markets now exist or might exist? What are the costs of alternative possible insurance 'premia' – national or international buffer stocks, foreign exchange reserves or international borrowing, forward markets and long-term contracts? The optimal form of insurance is bound to vary with the commodity and with the country (see, for instance, Gemmill,1985). It will also vary (from the standpoint of the developing countries) with the willingness of the international community to contribute to the cost of one form of insurance rather than another; and that willingness is likely to vary with that community's perception of its ideological, economic and political interests in alternative proposals. The political economy of international commodities and related policies might well receive more attention from public choice economists; to date it has primarily been left to political scientists.

Despite considerable academic interest and obviously increased need, there has been very little innovation in the markets for information and/or insurance (or risk-bearing) as they relate to primary commodities. International commodity markets thus remain seriously 'incomplete'. Indeed, so even do domestic US commodity markets; it remains difficult to write a contract more than 18 months in the future in either domestic or international commodity markets. Commodity-linked bonds, so far relating typically only to gold or oil, have still not taken off. Production and processing of many primary products involve heavy fixed costs and long gestation periods, notably in energy, minerals and, to a lesser degree, tree crops. More information and more stable incentives would undoubtedly improve the overall efficiency of worldwide investment allocations. Just as there is evidence that stability, and not just the average level of incentives, increases the volume of non-traditional exports in boom-and-bust Latin American economies, one can expect that increased stability of commodity markets would, all else being equal, increase investments in primary production relative to other outlets. The decline in internalized and centralized private management systems in the resources sector may have reduced the rationality of longer-term investments and increased the prospects for instability and cobweb phenomena; this is an issue deserving more investigation. The current heavy overcapacity in the metals sector is attributed by some to the fact of continued independent developing-country investments undertaken in the face of weak market prospects; but a complete explanation either of the overcapacity phenomenon or of developing countries' investment behaviour is unavailable. Contrary to mythology, it appears that, at least in copper, state ownership has nothing to do with it (Markowski and Radetzki,1986). Increased price stability, all else being equal, might also raise demand for the more stable products.

Issues in Income Enhancement for Developing-country Primary Commodity Exporters

The developing countries are not without some accomplishments in international commodity policy discussion, but they have fallen far short of their objectives. Their principal, modest, victories were in achieving some compensatory financing (in the IMF and the Lomé Convention), agreement that consumers should share the costs of buffer stocks (although the tin débâcle suggests that this was pretty tenuous), and legitimacy for producer associations.

Acting unilaterally, developing countries succeeded in substantially increasing their share of rents and quasi-rents in petroleum and mineral production, and thereby retained value from exports, in the 1960s and 1970s. Thereafter, their capacity to realize further gains proved limited, and some governments substantially 'overshot' their revenue potential – for example Jamaica with bauxite – with several negative consequences.

The potential for successful cartel activity in primary commodity markets proved less than many (see, for example, Bergsten,1983) had hoped or feared, foundering on high demand elasticities, low market shares, high supply elasticities in non-members and a variety of political and other difficulties. There has been academic enthusiasm for cross-country uniform export duties to overcome some of the difficulties of quota assignments and enforcement: to be effective, however, such duties would have to be translated into appropriate producer prices and, in a world of disequilibrium exchange rates, marketing boards and other official 'interferences' in markets, this may not be easy to do. Why uniform export duties should be any easier to agree and police than more direct restrictions is by no means evident, and the enthusiasts should be encouraged to develop their proposals more realistically than they have so far done. No doubt there are nevertheless unexploited opportunities for efficient joint producer activities in research, marketing and other downstream efforts.

If it is true that income elasticities for tropical beverages and some other primary products are higher in developing than in industrialized countries, as available evidence suggests, and if population growth continues to be higher in the former than in the latter, as seems likely, Southern markets will be increasingly important outlets for world primary products. There is potential here for efficient and expanding South–South trade, and there is room for research as to how best to facilitate it. One must presume that the increasingly common use of barter and various forms of countertrade is a sub-optimal approach. Similarly, there may be underutilized market potential in the centrally planned economies.

Among the other principal areas for further exploration and policy consideration in this sphere are the following:

- the implications of current and prospective technical change – much of it already of major significance in other spheres of economic activity – for future demand for particular primary commodities;
- new means of financing productive investment in the developing countries, not only in primary production but also in processing, transport, and marketing – and, in particular, financing for mineral exploration and other highly uncertain pre-investment activities in the resource sector;
- the relative roles of the various 'artificial' impediments to the adding of value to primary products in developing countries – for example, tariff and non-tariff barriers, restrictive business practices, and inappropriate freight rate structures – and the prospects for their reduction or removal;

- the influence of the various 'more natural' barriers to entry by developing countries into downstream activities in the primary commodity sector – for example, scale economies, location factors, technological weakness, lack of marketing expertise or established market contacts, and other sources of potential economic disadvantage

Issues in the Positive Analysis of Commodity Markets

As has been seen, the endless discussion and debate concerning the interrelationship between price instability, earnings instability and overall earnings has now happily eased as understanding of the issues has increased. What were once regarded as straightforward propositions – for example, that price stabilization would destabilize and raise producer incomes when instability arose from the supply side, and stabilize and lower them when it arose from the demand side – are now recognized as dependent on a battery of (not particularly plausible) assumptions with respect to the nature of demand and supply functions. The assumption of 'normal' competitive markets, however convenient it may be, is frequently difficult to employ in primary commodity markets characterized by concentration on either the buying or the selling side (or both), segmentation, intrafirm trade, state-to-state trade and/or countertrade, and long-term contracts. 'Free' markets, where they exist, often account for very small shares of total trade (and even smaller shares of production). There is plenty of room for more theoretical and empirical analysis of the functioning of *actual*, rather than conveniently simplified models of, specific commodity 'markets', and of investment and trading decisions relating to them (see, for example, Labys,1980; Maizels,1984). There have been major changes in recent times in various elements of commodity market structure and practice; for example, the degree of resort to internalization, countertrade and so on, providing opportunities for comparative analyses. As in other areas of the economics of international trade, there may be rich returns from the deployment of industrial organization approaches to primary commodity issues.

REFERENCES

Adams, Gerard F. (1983), 'The Impact of Petroleum and Commodity Prices in a Model of the World Economy' in Bert G. Hickman (ed.), *Global International Economic Models*, Amsterdam: North-Holland.

Adams, Gerard F. (1985), 'Commodity Export Instability, Micro and Macro Policies and Economic Development', Paper prepared for the Colloquium for Executive Directors on Primary Commodity Problems and Prospects, 27–29 March, Maryland, processed.

Adams, Gerard F. and Jere R. Behrman (1978), *Econometric Modelling of World Commodity Policy*, Lexington, Mass: D.C. Heath.

Adams, Gerard F. and Jere R. Behrman (1982), *Commodity Exports and Economic Development: The Commodity Problem and Policies in Developing Countries*, Lexington, Mass: D.C. Heath.

Adams, Gerard F. and Sonia A. Klein (eds) (1978), *Stabilizing World Commodity Markets*, Lexington, Mass: D.C. Heath.

Adams, Gerard F. and T. Priovolos (1981), *Coffee and Brazil*, Lexington, Mass: D.C. Heath.

Beckerman, W. and T. Jenkinson (1982), 'What Stopped the Inflation? Unemployment or Commodity Prices?', *Economic Journal*, March.

Behrman, Jere R. (1979), 'International Commodity Agreements' in William R. Cline (ed.), *Policy Alternatives for a New International Economic Order: An Economic Analysis'*, Praeger for Overseas Development Council.

Bergsten, Fred C. (1973), 'The Threat from the Third World', *Foreign Policy*, no. 11.

Chu, K.Y. and T.K. Morrison (1984), 'The 1981–82 Recession and Nonoil Primary Commodity Prices', IMF *Staff Papers*, March.

Chu, K.Y. and T.K. Morrison (1986), 'World Nonoil Primary Commodity Markets: A Medium-Term Framework of Analysis', IMF *Staff Papers*, March.

Dell, Sidney (1985), 'The Fifth Credit Tranche', *World Development*, February.

Drucker, Peter (1986), 'The Changed World Economy', *Foreign Affairs*, Spring.

Fleisig, Heywood and Sweder Van Wijnbergen (1985), 'Primary Commodity Prices, the Business Cycle and the Real Exchange Rate of the Dollar', Discussion Paper no. 90, Centre for Economic Policy Research, December.

Gemmill, Gilbert (1985), 'Forward Contracts or International Buffer Stocks? A Study of their Relative Efficiencies in Stabilizing Commodity Export Earnings', *Economic Journal*, September.

Helleiner, Gerald K. (1986), 'Outward Orientation, Import Instability and African Economic Growth: An Empirical Investigation' in Sanjaya Lall and Frances Stewart (eds), *Theory and Reality in Economic Development*, London: Macmillan.

International Monetary Fund (1986a), *World Economic Outlook*, Washington, April.

International Monetary Fund (1986b), *Primary Commodities: Recent Developments and Outlook,* Washington DC: IMF Commodities Division, Research Department.

Kaldor, Nicholas (1976), 'Inflation and Recession in the World Economy', *Economic Journal*, December.

Kanbur, Ravi S.M. and David Vines (1984), *North–South Interaction and Commodity Control*, Discussion Paper no. 8, Centre for Economic Policy Research, March.

Labys, Water (1980), *Market Structure, Bargaining Power and Resource Price Formation*, Lexington, Mass: D.C. Heath.

Lasaga, M. (1981), *The Copper Industry in the Chilean Economy*, Lexington, Mass: D.C. Heath.

Maizels, Alfred (1984), 'A Conceptual Framework for Analysis of Primary Commodity Markets', *World Development*, January.

Markowski, A. and M. Radetzki (1986), *State Ownership and the Price Sensitivity of Supply: The Case of the Copper Mining Industry*, Seminar Paper no. 351, Stockholm: Institute for International Economic Studies, April.

McKinnon, Ronald (1979), *Money in International Finance*, Oxford: Oxford University Press.

Newberry, David M.G., and Joseph E.Stiglitz (1981), *The Theory of Commodity Price Stabilization*, Oxford: Oxford University Press.

Obidegwu C. and M. Nziramasanga (1981), *Copper and Zambia*, Lexington, Mass: D.C. Heath.

Priovolos, T. (1981), *Coffee and the Ivory Coast*, Lexington, Mass: D.C. Heath.

Rostow, Walter W. (1984), 'Development: The Political Economy of the Marshallian Long Period' in Gerald M. Meier and Dudley Seers (eds), *Pioneers in Development*, Oxford: Oxford University Press for the World Bank.

Sachs, Jeffrey D. (1985), 'The Dollar and the Policy Mix: 1985', *Brookings Papers on Economic Activity*, no. 1, Washington.

Spraos, J. (1980), 'The Statistical Debate on the Net Barter Terms of Trade between Primary Commodities and Manufactures', *Economic Journal*, March.

Thirlwall, Anthony P. and J. Bergevin (1985). 'Trends, Cycles, and Asymmetries in the Terms of Trade of Primary Commodities from Developed and Less Developed Countries'. *World Development*, vol. 13, no. 7, July.

UN Conference on Trade and Development, 1986, *Trade and Development Report*, Geneva: UNCTAD.

World Bank (1986), *World Development Report*, Washington, DC: The World Bank.

11. Industrial Organization, Trade and Investment in Developing Countries

INTRODUCTION

There has been ferment in the recent North American and European literature of international trade theory. Having already captured the analysis of direct foreign investment and multinational enterprise, industrial organization theory is now bidding to take over the analysis of international trade as well. Little of this excitement has so far percolated through to theoretical or policy discussions in the developing countries. Thus far, the 'new theories' of trade have been considered almost exclusively with reference to trade among OECD countries. It is surely time to consider current 'frontier' trade theory issues in the context of the problems of the newly industrialized and other poorer countries. This chapter is exploratory – seeking no more than a 'first pass' at the interrelationships between the new trade theory and the current literature of economic development.

THE 'NEW' APPROACHES TO TRADE THEORY

Economies of scale have always created problems for orthodox trade theory. Economies of scope – relating to the range of activities across products and space – complicate matters still further. The absence or imperfection of arm's-length markets for firm-specific intangible assets and the transnational firms that result, and, more generally, barriers to international market entry, also require incorporation into an analytical framework that adequately represents the international trading reality. So does the fact of two-way trade in products of the same industry. Trade theoreticians have begun to address these issues systematically in recent years.

The literature on international monopolistic competition and intra-industry trade, for example, is by now quite extensive. Product differentiation, scale economies and Schumpeterian considerations are deployed to explain trade among similar countries in most up-to-date accounts, while traditional factor endowment approaches are retained to explain interindustry trade among dissimilar ones. North–South trade fits into the latter category, and there may therefore be a temptation to downplay the potential significance of the 'new' issues for the analysis of this type of trade (Frances Stewart (1984) has considered their relevance, however, for South–South trade). This would be a mistake.

The bulk of the formal literature of trade theory has been concerned with explaining the volume and the pattern of international trade. The gains from trade have been endlessly analysed in terms of comparison between a world with trade and a world of autarchy. Recent innovative theorizing, drawing on the literature of industrial organization, proceeds in the same way. The systematic insertion of market structure and scale economy considerations into the formal structure of trade theory, for instance by Helpman and Krugman, generally supports ' a basic view in which trade patterns reflect comparative advantage plus additional specialization to realize scale economies' (Helpman and Krugman, 1985:262). They conclude that there are potential extra gains from trade where there are economies of scale and imperfect competition, and at least a presumption that the beneficial effects of trade will outweigh losses for all factors of production.

But are these the issues that matter? Does anyone consider autarchy realistic? Outside the confines of academe, who is interested in tests of the 'ultimate' determinants of observed trade patterns at a point in time? Policy-makers work in the confusing real world of constant change, innumerable market imperfections and governmental interventions, both foreign and domestic. They are interested in the evolution of so-called 'dynamic comparative advantage' and the sources of economic progress. They seek to utilize international exchange 'optimally' so as to foster development rather than simply to allocate efficiently in static terms (Chenery, 1961).

The new literature on 'strategic' trade policy aspires to greater realism in the theoretical analysis of government (and firm) policies. Multinational firms in oligopolistic environments must calculate the effect that their actions may have on the behaviour of those rival firms and governments with which they interact. Governments must also allow for responses and reactions from other governments and from firms as they seek to influence economic events. Neither firms nor governments can assume that the world will remain unchanged following their own actions, in the way that a pure competitor can. Global markets, investment locations and trade advantages are the 'prizes' for which governments and large firms struggle. Market outcomes are the product of complex 'games' involving both private firms and governments. Traditional tenets of orthodox trade policy no longer obviously apply in the context of strategic economic conflict. Trade policy may not only influence the degree of 'distortion' engendered by domestic market imperfections, but, more interestingly, it may also alter the behaviour of oligopolistic firms and thus – allowing for foreign firms' and governments strategic responses or 'retaliation' – influence national welfare. It is revealing that trade theoreticians in the USA only became interested in these issues 'as US dominance...declined and its international dependence...deepened' (Grossman and Richardson, 1985: 5). Smaller nations have groped for more realistic approaches to these issues for much longer, although the underlying theory has characteristically been weak. What seems to have been happening is a mainstream theoretical rationalization of longstanding perceptions and practices which have previously been seen as unorthodox, or even perverse.

Three major strands of the emerging trade and development literature deserve highlighting – and strengthening. The first relates to the primary sources of growth in the newly industrializing countries (and developing countries more generally), the sources of dynamic comparative advantage and the role of trade and industrial policies therein. The second concerns the relevance of strategic trade policy to the developing countries. The third relates to the determinants and implications of alternative forms of organization in global industries. There has been considerably more written on the first than on the latter two issues.

TRADE, GROWTH, LEARNING AND DYNAMIC COMPARATIVE ADVANTAGE

Good development economists are deeply sceptical of simplistic recommendations for the achievement of more rapid growth. As conscious as any of the potential costs of static misallocation (and probably more so since they usually see more of it), they recognize the early limits to that which is known about dynamic processes. The purported link between proper static allocation and growth remains – both in the World Bank, where it has been most popular, and in pure economic theory – a 'black box' about which it is best (and most honest) to be cautious. Indeed, there are good reasons for questioning whether there indeed exist any such links, either in theory or in history.

Growth accounting exercises in developing countries, as in industrialized economies, invariably assign major importance to an unexplained residual which, for want of other explanations, we describe as 'technical change' – although increased inputs are typically of greater relative significance in developing, rather than industrialized, countries. In the literature of development economics, increasing total factor productivity is therefore absolutely central; and international trade and trade policy can only be analysed in the context of that central concern. It should immediately be evident that a focus on 'trade', narrowly defined as that which is recorded in traditional trade statistics (basically merchandise trade), does not begin to approach the range of possible international influences – both positive and negative – on domestic productivity increase. Technology imports, the terms of relationships with foreign buyers or sellers, the role of direct foreign investment and 'new forms' of international investment (Oman, 1983) are among the international issues that also matter. While there may be periods of pure 'export-led growth' – for instance, following those of underutilization of domestic resources or gross misallocation of an anti-tradable or anti-export kind – they are unlikely to be sustained. Arthur Lewis has put this point well in a passage that has been widely cited and will undoubtedly endure:

> The engine of growth should be technological change, with international trade serving as a lubricating oil and not as fuel. The gateway to technological change is through agricultural and industrial revolutions, which are mutually dependent (Lewis, 1978:74).

In developing countries, the complexities of 'frontier' innovations and the need for incentives for Schumpeterian entrepreneurs – the preoccupation of trade theoreticians analyzing Western high-technology sectors – are typically less important than the means of absorbing and adapting existing scientific knowledge to their own developmental context (Katz, 1984; Lall, 1984; Teitel, 1984).

It is obviously desirable to understand better the role of international trade and other international influences upon domestic productivity change, because productivity increase *is* what is ultimately at issue. But the evidence on the costs of 'inappropriate' trade policy does not obviously support heavy emphasis upon its 'reform'. Even in the static terms in which economists prefer to measure, and neglecting their ignorance of what appropriate allocation for growth might be, allocative efficiency has rarely been found to be as important as other dimensions of efficiency.

'Technical inefficiency', in the sense that performance is inferior to feasible (and sometimes existing) domestic practice, has generally been found more important than 'allocative inefficiency', in the sense of 'welfare triangles'. Inappropriate trade (and other) policies can breed technical inefficiencies, as well as allocative ones, as domestic firms and factors earn rents rather than adopt 'best practices' in industries in which they possess inherent comparative advantage. But other policies, practices and influences are likely to dominate trade policies. In a recent survey paper Pack concludes:

> ...to date there is no clear cut evidence that countries with an external orientation benefit from greater growth in technical efficiency; combined with the relatively small static costs of protection, this finding leaves those with a predilection towards a neutral regime in a quandary. (Pack, 1989:353)

He calls for the assessment of the contribution of export orientation in countries like Korea in terms of a comparison between actual total factor productivity growth with that which would have occurred if expanded sales had to be made primarily on domestic markets, however difficult such counterfactual analysis might be; and offers reasons for expecting that export orientation would perform well in such tests.

Policies and practices relating to matters other than intersectoral or interindustry allocation may be far more important: for example, those relating to technology imports and local technical adaptation and development; research and technology policy more generally; managerial experience and training; choice of product mix and product design; worker and management incentives; domestic market structure; availability of education, nutrition, health, and other welfare benefits for the labour force. As Streeten has put it:

> The ultimate test of the respective merits of...strategies is not their ability to allocate resources between sectors, but their power to mobilize domestic resources and skills and to create and activate incentives, attitudes and institutions for development. (Streeten, 1982:163)

External ties may be just as important, or conceivably even more important, on the importing side – technology, expertise, product design and marketing, management, and so on – as on the export side, although exports have received much more theoretical attention. Trade's historical role as an 'engine of growth' may be replicated today through new institutional arrangements in international exchange, and through channels that are not always related to exporting.

The incorporation of learning within the new theories of international trade remains incomplete. The analysis of static scale economies in trade has seen important theoretical advances but probably has less policy significance than a full analysis of the learning phenomenon. Much of the rationale for forced import substitution strategy and for individual infant industry protection was the notion that productivity increases with experience (usually proxied by cumulative output or time). Casual empiricism and anecdotal accounts suggest, however, that learning has often been disappointing, that infant firms and industries typically fail to mature; and there is a vast literature on the failures of import substitution policies. Yet there have been remarkably few careful industry-level empirical tests of the 'learning' phenomenon and its relationship to industrial or trade policies (Bell *et al.*, 1984; Krueger and Tuncer, 1982).

'Technological mastery' can undoubtedly be acquired through learning-by-doing and, in a continuous process of adaptation and experimentation, its acquisition can dramatically increase firm or industry productivity. When such learning is absorbed by nationals (individuals and firms) and becomes part of the indigenous base of human capital and technological infrastructure, rather than being retained within the operations of foreign firms (even if some leakage in such cases is likely), it can enhance *overall* national industrial competitiveness. Most of Korea's industrial exports have been produced by wholly nationally owned firms that received substantial official support. It may be that the promotion of 'infant industry exports' is a particularly effective means of developing international industrial competitiveness (Westphal, 1982).

Learning-by-doing and scale economies do not, in themselves, create a presumption of the need for active government policy. Information imperfections and imperfect insurance systems are required to tip the balance towards it. Superior government information and greater government willingness (or capacity) to bear risk, together with the existence of externalities, are the logical roots of interventionist trade policy.

That part of technology acquired through learning-by-doing is only imperfectly tradable, if it is tradable at all. When traded, technology is, in any case, subject to non-competitive pricing – and prices are generally believed to fall with increasing technological knowledge on the part of the purchaser. Not only is foreign technology an imperfect substitute for domestically owned technology, then, but there may also be a case for policy intervention in support of the latter's development, particularly in the light of frequent informational and insurance imperfections. (These issues are explored in greater detail by Pack and Westphal, 1984.) However, none of this argument should be taken as dismissive of the importance of continuing to draw upon foreign sources of technology.

STRATEGIC TRADE POLICY AND DEVELOPING COUNTRIES

It may be possible for governments to influence oligopolistic equilibria through trade (and other) policy by undertaking credible threats and precommitments in the sphere of export or import subsidies or taxes, which ultimately raise or lower national firms' shares of global oligopolistic markets and profits. There is no presumption, however, that such policies will increase national welfare. The same goes for other industrial policies. Whether they do depends, above all, upon the hypothesized counterfactual 'conjectures', and thus behaviour, of oligopolistic national firms – whether they systematically underestimate or overestimate foreign firms' reactions to their own actions (Grossman and Richardson, 1985). Also still relevant, of course, are the traditional optimal tariff arguments for government intervention in international trade, always allowing for foreign retaliation, which have to be factored into what is already a complex set of calculations. A complete assessment of national welfare would also require consideration of indirect effects of reallocations upon the rest of the economy in a general equilibrium framework.

These arguments hinge on the identification of 'national' firms and their earnings as coincident with the 'national' interest. Who actually earns the supernormal profits in oligopolistic global industries is of crucial significance. As transnational corporations expand their activities into a variety of 'new forms' of rent-extracting international investment – such as joint ventures, licensing, management and marketing contracts, turnkey plants, international subcontracting (Oman, 1983) – it becomes increasingly difficult to trace the eventual beneficiaries of and losers from changing global market shares. Where, as in the more poorly endowed developing countries, there may be doubt as to the degree to which their nationals share in oligopolistic super-profit, the changes in market share generated by domestic policy change or other influences are more likely to be assessed in terms of the altering externalities created. In the newly industrialized countries, however, there are already many examples of dynamic, internationally competitive and expanding domestic firms (Lall, 1984). Policies based on the encouragement of local firms ('national champions') may be just as important in these countries as they are in the OECD.

Dunning (1981) has suggested that there may be national characteristics of transnational firms based on the factor endowment and other characteristics of their countries of origin. Kojima (1985) has long argued that Japanese firms, for instance, behave fundamentally differently from US firms in respect of their effects on international trade. More recently, Lipsey and Kravis (1985) have analysed the performance of US manufacturing firms and found that, despite the reduction in US trade shares between 1966 and 1977, the share of world manufactured exports produced by US multinationals (whether in US or overseas locations) actually rose. This suggests that determinants of location – including host government policies – played an important role in US firms' performance and practice, and not, as some have suggested, declining US technological leadership. These approaches all suggest that it is important to differentiate between policies that relate to national *firms* and policies that relate to national *location* of economic activity.

If strategic behaviour and interfirm and intergovernmental bargaining *are* important elements in some parts of the international trading scene – as many have long argued, particularly, as has been seen in Chapters 2 and 10, in the debates over primary commodity trade – it will be necessary to develop improved theoretical frameworks for understanding these phenomena, and to establish, at the level of individual countries, which sectors are best analysed in these terms. In the recent Northern theoretical literature, disproportionate attention may have been devoted to 'high-tech' industries in which early commitment to R and D and the development of productive capacity and marketing seem most obviously relevant to the development of 'dynamic comparative advantage'.

Developments in these frontier industries are not without interest to developing countries. Witness the Brazilian effort to develop its own informatics sector, the growing Southern concern over the implications for them of the information revolution, and the South's caution regarding US attempts to liberalize world trade in services. But the new theories are of potentially much wider relevance to developing countries' trade and trade policies. Wherever there are high fixed costs, high risks and, consequently, market concentration, similar issues arise – and these are not new issues. Who would deny the importance of oligopoly and 'small numbers' bargaining in the development of trading patterns in primary metals, petrochemicals, bauxite, copper, bananas and many other primary commodities? Stuckey's (1983) deployment of industrial organization theory in the analysis of vertical integration and joint ventures in the international aluminum industry illustrates the possibilities of innovative and insightful research in this area (see also Labys, 1980; Maizels, 1984).

Even in relatively standardized and 'low-tech' manufacturing, where there is often more international competition, there are frequently both scale economies and learning-by-doing potential for local firms. Governments in the industrialized countries have been most active with protectionist trade policies in those sectors where their national firms are unable to control overseas new investment and trade patterns – for example textiles and clothing, footwear, consumer electronics, steel, agriculture and so on. In the ensuing context of worldwide excess capacity, oligopolistic games among private firms are replaced by oligopolistic games among governments. Threats of trade barriers or subsidies can deter investment and alter trade patterns even if never actually carried out. Indeed a 'successful' threat will render its implementation unnecessary. In this sense, the measured costs of protectionism to trading partners may be vastly understated (Bhagwati, 1977). 'Collusion' on prices, output and market shares – all in the interest of minimizing disruption – can be negotiated among governments as well as private firms, and it can be just as socially costly. The bargaining strength of the developing countries in these trade policy 'games' has obviously always been weak; but, for some of them, it has recently been rising; and the debt problem may have strengthened their hand further. In the competition for access to governmentally restricted Northern markets some of these games are played by developing countries against one another; in such cases the smallest and poorest are at a significant disadvantage.

Oligopolistic games are inherently unstable. The pressures for attempted strategic thrusts on the part of governments are at present unusually great, and the risks of non-cooperative beggar-thy-neighbour strategic policies leaving all parties worse off than they could be with cooperative behaviour unusually high. Resort to non-cooperative policies (sometimes surreptitious) simultaneous with the maintenance of the 'rules' of cooperative behaviour in the formal trade regime challenges the survival of the latter. Such 'two-track' practices must either result in a much broader and stronger system of rules (together with better enforcement and dispute settlement procedures) or the relative spread of non-cooperative behaviour. The need for a credible and effective 'trade and investment regime', based upon the new perceptions and new realities of global industrial organization, and determined by relatively small numbers of firms and governments in particular sectors, should be obvious. Particularly deserving of more analytical attention, as Grossman and Richardson point out, are the merits and costs of alternative coalitions among countries and firms (Grossman and Richardson, 1985:29).

Strategic approaches may be relevant in some sectors and irrelevant in others. It has been suggested, for instance, that in the US case, strategic approaches might be useful in semiconductors (where small numbers of Japanese firms conduct cooperative R and D activities with official backing while US firms vigorously compete with one another) and larger civilian aircraft (where Boeing faces Airbus), but not in telecommunications equipment, steel or automobiles. Even in the former two cases, the absence of supernormal profits in these industries suggests that the gains might be small (Richardson, 1985). A sector-by-sector analysis, based on detailed knowledge of both the structure of the global industry and the make-up and prospects of national industries, seems necessary before any national-level (or, for that matter, global) policy implications can be derived.

Infant industry and infant firm protection in support of the expansion of manufactured exports looks like being a major issue of the 1990s (see Chapter 12). Westphal and others have described the considerable success realized by Korea with targeted policies of this type. Brander and Spencer, among others, have presented theoretical models showing that terms-of-trade losses from export subsidies may be more than offset by other gains from increased market shares in oligopolistic global industries. Krugman (1984) offers a model of oligopoly in which protection against imports permits firms facing internationally segmented markets to avail themselves of increasing returns and thus more effectively to penetrate external markets. He is careful not to recommend such policies but only to demonstrate that under reasonably plausible assumptions they can be defended as logically coherent. In the context of developing countries, export subsidies may simply compensate for overvalued domestic currencies and other distortions, and thus contribute to the overall neutrality of the incentive structure; in this context, there are also further gains from employment and other externalities to consider. A stable international trade regime will have to leave room for 'legitimate', as opposed to 'predatory', export subsidies. Needless to say, the industries in which developing countries are competitive are not always oligopolistic. But the governmental trade policies with which they must deal to penetrate Northern markets may nevertheless be strategically determined.

GLOBAL INDUSTRIAL ORGANIZATION AND THE DEVELOPING COUNTRIES

The organization of global industry has not been a subject of much analytical attention or empirical research. Yet in terms of economic distance (transport and communications costs relative to total costs) the global market has by now shrunk to a size comparable to that of many national markets only a few decades ago. The issues of industrial organization theory begin to merge with those of trade theory in modern efforts at positive analysis of investment decisions, the location of economic activities and trading patterns within global industries. Sound national and international policies require that we seek a better understanding of the evolution of firms and market structures at the global level and over time. The key issues include the following:

- What determines investment locations for various stages of production and types of plant within the industry?
- What determines the nature of relationships – contractual or hierarchical or whatever – among plants and firms in the industry, and what are their welfare implications?
- What determines the degree of competition among firms in the industry and what are the welfare implications of alternative market structures?
- What are the implications for all of the above issues of nationally segmented markets and independent national policy-making units?

Policy issues are obviously never far behind. Not only are there the traditional issues of optimal national industrial and trade policies, but one can also now envisage the concept of optimal *global* industrial policies. International policies, or at least regularized consultations, already exist for various primary commodities and, to a lesser extent, in such industries as steel, textile and automobiles. The desirability and efficacy of controlling international restrictive business practices are also obvious matters to pursue (Schachter and Hellawell, 1981; Casson, 1984).

Global industrial organization studies should clarify the process of firms' adjustment to structural change, such as that represented by the industrialization of the developing countries. What influences are most significant in determining the variety of possible firm responses – exit, diversification, merger, defensive investment, internationalization? Efforts to ease trade adjustment processes for firms and their workers have not as yet drawn noticeably on industrial organization approaches or research.

Approaches to the study of global manufacturing industries, or important parts of them, have been made (for example, UNCTAD, 1980; UNCTC, 1983; Altschuler *et al.*, 1984, Encarnation and Wells, 1984; Toyne *et al.*, 1984; Grunwald and Flamm, 1985; Guisinger, 1985; Newfarmer, 1985; Walter, nd). But much more could be done.

An important element in such studies is the role of transnational corporations and intrafirm trade. In 1977 the USA imported 71 per cent of the manufactures it received from Mexico on a related-party basis; in electrical machinery it was 96 per cent, whereas in textiles it was only 10 per cent (Helleiner and Lavergne, 1979:307). In the same year majority-owned foreign affiliates of US firms accounted for 55 per cent of US manufactured imports from Canada (27 per cent excluding the Auto Pact) (Lavergne and Helleiner, 1985:74).

Intrafirm international trade may be seen as a happy device for overcoming market segmentation and other imperfections, stimulating information, technology, goods and factor flows between countries. On the other hand, when only some sectors are so transnationalized because of other influences, overall trading patterns may be distorted relative to some conceptually 'efficient', even 'dynamically efficient', solution. Moreover, and more fundamentally, there is no assurance that the international distribution of the gains from trade will be such as to make transnationalization attractive to all host countries. Where high proportions of international trade in goods, factors and services are undertaken on an intrafirm basis, it is not obvious that traditional competitive market analysis of trade will be very illuminating. Government policies based on market instruments may work, but those based on non-market interactions with firms may be more cost-effective.

Host government policies have undoubtedly been important influences in the location, sourcing, organizational and financing decisions of multinational firms. Incentive systems at the national level clearly do matter both to domestic and to international decision-makers (Guisinger, 1986). 'Market access' disputes now relate not merely to goods trade and traditional protectionist instruments but also to investment, technology and services flows. Transnational firms can be expected to prefer international *laissez-faire* but, in the real world of pervasive government interventions, it may be immaterial to them whether they serve particular national markets through exports, direct investment or technology sales.

US trade policy increasingly reflects the new perceptions of these interrelationships.

There can be no guarantee that projects attractive to private foreign investors will be socially desirable. Particularly where projects cater to protected local markets and/or where input prices (for example, energy) are significantly 'administered', there may be heavy (static) social costs from privately profitable undertakings. As long as the 'distorted' incentives simply redistribute income among nationals it may be possible to find a 'dynamic' or other rationale for them. When, however, they simply generate rent for foreigners, there can be none. Reuber *et al.* (1973), Lall and Streeten (1977), and Encarnation and Wells (1986) all have found a sizable minority of foreign direct investment (FDI) projects that reduce the host country's national product. If domestic incentive systems are not easily or quickly altered, administrative screening, performance requirements and bargaining arrangements – with all their difficulties, and risks of bureaucratic muddles and corruption – may help to keep the rents from domestic incentive arrangements at home (Guisinger, 1986). Encarnation and Wells (1986) warn that even export-oriented projects can waste national resources.

Thus, inducements to investment are regularly

> ...accompanied by constraints which national governments place on global decision making. Limits on ownership in local subsidiaries, rules on how much they must export or buy locally, whom they must employ and how they must finance their operations apply almost everywhere. These so-called performance requirements are supposed to ensure that the firm provides desired benefits to the host country, but they can impose significant costs on the firm facing global markets. (Encarnation and Wells, 1984:3).

The most developed empirical literature of international economic bargaining in the developing countries relates to the interaction between transnational corporations and host governments. This is not the place for a review of that literature (see Helleiner, 1989), but it may be helpful to compare briefly the relatively successful Korean policies on multinational firms, trade and market structure with the relatively unsuccessful ones of India. These accounts draw heavily on analyses by Bohn-Young-Koo (1985) and Lall (1985).

Korea represents a case in which an interventionist government has played a major role in *directing* foreign investors and domestic firms towards particular (and changing) *structural* and developmental objectives. At first, government policies favoured import substitution. From the early 1960s to the early 1970s the government emphasized exporting; from 1973 until 1980 it promoted a 'second round' of capital-intensive and skill-intensive import substitution and eventually exports from such industries as tyres, steel, ships, electronic products and fabricated metal products. The government exercised tight control over imports and implemented quite specific targets for exports. Until 1980 it also employed restrictive policies on foreign investment with careful approval procedures confining foreign direct investment (majority ownership) almost entirely to export-oriented and high-technology projects, or those substituting for imported raw materials (chemicals, fertilizers, petroleum products and so on). Foreign domestic investment in differentiated oligopolies catering to the local market in which foreign firms possessed owner-specific advantages have been the exception in Korea, because government policy obstructed such 'natural' tendencies.

Westphal suggests, on the basis of Korean experience, that '...the selectivity with which infant industries are promoted appears to be of far greater consequence than the relative magnitude of the effective incentives initially granted to them' (Westphal, 1982:268). Selectivity in the import of technology was also characteristic of the Korean 'success story'. Drawing knowledge liberally from input and capital equipment suppliers and from buyers of their output, and developing their own expertise, Korean firms 'could unbundle the elements of imported technological packages...[and] not waste money unnecessarily on the excessive baggage that often is a part of such packages' (Rhee, Ross-Larson and Pursell, 1985:49).

Government intervention in pursuit of broadly similar aspirations took rather a different turn in India, which may be regarded as the polar opposite of Korea's experience. In India, governmental controls on foreign direct investment and technology imports have been pervasive at the same time that trade policies have been basically inward-oriented, with imports controlled so as to supply only those inputs that could not be physically produced at home. Major sectors of the economy were run by a public sector that was 'grossly inefficient, overmanned and mismanaged' (Lall, 1985:310), while the domestic private sector was shackled by irrational and counterproductive anti-monopoly regulation. When India shifted to export promotion it was forced to do so 'by giving subsidies to counter the high costs, rigidities and difficulties of producing and selling from a fragmented, technologically obsolescing, managerially slack, and infrastructure-starved production system.' (Lall, 1985:310).

'There is no market economy in the Third World with a substantial industrial sector which has constricted MNE entry to anywhere near the extent of India' (Lall, 1985:318). The uniquely low level of external technological dependence stimulated considerable local technological effort and eventually even significant exports of more 'appropriate' technologies (simplified, sturdier, descaled, and otherwise adapted to local conditions), but it also led

> ...to a lot of second-rate technology being imported and to growing technological lags in Indian industry. More important in the long run, the combination of total protection against imports, substantial protection against MNE entry, and restriction on licensing, in a market characterized by slow growth..., conspired to reduce the *demand* for new technologies within the country, exacerbating the inefficiencies and uncompetitiveness of Indian industry. (Lall, 1985:311)

It should be evident, from these examples, that carefully targeted policies, based on a sophisticated understanding of the relevant global industries, can succeed, but also that inappropriate and overly crude deployment of policy in pursuit of what seem to be similar objectives can also be extremely costly. Policy failure has been analysed to death in orthodox economics departments in recent years, and one can sometimes gain the impression that it is inevitable. Market failure also exists; 'market solutions' have not always been successful. More research might well be undertaken on those cases of apparent policy success, where market failures were overcome.

In the analysis of the prospects for successful manufacturing for export, the new trade theories are at least as important as the old. Comparative advantage obviously still matters. But so does industrial organization. Barriers to the entry of new firms from developing countries derive from incumbents' advantages of scale, experience, reputation and influence over governmental policies. Incumbents may undertake defensive, pre-emptive investments, particularly if encouraged by their governments' trade and industrial policies, to dissuade expansion by more efficient newcomers. (For a small, industrialized country perspective on these issues, see Harris, 1985.)

Marketing, distribution and after-sales servicing networks may be of major significance in the development of industrial exports. Their links to production systems may be crucial to the generation of potential scale economies, the effective transfer of technology and thus indigenous 'learning', and rapid adjustment to market change. While hierarchical intrafirm arrangements are not the only way of ensuring strong links of this kind, they clearly facilitate them. Moreover, restructuring of Northern industry is likely both to be resisted less and to be more orderly when Northern-based firms are directly involved in the new production in the South than when independent Southern firms try to break into Northern markets. Add to this the potential for tapping into already existing marketing and distribution systems and the pressure for utilizing traditional foreign direct investment in export-oriented manufacturing, even in countries with a strong preference for independent firms, may be irresistible. Certainly host governments have been forced by global competition to be far more accommodating to foreign investment with export-oriented manufacturing projects than with others; indeed they may sometimes have been led to overbid with incentives for foreign investors. Not only may there be alternatives to FDI; they may also, in some dimensions, be developmentally superior. Unfortunately they are almost certainly riskier. Nationally owned exporting firms seeking to enter foreign markets for the first time will have to work at developing effective alternatives and/or developing transnational marketing/production links of their own.

So far as governmental strategic trade policy possibilities are concerned, some agreed means of mutual disarmament through the establishment and enforcement of rules (not necessarily liberal ones) seems most likely to generate predictable outcomes, whatever trade theory one is using. How beneficial these outcomes are for the developing countries – the new entrants to world markets – depends on the nature of the rules and thus on a bargaining process, the modelling of which represents still another research frontier.

CONCLUSIONS

As promised, this chapter has been no more than exploratory. It has sought to capture some of the ferment and excitement of recent trade-theoretic literature and to consider its relevance to the development literature. It has offered few answers but has sought to open up a new research frontier in the international dimensions of development. It has consciously downgraded the importance of much of the 'traditional' trade and development literature, without advocating any dismissal of the traditional virtues of (dynamic) comparative advantage. Scale, learning and technical change have been emphasized in considering development processes; barriers to entry, oligopoly and strategic behaviour in considering trade and other international policy. The determinants and implications of industrial organization and change therein at the level of global industries must be better understood if the prospects for the development of sound policies and for developing countries' entry and survival in global markets are to be encouraged. If the overall account has been somewhat uncertain and agnostic, that is as it should be. That is, at present, the state of the art.

REFERENCES

Altschuler, Alan *et al.* (1984), *The Future of the Automobile, The Report of MIT's International Automobile Program*, Cambridge:MIT Press.

Bell, Martin, Bruce Ross-Larson and Larry E. Westphal (1984), 'Assessing the Performance of Infant Industries', *Journal of Development Economics*, vol. 16, nos. 1–2, September–October.

Bhagwati, Jagdish N. (1977), 'Market Disruption, Export Market Disruption, Compensation and GATT Reform' in Jagdish N. Bhagwati (ed.), *The New International Economic Order: The North–South Debate*, Cambridge: MIT Press.

Bohn-Young-Koo (1985), 'Korea' in J.H. Dunning (ed.), *Multinational Enterprises, Economic Structure and International Competitiveness*, Chichester and New York: John Wiley and Sons.

Brander, J.A. and B.J. Spencer (1985), 'Export Subsidies and International Market Share Rivalry', *Journal of International Economics*, vol. 18, nos. 1–2, February.

Casson, Mark (1984), 'Multinational Monopolies and International Cartels' in P.J. Buckley and M. Casson, *Theory of the Multinational Enterprise: Selected Papers*, London: Macmillan, Chapter 4.

Chenery, H.B. (1961), 'Comparative Advantage and Development Policy', *American Economic Review*, March.

Dunning, John H. (1981), *International Production and the Multinational Enterprise*, London: George Allen and Unwin.

Encarnation, Dennis J. and Louis T. Wells (1984), 'Competitive Strategies in Global Industries: A View from the Host Country', mimeo., Harvard Business School Colloquium on Competition in Global Industries.

Encarnation, Dennis J. and Louis T. Wells Jr. (1986), 'Evaluating Foreign Investment', in T.H. Moran *et al.*, *Investing in Development: New Roles For Private Capital*? Washington DC: Overseas Development Council.

Grossman, Gene M. and David J. Richardson, (1985), 'Strategic Trade Policy: A Survey of Issues and Early Analysis', *Special Papers in International Economics*, Princeton University, no. 15, April.

Grunwald, Joseph and Kenneth Flamm, (1985), *The Global Factory: Foreign Assembly in International Trade*, Washington DC: Brookings Institution.

Guisinger, Stephen (1985), *Investment Incentives and Performance Requirements*, New York: Praeger.

Guisinger, Stephen (1986), 'Host Country Policies to Attract and Control Foreign Investment', in T.H. Moran *et al.*, *Investing in Development: New Roles for Private Capital?*, Washington DC: Overseas Development Council.

Harris, Richard (1985), *Trade, Industrial Policy and International Competition*,

Toronto: University of Toronto Press.

Helleiner, G.K., (1989), 'Transnational Corporations and Economic Development' in H.B. Chenery and T.N. Srinivasan (eds), *Handbook of Development Economics*, Amsterdam: North Holland.

Helleiner, G.K. and Real Lavergne (1979), 'Intra-firm Trade and Industrial Exports to the United States', *Oxford Bulletin of Economics and Statistics*, vol. 41, no. 4, November.

Helpman, Elhanan and Paul R. Krugman (1985), *Market Structure and Foreign Trade, Increasing Returns, Imperfect Competition and the International Economy*, Cambridge: MIT Press.

Katz, J. (1984), 'Domestic Technological Innovations and Dynamic Comparative Advantage: Further Reflections on a Comparative Case Study Program', *Journal of Development Economics*, vol. 16, nos. 1–2, September–October.

Kierzkowski, Henryk (ed.) (1984) *Monopolistic Competition and International Trade*, Oxford: Clarendon Press.

Kojima, K. (1985), 'Japanese and American Direct Investment in Asia: A Comparative Analysis', *Hitotsubashi Journal of Economics*, vol. 26, no. 1.

Krueger, Anne O. and Baran Tuncer (1982), 'An Empirical Test of the Infant Industry Argument', *American Economic Review*, vol. 72, no. 5, December.

Krugman, Paul (1984), 'Import Protection as Export Promotion: International Competition in the Presence of Oligopoly and Economies of Scale' in H. Kierzkowski (ed.), *Monopolistic Competition and International Trade*, Oxford: Clarendon Press, Chapter 11.

Labys, W.C. (1980), *Market Structure, Bargaining Power and Resource Price Formation*, Lexington, Mass: Lexington Books.

Lall, Sanjaya (1985), 'India' in J.H. Dunning (ed.), *Multinational Enterprises, Economic Structure and International Competitiveness*, New York: John Wiley and Sons.

Lall, Sanjaya (ed.) (1984), 'Exports of Technology by Newly Industrializing Countries', *World Development, Special Issue*, vol. 12, nos. 5–6, May–June.

Lall, Sanjaya and Paul Streeten (1977), *Foreign Investment, Transnationals and Developing Countries*, Boulder, Col.: Westview Press.

Lavergne, Real and G.K. Helleiner (1985), 'United States Transnational Corporations and the Structure of United States Trade Barriers: An Empirical Investigation' in UNCTC, *Transnational Corporations and International Trade: Selected Issues*, New York.

Lewis, W. Arthur (1978), *The Evolution of the International Economic Order*, Princeton: Princeton University Press.

Lipsey, Robert E. and Irving B. Kravis (1985), 'The International Competitiveness of US Firms', *NBER Working Paper*, no. 1557.

Maizels, Alfred (1984), 'A Conceptual Framework for Analysis of Primary Commodity Markets', *World Development*, vol. 12, no. 1, January.

Newfarmer, Richard S. (ed.) (1985), *Profits, Progress and Poverty, Case Studies of International Industries in Latin America*, Paris: University of Notre Dame Press.

Oman, Charles (1983), *New Forms of International Investment in Developing Countries*, Paris: OECD Development Centre.

Pack, Howard, (1989), 'Industrialization and Trade' in H.B. Chenery and T.N.

Srinivasan (eds), *Handbook of Development Economics* Amsterdam: North-Holland.

Pack, Howard and Larry E. Westphal (1984), 'Industrial Strategy and Technological Change: Theory versus Reality', mimeo., UNU Conference on New Directions in Development Theory, Cambridge, Mass.

Reuber, Grant *et al.* (1973), *Private Foreign Investment in Development*, Oxford: Clarendon Press.

Rhee, Yung Whee, Bruce Ross-Larson and Garry Pursell (1985), *Korea's Competitive Edge, Managing the Entry into World Markets*, Johns Hopkins University Press, for the World Bank.

Richardson, J. David (1985), 'Annual Research Conference–I: Trade Policy In a Volatile World Environment', *NBER Reporter*.

Schachter, Oscar and Robert Hellawell (1981), *Competition in International Business, Law and Policy on Restrictive Practices*, New York: Columbia University Press.

Stewart, Frances (1984), 'Recent Theories of International Trade: Some Implications for the South' in H. Kierzkowski (ed.), *Monopolistic Competition and International Trade*, Oxford: Clarendon Press, Chapter 6.

Streeten, Paul (1982), 'A Cook Look at 'Outward-Looking' Strategies for Development', *The World Economy*, vol. 5, no. 2.

Stuckey, John A. (1983), *Vertical Integration and Joint Ventures in the Aluminum Industry*, Cambridge, Mass: Harvard University Press.

Teitel, Simon (1984), 'Technology Creation in Semi-Industrial Economies', *Journal of Development Economics*, vol. 16, nos. 1–2, September–October.

Toyne, Brian *et al.* (1984), *The Global Textile Industry*, London: George Allen and Unwin.

UNCTAD (1980), *Fibres and Textiles: Dimensions of Corporate Marketing Structure*, Geneva.

UNCTC (1983), *Transnational Corporations in World Development, Third Survey*, New York: UNCTC.

Walter, Ingo (ed.) (nd), *World Industry Studies* (series), London: George Allen and Unwin.

Westphal, Larry E. (1982), 'Fostering Technological Mastery by Means of Selective Industry Promotion' in M. Syrquin and S. Teitel, (eds), *Trade, Stability, Technology and Equity in Latin America*, New York: Academic Press.

12. Direct Foreign Investment and Manufacturing for Export in Developing Countries: A Review of the Issues*

INTRODUCTION

The precarious condition of the global financial system has generated a wide range of suggestions for reform, and continuing advocacy of 'adjustment' for the developing countries. Among the most consistent instruments suggested for achieving the twin objectives of more stable development finance and structural adjustment in production is a quite traditional one: direct foreign investment. It is argued that too much reliance was placed upon debt finance in the 1970s, particularly short-term debt, which has proven highly unpredictable both in its servicing obligations and in its gross flow to the developing countries (see Chapter 9). Now, its future is very much in doubt, except for those few creditworthy countries (such as India and Malaysia) who 'underborrowed' in the past, as commercial banks attempt to restructure their portfolios in response to the adverse experience of the post-1981 period. At the same time, the urgent need for key inputs of management and marketing skills, technology, and know-how in 'non-traditional' tradable goods and services sectors – into which the balance of payments pressures of recent years are driving the developing countries – seem most readily available in the familiar and traditional 'packaged' form of direct foreign investment, however desirable it might be to 'shop' for individual components thereof in less desperate and more leisurely times. Efficiency considerations have led most analysts to place greater emphasis upon 'non-traditional' exporting – notably from the manufacturing sector – than upon the new areas of import substitution.

* I am most grateful to Vincent Cable, Sidney Dell and Louis Wells for their comments on an earlier draft.

To the longstanding advice to improve incentives for export-oriented manufacturing has now been added widespread calls for the relaxation of screening procedures, and the provision of fresh incentives for foreign investors in developing countries. At a Western Economic Summit Conference in London for instance, this new conventional wisdom was vigorously expressed again, as the leaders spoke of

> ...encouraging the flow of long-term direct investment: just as there is need for industrial countries to make their markets more open for the exports of developing countries, so these countries can help themselves by encouraging investment from the industrial countries.

The more internationalist of recent commentators recommend strengthened efforts to complete the UN's code of conduct for transnational corporations to ensure a more stable and balanced policy regime within which investors and governments can confidently encourage increased investment flows. There has already been some relaxation in host country policies on direct foreign investment (UNCTC, 1983: 9–11).

Questions must nevertheless be asked about the efficacy of the suggested new reliance upon direct foreign investment. By now there has been sufficient experience with this form of international economic interaction that it may be possible to anticipate some of the problems that will arise were there to be a significant policy shift back to it. Particularly relevant, when every developing country is at the same time being urged to expand its exports, is the experience with export-oriented direct foreign investment.

A major initial constraint upon the use of foreign direct investment – analogous to that for other commercial sources of finance – is the geographic concentration that has always characterized it. Eleven NICs were the destination for more than half of total OECD direct investment flows to developing countries in recent years. Low-income countries (as defined by the OECD) received only 4 per cent of the 1981 flow of OECD direct investment to developing countries and accounted for 7 per cent of the end-1981 stock (OECD, 1983: 21–5). (Foreign investment may nevertheless account for a significant share of a small or poor country's total external resource inflow.) According to the OECD, its direct investment has gone primarily to countries 'with a dynamic and outward looking economic stance, sustained by appropriate financial and economic policies, a disciplined labour force and, at the time of transaction, a good international credit standing' (OECD, 1983: 8).

Where there are scale economies, learning effects, other countries' trade barriers, investment incentives and trade-related performance requirements, and where oligopolistic multinational firms are key decision-makers, it would be foolhardy for a developing country to proceed with policy on the basis of traditional models of pure competition, perfect markets and comparative advantage. On the other hand, the state of the policy art in these real-world circumstances is still distressingly weak. What is clear is that investment and trade policies must be considered together as 'codeterminants of the location of production and pattern of trade' (McCulloch and Owen, 1983: 353).

ALTERNATIVE APPROACHES TO ANALYSIS OF DIRECT FOREIGN INVESTMENT POLICIES

Consideration of the merits and demerits of direct foreign investment for the expansion of manufactured exports (or any other productive activity) requires a norm against which comparisons are to be made. Different analyses of these issues frequently employ quite different standards of comparison.

Much of the new international emphasis upon direct foreign investment flows from disaffection with, and gloomy forecasts of, commercial bank lending as a source of external capital for developing countries. Direct foreign investment is thus seen primarily, although usually not exclusively, in terms of its role as a source of international capital. But is this new foreign investment to provide *additional* capital? It is not always clear how this widely recommended expansion of transnational corporate investments is to be financed.

Some may be financed from the firms' own earnings, although significant expansion would seem to be predicated upon substantially increased earnings (above previous 'normal', non-recession, rates) which do not currently seem to be in prospect. The bulk of any expansion would presumably have to be financed through new issues of equity or debt. An OECD-sponsored survey of 68 projects in which new capital was raised by direct foreign investors in the pre-banking-boom period found that almost half of the new capital was made up of debt rather than equity issues. Over half of the debt capital (54 per cent) and 40 per cent of the equity was raised in the developing countries themselves (Reuber, 1973:67). By no means all of any expansion in direct foreign investment would therefore constitute net additions to local savings. Some governments inhibit and others encourage resort to local finance on the part of foreign enterprises; local equity is usually favoured relative to local debt.

Transnational corporations have nevertheless traditionally played an important intermediary role in international capital markets. Earlier analysts have noted that:

> Measures that prevent private foreign corporations from doing business at all or that restrict their activities, either preclude or restrict access to international capital markets in developed countries via the most important international financial intermediaries functioning today and the intermediaries that are largely responsible for the large increase in international capital flows that have occurred during the past decade. (Reuber, 1973: 67.)

Is it contemplated that transnational corporations (and their subsidiaries) are now again to intermediate between cautious Northern investors, including commercial banks, and developing country borrowers?

So far as debt issues are concerned, such intermediation should be seen principally as a device to keep commercial bank lending to developing countries a little higher and perhaps a little cheaper than it would otherwise be, by assigning more of the risks in particular sectors and cases to direct investors and less to banks. Such financing might result in a somewhat wider spread of borrowing countries, a somewhat narrower range of activities and, conceivably, sometimes longer terms to maturity, notably when bond finance is involved, than was the norm for commercial bank finance in the developing countries in the 1970s. But otherwise little would be changed by redirectlng bank flows through transnational corporate intermediaries. A relevant norm for comparison, if short- to medium-term debt finance is seen as a major source of expanded direct foreign investment in developing countries, is the cost, country mix, sector mix and maturity of the financial flows that would follow from expanded World Bank or other official intermediation or co-financing activity instead.

New equity and bond issues, to the extent that they are taken up in developed rather than in the developing host countries, are a highly desirable means of acquiring expanded external flows to developing countries. Such flows seem to be what most financial commentators who speak of the need for expanded direct foreign investment in developing countries in the 1980s and 1990s actually have in mind. But how great are the prospects of significantly expanded flows? Are they significantly responsive to governmental policies towards foreign investment in the developing countries? Are direct foreign investment and commercial bank borrowing substitutes for one another? What other means may be found for mobilizing development capital and/or sharing risks in more acceptable ways than in current commercial bank lending arrangements? What about, for instance, developing the proposals for insuring bank lending to developing countries? (An excellent summary of the issues surrounding such insurance schemes can be found in Wallich, 1984.) What are the relative merits of co-financing of various kinds and direct foreign investment? What can be done to ensure that any new gross inflows of foreign equity or bond finance will not be offset, as was so much bank credit to Latin America in the 1970s, by private speculative outflows?

A quite different strand of the literature relates not to the alternative forms or means of acquiring external finance but, rather, to alternative forms of economic organization. In this approach, direct foreign investment represents an internalized or hierarchical form of trade in goods and services – a form with certain advantages and disadvantages relative to the market alternative (see, for example, Casson, 1979; Dunning, 1981). In the relevant literature a variety of non-equity forms (or 'new forms', in some sources; for example, Oman, 1983) of interaction are considered: for example, licensing; subcontracting; franchising; management contracts; marketing contracts; technical assistance contracts; joint ventures; turnkey plant sales; co-production or production-sharing agreements and so on.

Although the data are imperfect there seems to have been an overall shift away from traditional majority-owned foreign investment towards 'new forms' of investment in developing countries, notably joint ventures and licensing agreements, during the 1960s and 1970s. Most dramatic in the petroleum and metals industries, it was also found in manufacturing and particularly in manufacturing for host country markets (import substituting activities) and in those with mature technologies, although there was considerable intercountry variation in manufacturing sector experience (Oman, 1983: 201–4, 227–8; UNCTC, 1983: 40–6). There is also evidence of similar organizational restructuring in export-oriented agriculture (Glover, 1983).

This trend has been less noticeable in manufacturing for export than in other traditional areas of foreign direct investment activity. That direct investment is by no means necessary for successful export-oriented manufacturing is illustrated by the Korean case where the bulk of the exporting has been done by local firms (Westphal *et al.*, 1979). The UNCTC has noted that transnational corporate involvement has been unnecessary and relatively limited in the export of standardized labour-intensive goods; it has been much more important in the export of differentiated products and inputs to industries making them, and, in the Japanese case, in capital-intensive raw material processing (UNCTC, 1983: 182–3; see also Keesing, 1983). In large part, the changes towards non-equity forms of foreign investment or involvement were a response to governmental policies in the host countries. To the extent that government policies generated the alternative forms, their 'liberalization' could be expected to induce some return to the original direct investment mode. To some degree, however, the new forms involved an independent evolution of investment and international business practices relating to risk-sharing, management and financing, and the appearance of smaller internationally-oriented firms, the product of business evolution and decision-making rather than government policies.

A careful consideration of the benefits and costs of alternative forms of interaction with foreign firms, including direct foreign investment of the traditional kind, is desirable, whatever the prospects for expanded finance of one kind or another. Some of the advocates of expanded direct foreign investment (particularly those in chambers of commerce and business) clearly feel that the direct foreign investment form is a superior one, whether for their own self-interested purposes or in the broader interests of social efficiency. More particularly, what they frequently mean to advocate is less governmental restriction of the range of business choice. Typically, they are interested in a favourable 'investment climate' that provides firms with maximum predictability and freedom. As the OECD has put it,

> Stability of investment conditions, non-discrimination ('national treatment'), freedom of capital movements, and satisfactory arrangements for the settlement of investment disputes are features of investment security to which foreign investors attach particular importance. (OECD, 1983: 8)

By confusing the discussion of finance (everyone is for more of it) with that of economic organization, they seek to alter previous governmental policies with respect to the latter. They imply that easing policies towards direct foreign investment – an improved 'investment climate' – will, in fact, increase the flow of external capital. But this link is by no means self-evident. Only when previous *prohibitions* are removed can there be a reasonable presumption of increased foreign investment, and even that may not involve flows from abroad. Prohibitions have not typically been found in manufacturing activities likely to be competitive in world markets; indeed, restrictions on foreign investors have generally been smallest in manufacturing for export.

Direct investment flows are, in any case, overwhelmingly the product of more fundamental determinants of profitability – the overall state of the host country and the world economy.

THE SUPPLY OF DIRECT FOREIGN INVESTMENT

The most fundamental issue concerning the proposed new policy orientation towards direct foreign investment (DFI) is its supply elasticity. How much expansion can one sensibly anticipate in response to altered policies, either at the national or global level? There has long been controversy about the nature of the supply schedule for foreign investment, always assuming that one can analyse the market for the foreign investment 'package' rather than breaking it down into its constituent markets for capital, technology, management and so on.

No doubt each global industry possesses its own peculiar characteristics, and the supply schedule for DFI can be expected to look different from industry to industry. One study hypothesized that the 'market' for DFI in manufacturing oriented to worldwide export markets is separable from 'markets' for DFI geared to national or regional product markets (Guisinger, 1985). Equally, individual country characteristics vary greatly, with the result that 'price' variations are also likely to influence the supply of foreign investment differently from country to country. No less important is the stage at which the foreign investor is in his relations with the host country. Responsiveness can be much greater at the point when an investor is still contemplating putting resources into a 'green field' investment than after he has already made a commitment and is, in some respects, 'trapped' in his elected environment. (In some instances, however, the build-up of local political allies can increase firms' resistance to governmental pressures as time goes on (Newfarmer, 1983: 86–7). Thus the supply elasticity of direct foreign investment is most usefully considered in terms of the specifics of a particular industry in a particular country at a particular point in time.

Generally, investment incentives have been considered to play a minimal role in foreign investment decision-making. For instance, an OECD survey notes that:

> Experience has shown that measures undertaken by home and host governments to improve the flow of foreign direct investment or to direct it to specific sectors and locations influence investment decisions only marginally. Such incentives

> can never substitute for the 'fundamentals': the investment climate, political security and profit opportunities (OECD, 1983: 8).

Profit prospects typically dominate foreign firms' decisions to locate in particular countries – as determined by such needs as resource availability, access to or defence of significant markets, together with the necessary security and political stability. A survey of 52 major international corporations based in 12 countries, undertaken by the Group of Thirty, confirmed that the dominant influences on their foreign direct investment decisions were, overwhelmingly, the need to gain access to local or regional markets and to avoid trade barriers. This was as true of investment in developing countries as elsewhere although 'In the case of LDCs, higher risk and lower-than-expected growth rates were beginning to offset the desire to gain access to new markets' (Group of Thirty, 1984: 31.)

Most striking in this survey, from the standpoint of current concerns (and the concerns of this chapter) were its findings with respect to (a) government policies and (b) export prospects. Tax and other inducements offered by host countries were regarded as

> . . . unimportant influences on investment decisions, though some companies stressed that specific inducements could, on occasion, tip the balance of a decision in favour of investment in a particular country if all other conditions were satisfactory – which was, however, rare. (Group of Thirty, 1984: 32)

No single respondent listed tax advantages in the top three influences upon investments in developing countries. So far as DFI for exporting was concerned, comparative labour costs were mentioned by relatively few firms in the survey (although twice as high a proportion with respect to investments in developing countries as elsewhere); it was not mentioned at all by firms in high-technology industries, chemicals, food and drink, electrical or pharmaceutical industries, or even some labour-intensive industries; and 'The idea of using LDCs as exporting bases was not attractive to most companies' (ibid.).

However, this survey did not include within its definition of direct foreign investment any international subcontracting to independent companies or what the report itself calls 'direct investment without investment' (ibid.: 12), in which frequently 'the local company has in effect been brought into existence and is kept in being by the international company (ibid.); and 'the economic and balance of payments effects are almost identical to those of FDI' (ibid.: 13). Foreign firms engaging in international subcontracting achieve these results 'without going through the motions of conventional foreign direct investment or incurring the same kind of risks as those attaching to conventional DFI' (ibid.: 12). Growing resort to such non-DFI forms may seriously distort interpretations of foreign firms' interest in exporting that are based on questions relating purely to conventional ownership modalities.

Against the substantial body of survey and theoretical evidence of the limited impact of governmental inducements to foreign investors, one World Bank study (Guisinger, 1985) appears to argue quite differently – at least with respect to the industries and countries studied: automobiles, computers, food products and petrochemicals, in 10 countries of which seven were developing (Brazil, India, Indonesia, Kenya, Mexico, Philippines, and Singapore). While the impact is certainly uneven across industries and countries, and it is recognized that incentives may not be the most important influences upon foreign investment in particular locations, this study purports to find that incentives *do* matter to foreign investment decisions and that countries compete in (differentiated) markets for foreign investment. In two-thirds of the 74 cases studied, host country government policy influenced the investors' choice of country. The enormous variety of possible policy instruments (far beyond the tax issues that typically dominate debate) makes it extremely difficult to ascertain the exact overall net impact of any individual government's policies; it also permits a high degree of 'product differentiation' on the part of governments seeking to attract investors and a low degree of transparency regarding their policies. Governments are also found to be offering firm-specific incentives and thereby effectively practising price discrimination. However, since tariff protection is included among this study's 'incentive policies', it is not obvious that its results are, after all, inconsistent with earlier ones. Indeed, where investment flows are stimulated by protectionist policies, they may even reduce national income in the host country (Brecher and Diaz-Alejandro, 1977).

The study argues that there are three separate markets for foreign investment: one for investments directed at the markets of individual host countries; one for those relating to common markets; and one for investments geared to production for export – and there is competition in each. In the competition for foreign investment, the effectiveness of any individual countries' policies clearly depends upon other countries' reactions, and these may themselves depend upon the direction of change. Increases in incentives are more likely to be followed by competitors than are decreases. The existence of competition among countries such that all offer more or less the same incentives could explain why firms so frequently say that investment incentives do not influence their location decisions; yet if just one country were unilaterally to abandon its incentives there would indeed be effects upon the geographic pattern of investments. These results accord with casual empirical observations of intergovernmental bidding for foreign investment projects, and with the views of those who have predicted 'investment wars' for the future (Bergsten, 1974).

None of this evidence of competition among countries for foreign investors offers any guidance as to whether increased incentives will increase the aggregate flow of direct foreign investment to developing countries. Since there was very little direct competition for investments observed between developing and developed countries – although there was some indirectly, via the erection of trade barriers – there is still no presumption that improved incentives will increase the flow of direct investment to the developing countries. Increased incentives on the part of developing countries, inevitably matched by others in the competitive struggle for foreign investment, may simply reduce their earnings from it without significantly increasing its flow. It may nevertheless be true that, 'With better general economic policies and a better entry system, the same amount of investment could be attracted at a lower cost' (OECD, 1983: 14). There would also seem to be scope for joint, or at least coordinated, approaches to the provision of incentives to foreign investors. Such approaches need not require total uniformity of policies, which is probably an impossible attainment anyway, but they could provide explicitly for differential incentives – for instance, to offset the disadvantages of the poorest countries.

Radetzki has shown that one can be seriously misled about the response of foreign firms to changing investment regimes and Third World overall market shares if one relies purely upon traditional data sources. What at first looks like supply response and deteriorating market shares may in fact merely be altered forms of involvement (Radetzki, 1982). Although this was written with reference to minerals development the point is a general one. The great variety of institutional forms of foreign firms' involvement in developing countries' manufacturing for export has always made the interpretation of data on the degree of transnationals' involvement and the role of direct foreign investment in this activity very difficult (see, for example, Nayyar, 1978). Alternative forms of foreign involvement are considered in the following section.

There must, in any case, continue to be doubt as to *how much* and *what kind* of incentive is necessary to induce the desired expansion in *net* foreign investment at the national level. It would certainly be wrong to consider that all of the investment that benefits from incentive programmes is additional to the investment that would otherwise have occurred. There is bound to be some 'redundancy' in incentive programmes: that is, investors receive subsidies they do not require in order to invest. Indeed, the selectivity and discrimination observed in actual programmes undoubtedly reflects governmental attempts to reduce such 'redundancy'. Even so, some of the additional foreign investment apparently successfully induced by selective incentives may simply displace investment by others, both foreign and local. (See Usher, 1977.) There are also differential effects created by different kinds of incentives: product-oriented incentives, factory-oriented incentives, tax incentives of various types and so forth. While such incentive arrangements may, in some sense, be aggregated in firms' calculations as to the desirability of alternative locations, they do not all generate the same structure of investments, the same product mix, or the same technologies in the incentive granting country. These issues deserve more careful theoretical and empirical investigation.

DIRECT FOREIGN INVESTMENT AND ALTERNATIVE FORMS OF ORGANIZATION

According to conventional industrial organization theory, vertical integration (internalization) is more efficient than market exchange when the relationship is ongoing, but complex and subject to frequent change. Internalization improves the flow of information between transactors, reducing the possibilities for the provision of untruthful and misleading data, and reduces the prospect of small numbers bargaining problems. The purchasing firm, in addition to such savings in transactions costs, may also benefit from reduced supply uncertainties, protect itself from foreclosure by vertically integrated rivals, and derive increased scale economies via increased intrafirm specialization (Williamson, 1975). Internalization and its capital requirements may also generate significant barriers to others' entry to particular industries.

Foreign ownership thus carries certain potential advantages in entering world markets. Apart from foreign firms' ownership of particular technology and management not readily available to local firms, they can bring information about foreign markets, experience and expertise in the many complex facets of international marketing and influence upon commercial policy-makers and customs authorities in home markets (de la Torre,

1974). They may also benefit from scale economies associated with their worldwide operations. (In some instances, foreign firms may restrict exports in order to protect the established markets of the parent firm or other subsidiaries; but this is unlikely to be important in cases where 'fresh' DFI is brought specifically to expand exports.)

The advantages of foreign firms over local ones are obviously most marked in industries where technology is least standardized, scale economies are prevalent and marketing is most difficult. In other industries they may not possess significant advantages over local firms. Aggregative data comparing foreign firms' export performance with that of local firms may therefore be quite misleading with respect to the potentially important role direct foreign investment and foreign firm participation may play. At the industry level, foreign firms have frequently been found to be relatively effective exporters (see, for example Lall and Mohammad, 1983; see also references in Newfarmer, 1983).

Foreign direct investment of the traditional type, by linking control over investment with a measure of control over international markets, provides some protection to the prospective exporting country against gross miscalculation. Where foreign firms are not directly involved in the profitability of new enterprises they may happily sell equipment or technology to more competitors than can eventually be accommodated in world markets – especially if the sales are backed and insured by governments. The dispersed and uncoordinated investment activities of a variety of national firms in developing countries, all competing with one another, may generate excess capacity, worsened terms of trade and, eventually, some losers (Cline, 1982).

Oman has pointed out (1983: 202) that 'the long-term global investment planning perspective which multinational firms are relinquishing may be assumed by multinational banks and international financial organisations, at least to the extent that host countries require foreign loans to undertake their investment projects'; but there are limits to their capacities in this regard. Besides, from the standpoint of individual national interest, the objective of 'non-traditional' approaches ('new forms') is presumably to get loose from external control over domestic investment decisions, marketing policies and the like. The substitution of external bankers for external producing firms, as controlling institutions, would seem to constitute rather limited progress towards the goal of greater independence.

The moves towards global industrial organization and cartelization *outside* the transnationals clearly involve major risks for the developing countries. At their worst they may lead to more MFAs, explicitly and unashamedly discriminating against 'low-cost' producers. Still, there is undoubtedly considerable room for further experimentation and development of non-DFI manufacturing for export.

Some firms, notably some Japanese trading companies and recently others based in Hong Kong, already specialize in the assembly of efficient 'packages' of equipment, know-how, management and marketing skills from a variety of sources. As far as DFI is concerned, Third World multinationals may play an expanding role in manufacturing for export not only within the South but also to the North. Some Third World multinationals have developed considerable specialized knowledge of small-scale and labour-intensive production procedures in the manufacture of standardized products (Wells, 1983; Lall, 1983).

The specifics of relationships between separate contracting firms or between parents and subsidiaries are governed by traditions that vary from country to country. International trading and investment relationships may be formally constrained by international laws, codes and guidelines; but these do not begin to tell the complete story as to how these relationships were built or the conventions by which they are maintained. A complex web of law, economics and custom operates to determine the details of particular relationships and contracts.

In the USA it is traditional to deploy batteries of lawyers to work out voluminous contracts specifying in enormous detail how hypothetical circumstances may in future be handled. Changing or unexpected circumstances require altered contracts – and more lawyers. In East and Southeast Asia, where litigation does not play so prominent a role, there is typically greater care taken in the early stages to investigate the overall circumstances, rather than the strict legalities, of a possible agreement. Once made, there is implicit agreement that the relationship must be flexible, that risks must be shared, and that the details can be worked out when required, provided that there is mutual trust and genuine commitment; if trust is breached, it is understood that the relationship will be terminated.

> Many overseas Chinese firms have no truck with written contracts, feeling that if you need a contract to hold a man to his obligations you ought not to be doing business with him at all... A company places a small order with a new supplier or sub-contractor as a test of reliability and integrity. Ample opportunity is often deliberately left for cheating. Trust, and the size of the orders, builds up gradually over many years. . . . Lacking enforceable contracts, overseas Chinese businessmen cannot afford to be aggressive competitors who seek to

> screw the best deal they can out of their suppliers and customers. They need instead to negotiate deals where both parties benefit, if possible equally. This, above all, is why western and overseas Chinese businessmen find themselves talking a different language. The idea that everybody can be a winner is strange to western firms – and western business schools. (*The Economist*, 28 April 1984: 82–3.)

All else being equal, trust is probably maximized through internalized transactions – that is, through relationships of ownership or family ties. In large and more Western-oriented firms, where family or traditional modes of interaction are of limited relevance, ownership ties are a prime means of reducing risk and uncertainty, lowering transactions costs and frequently also deriving economies of scale in information, marketing, sourcing and production systems. As information and management systems become more sophisticated and computerized there is likely to be an ever higher efficiency premium upon reliability. Tight control systems seeking to reduce the capital tied up inefficiently in inventories, while necessarily incorporating back-up procedures, build upon absolute reliability of delivery and quality. Modern management and information technology may therefore generate increased tendencies for more centralized control and, quite possibly, internalization and direct investment.

In principle, the exporting country that is host to a subsidiary engaged in exporting may gain both from the increased stability and from the increased income created by the foreign firms via such internalized organizational arrangements. But there is no guarantee that it will. Moreover, other exporting firms and countries may suffer from lower income and increased uncertainty and instability in consequence of one country's 'success' with such approaches, as they are relatively 'residualized' in what are often fairly thin and sometimes oligopolistically organized markets.

It is striking that there has not been more independent study of the relative advantages of different forms of investment, different governmental policies and performance requirements, and different general relationships between host countries and foreign firms in particular industries, both for firms of varying characteristics and for various actors in different kinds of host countries. Business schools have addressed some of the issues in terms of firms' interests, but little research has been done on others' interests.

GOVERNMENT POLICIES

Developing (Host) Countries

Far more important to the prospects for successful manufacturing for export than whether or how foreign firms participate is the overall profit potential from export activities in particular countries and industries. To a substantial degree the short-run determinants of profitability are the product of nature, factor endowment, location, history and other uncontrollables. Governmental policies with respect to exchange rates, tax systems, subsidies, infrastructure provision, licensing and other bureaucratic requirements are usually nonetheless an important element in the determination of such profitability; and they, of course, are likely to impact upon both foreign and local firms. If exports are to be expanded, government policies must be directed at the provision of the required incentives.

If the desired future trade balance is to materialize from expanded investment activities, whatever their nature, the structure of incentives must encourage import-substituting and exporting activities. There is a vast literature on incentive structures in developing countries, the bulk of which concludes that they have typically been characterized by an anti-export bias and frequently also an anti-tradables bias (from overvalued currencies). Appropriate exchange rates and a fairly uniform tariff structure is the conventionally recommended recipe for maintaining efficiency and external balance, although due account is also to be taken of the possibility of terms-of-trade gains through targeted restrictions upon trade, learning effects, infant industry encouragement, and irrational consumer preferences for imported goods and services, all of which are justifications for departures from unified exchange rate systems (Balassa, 1982: 66–71). There remains some disagreement concerning the significance and the potential for 'learning' and therefore about the appropriate degree and character of infant industry policies (see Chapter 11). Analogous arguments about learning can be deployed in support of the encouragement of infant national *firms*, presumably at the expense of foreign firms, some of which may be investors or potential investors in the protecting country.

Another set of policy instruments that has been deployed in support of trade objectives is that of performance requirements, either with respect to raising exports or lowering imports. They may, of course, offset the effects of some of the investment incentives. US data suggest that whereas

US affiliates overseas benefit from investment incentives with about the same frequency in developed and developing countries, they are subject to performance requirements (of various kinds, not all trade-related) four times as frequently in the latter countries as in the former. Fully 25 per cent of US affiliates in developing countries were affected by them in 1977; and there was wide intercountry variation (McCulloch and Owen, 1983: 342, Safarian, 1983: 614). A GATT panel has ruled that those relating to domestic procurement and the consequent limitation of imports contravene the GATT, whereas those requiring a certain level of export performance do not. This legal distinction, whether or not it is eventually upheld in other cases, seems to have no justification in economics. Performance requirements, unless they are redundant, deflect trade from the channels in which it would otherwise flow and are therefore equally 'distorting' of the market, regardless of their nature. Whether the 'free' market flows generated by imperfect markets are themselves socially efficient is a much larger question that the GATT has never addressed. It can be argued that some performance requirements move the trading outcome back toward the equivalent of the competitive equilibrium solution that is theoretically optimal, serving to offset restrictive business practices and other real-world distortions that obstruct efficient overall outcomes. The widespread existence of export restrictions – explicit or implicit – in technology contracts and subsidiary operations relating to import-substituting production is evidence that transnational corporate involvement can impede, as well as assist, the expansion of exports.

In some circumstances it may be possible to induce or require direct foreign investors who originally entered production in a developing country location to meet local markets to shift to exporting, but this is typically more difficult than the encouragement of 'fresh' export-oriented investors since it requires alteration of the firms' global production and marketing strategies (Bennet and Sharpe, 1979). It may also involve large government subsidies to overcome them.

Project-specific performance requirements, in the form of 'buy-back' agreements requiring investors to purchase specified volumes of the project's output, are also deployed to ensure desired trade effects from new direct foreign investments. With the growth in countertrade and state trading, this non-market means of overcoming early marketing problems seems likely to increase in importance.

The deployment of trade-related performance requirements for foreign firms is a matter of growing international concern. If the developing countries that have been most active in their use are to take informed positions in their defence, and if others are to benefit from their experience, it is essential that there be careful assessments of the degree to which they have worked. Have domestic sourcing, minimum export requirements and the like achieved the results that they were intended to achieve? What costs and difficulties have been experienced in their use? How do the costs and benefits of such performance requirements compare with those of alternative policies that could be directed to the attainment of the same objectives? In what circumstances (industries, countries, firms) are these policy instruments likely to be most effective or least effective?

There are many other possible objectives besides balance of payments improvements that might influence the nature of bargains struck with foreign investors: for example, employment creation, training, local R and D and so on. If development is seen in terms of technical change, productivity improvements and learning-by-doing, these elements of performance are far more important than those relating to relatively short-term trade effects. There have been very few empirical analyses of 'learning', total factor productivity change and their correlates in export-oriented manufacturing as compared with other activities, foreign-owned firms compared with local firms, or combinations thereof.

If capital, management, marketing skills and the like are required in particular export industries, government policy must be directed at their acquisition. But there is no *necessary* connection between these two sets of objectives (exporting and the acquisition of scarce inputs) and therefore no necessity for linking them through the use of only one policy instrument. Some countries nevertheless seek particularly to steer foreign investment into export activities.

One much discussed means for so linking them are the so-called 'export processing zones' (EPZs). These zones typically provide strong incentives for export activity at the same time that they particularly encourage the participation of foreign-owned firms. They have proven highly controversial because of their enclave character and their obvious reliance upon an inflammable mixture of foreign capital and local low-wage (frequently teenage and female) labour. Their relative importance in manufactured exports from those developing countries that have created them is highly variable but is typically quite small: for example, 4 per cent in Korea, 12 per cent in the Philippines, 26 per cent in Sri Lanka, 41 per cent in Malaysia (Maex, 1983: 63). If there exists a conventional wisdom on the utility of EPZs in developing countries it is probably summarized as follows:

> Because the viability of the export-processing zones rests to such a considerable extent on the strategies and interests of transnational corporations and on technological developments and because the possibilities for domestic firms to expand operations in the zones are limited, an industrial development strategy relying on export-processing zones alone would not be prudent. In those developing countries for which the availability of unskilled labour is the main, and perhaps the only, economic resource, the export-processing zones may be of value in the initial phase of industrialization. In other developing countries they can be an important supplement to other industrialization efforts. In both cases, the export-processing zones can create employment opportunities and yield export earnings. In the long run, attempts should be made to further the integration of the zones into the overall industrial development process, for example by the establishment of forward linkages between semi-conductor production and the manufacture of certain consumer electronic products such as calculators, digital watches, and electronic games. The use of export-processing zones in conjunction with import-substitution oriented activities and export-oriented activities of a more general kind, would provide diversified and viable industrial capacity and capability in the developing countries. (UNCTC, 1983: 184–5.)

Despite considerable controversy over their role in development, there is a striking dearth of careful empirical economic analysis of their overall costs and benefits. Studies to date are either highly theoretical or purely descriptive – neither very helpful for policy-makers trying to decide whether to create EPZs or, if they do, how they should be structured. The results of one benefit–cost analysis of EPZs predictably showed considerable sensitivity to assumptions with respect to the opportunity cost of labour (Tsui, 1987; see also Basile and Germidis, 1984).

Developed (Home) Countries

Governments of the home countries of direct foreign investors have been concerned to encourage their firms with promotional activities, favourable tax treatment and the provision of protection against otherwise uninsurable risks, particularly political ones. These insurance and related arrangements typically cover loans, suppliers' credits, service sales and even some earnings remissions, as well as equity. (For more details on individual home governments' programmes, see OECD, 1983.)

But the importance of these home government policies can easily be exaggerated. The total share of the direct foreign investment stock in developing countries that is covered by governmental insurance arrangements is only about 9 per cent (OECD, 1983: 30–3). No doubt the percentage coverage of new direct investment flows is somewhat larger, but most direct foreign investors do not seem to be heavily dependent upon such governmental insurance and guarantee schemes. It is said that such insurance as is desired by direct investors is increasingly being obtained on private markets (UNCTC, 1983: 96; OECD, 1983: 117–18). Many elements of uncertainty concerning host country policies and circumstances are not readily covered by insurance contracts. Re-interpretation of the details of contractual arrangements, for example, are far more complex and difficult to consider or protect oneself against in advance than such obvious measures as expropriation, exchange controls or civil disturbances. But knowledge as to which types of firms seek which types of insurance in which industries and which countries is scarce.

Home governments providing insurance for their investing firms prefer to do so only for investments in countries with which they have intergovernmental agreements on foreign investment. Bilateral treaties providing for the protection of foreign investments are usually asymmetric in the obligations imposed upon the relevant parties. Foreign owners of capital benefit from 'national' treatment or most-favoured-nation provisions, assured convertability of earnings and capital repatriation, fair and prompt compensation upon nationalization and the like; the only return to the host country signatory is the increased likelihood that foreign investors will be insured by their home governments against the very events (plus wars and insurrections) which the treaties ostensibly forbid. Vernon has described these treaties as 'patently unbalanced . . . too unbalanced to provide the basis for a durable regime' (Vernon 1982: 10–11).

Home governments are also subject to other pressures regarding the nature of their promotional, insurance and overseas assistance programmes. The US government, for instance, is mandated not to extend favourable export credit terms to projects that are likely to compete with American products in home markets, and has exerted pressure upon the World Bank similarly to constrain its lending. 'Industrial cooperation' agreements and programmes, such as those run by the EEC through the Lomé Convention, routinely incorporate protectionist biases in their advice, technical assistance and other supports.

The longstanding efforts to construct a code for transnational corporations under UN auspices continue. Less comprehensive codes and guidelines have been negotiated or are under discussion in the ILO, UNCTAD, and OECD: and there have long been proposals for a 'GATT for investment'. An overall legislative and regulatory framework that seeks to minimize conflict and encourage accommodation in the general global interest remains a worthy aspiration. But what can be agreed in such a way as to cover all sectors and circumstances in a multilateral forum inevitably will be too general to carry many specific teeth. Few expect any of the new codes significantly to affect the flow of new direct investment to developing countries. (More information on their contents may be found in OECD, 1983 and UNCTC, 1983: 95–6, 107–21.)

The commercial policies of the industrialized countries, to which most Third World manufactured exports at present are directed, are obviously of crucial importance to the export prospects of the developing countries. As South–South trade in manufactures expands, the commercial policies of other developing countries will also become increasingly important.

In the former case, as argued in Chapter 9, there is reason to believe that commercial policy may be responsive to domestic political pressures in such a way as relatively to favour imports from subsidiaries or affiliates of home firms; much of this relatively favoured trade is likely to be intrafirm. On the other hand, developing countries' governments can be expected to exert disproportionate bargaining effort on behalf of their own home firms, those that are *not* owned by foreign investors. All else being equal, the influence of domestic political interests within the industrialized countries is likely to prevail over those of developing country governments, whose weak overall bargaining strength is indicated by the relatively poor results that they have achieved for their exports in developed country markets in successive GATT tariff bargaining rounds. Although econometric investigation of the US tariff is unable to confirm the hypothesis that imports from US-owned firms are particularly well treated in international tariff bargaining (Lavergne and Helleiner, 1984), it seems roughly to accord with observed practice with respect to US non-tariff barriers. Even 'neutral' reductions in trade barriers may disproportionately benefit international firms relative to national ones, particularly in the short term, since they are better able quickly to serve established markets via known external sources and to capture the potential efficiency gains from liberalization (McCulloch and Owen, 1983: 346).

Selective barriers to developing country exports, such as voluntary export restraints, apart from their direct effects upon current trade, can also influence the geographic pattern of further investments in the affected industries, as investors and buyers seek new 'uncontrolled' exporting bases and sources in which to expand the activities that are constrained in their original locations. These incentives for export-oriented direct foreign investment and sourcing in new locations are severely damped, of course, when the trade managing authorities show signs of imposing restraints upon newcomers as soon as they begin to succeed. In Canada, for instance, imports of cotton tailored shirts from Sri Lanka were described as 'disruptive' and restrained when they achieved a level of only 0.02 per cent of total Canadian imports of this product (Biggs, 1980: 85).

A particularly significant commercial policy inducement for transnational and other firms to locate export-oriented production in developing countries is the value-added tariff, offering customs duty relief on manufactured imports when inputs into the product in question originate in the country that imports the final product. Imports under these provisions constituted 7.5 per cent of total US imports in 1982 (USITC, 1984: 15). In the same year, 42.7 per cent of the value of US imports under tariff item 807 (the major relevant item) came from developing countries; since imported US inputs made up a much higher proportion of the total value of the exports in developing countries, their share of dutiable value was only 28.9 per cent. The EEC's scheme, unlike that of the USA, requires that the 'outward processing' be undertaken by a firm resident in the EEC in order to qualify for favourable customs treatment. Outside the USA, there has been very little information or research on the uses and effects of this important set of policies.

Also relevant are the GSP (although it is subject to unilateral withdrawal without compensation) and such regional preferential arrangements as the Lomé Convention and the Caribbean Basin Initiative. In all of these programmes the rules of origin are crucially important to the determination of their value to the affected developing countries.

The direct effects of home government trade barriers have received quite a lot of research attention. So, in recent years, has the structure of these trade barriers and its political determinants. Interactions between investment and restricted trade flows have not, however, been fully explored. Nor have available data permitted a full investigation of the role of direct foreign investment in the determination of the structure of trade barriers. The distribution of the 'rent' from non-tariff trade barriers and preferential schemes is also relatively unexplored research territory.

FURTHER RESEARCH REQUIREMENTS

Despite the new conventional wisdom that export-oriented manufacturing and direct foreign investment deserve significant new encouragement in the developing countries there is still distressingly little known about optimal policies relating to them. In a world of varied market imperfections and a myriad of governmental interventions, advice based on traditional models of pure competition is not persuasive. There is a need for simultaneous analyses of policies towards trade and policies towards investment since, together, they co-determine the location of global production and the pattern of future trade.

Analysis of direct foreign investment can proceed either in the context of concern with adequate levels and appropriate forms of development finance, or in that of consideration of alternative institutional arrangements for transacting with foreign firms. The research questions asked relate very much to which approach is being pursued. An investigation of financial issues will enquire as to the possibilities of sharing risks and tapping new sources of capital in ways other than through direct foreign investment, and ask whether new flows of direct foreign investment are likely, in fact, to be additional. Research focusing upon forms of economic organization will consider the benefits and costs of conducting whatever activities are favoured through a variety of 'new forms' of investment and contracting, relative to those carried out through direct investment packages.

The evidence on the supply elasticity of direct foreign investment is still fairly scanty and inconclusive. More detailed investigation of the 'markets' for different kinds of direct foreign investment – by industry, market orientation, or types of incentive-offering countries – could improve on recent World Bank research on investment incentives and performance requirements. Investigation of the effects of different types of incentives (or performance requirements) upon firm behaviour and the attainment of broader social objectives is also potentially productive. Particular attention should be paid to the possibility of developing countries' overdoing their incentive programmes through uncoordinated competition for a relatively inelastic supply of investment.

The analysis of advantages and disadvantages, and benefits and costs, of alternative forms of interaction between transnational corporations and host governments has received far more attention from those concerned with business decision-making than it has from those interested in social objectives in the host countries. Not only in the sphere of manufacturing for export but in other industries and activities as well, there should by now be enough developing country experience to permit a systematic empirical investigation of these issues.

There is room for further research on many other aspects of government policies towards foreign direct investment and towards export-oriented manufacturing both in developing and industrialized countries. The effects of 'infant industry' and other 'learning'-oriented policies towards industries and firms in developing countries have not been adequately documented. (Indeed, the correlates of productivity growth have generally received much less research attention than questions of intersectoral and interindustry allocation.) Neither have those of various kinds of trade-related performance requirement. Despite the burst of interest in export-processing zones, and the by now considerable experience with them, there have not been enough careful empirical analyses of their costs and benefits either. So far as home country policies are concerned, there is a need for research on the detailed impact of foreign investment insurance and related programmes, exploring the types of firms, industries and countries that are affected by them. Little is known about the effects of value-added tariff and outward processing arrangements in countries other than the USA. Nor has there been much research on the role of direct foreign investment in influencing the overall structure of trade barriers and other incentives and disincentives in the international arena, and in earning policy-created rents.

REFERENCES

Balassa, Bela *et al.* (1982), *Development Strategies in Semi-Industrial Economies*, Baltimore: World Bank, Johns Hopkins.

Basile, Antoine and Dimitri Germides (1984), *Industry in Free Export-processing Zones*, Paris: OECD.

Bennett, Douglas and Kenneth E. Sharpe (1979), 'Transnational Corporations and the Political Economy of Export Promotion: The Case of the Mexican Automobile Industry', *International Organization*, vol. 33, no. 2, Spring, pp. 177–201.

Bergsten, C. Fred (1974), 'Coming Investment Wars?', *Foreign Affairs*, October, pp. 135–52.

Biggs, Margaret A. (1980), *The Challenge: Adjust or Protect?* Ottawa: North–South Institute.

Brecher, Richard A. and Carlos F. Diaz-Alejandro (1977), 'Tariffs, Foreign Capital and Immiserizing Growth', *Journal of International Economics*, vol. 7, no. 4, November.

Casson, Mark (1979), *Alternatives to the Multinational Enterprise*, London: Macmillan.

Cline, William R. (1982), 'Can the East Asian Export Model of Development be Generalized?', *World Development*, vol. 10, no. 2, February.

de la Torre, J. (1974), 'Foreign Investment and Export Dependency', *Economic Development and Cultural Change*, vol. 23, no. 1, October, pp. 133–50.

Dunning, John H. (1981), *International Production and the Multinational Enterprise*, London: George Allen & Unwin.

Germides, D. (1984), *Policies to Attract Export-Oriented Investment: The Role of Free Export-Processing Zones*, Paris: OECD.

Glover, David (1983), *Contract Farming and the Transnationals*, PhD dissertation, University of Toronto.

Group of Thirty (1984), *Foreign Direct Investment, 1973–1987* New York.

Guisinger, Stephen (1985), *Investment Incentives and Performance Requirements*, New York: Praeger.

Keesing, Donald B. (1983), 'Linking up to Distant Markets: South to North Exports of Manufactured Consumer Goods', *American Economic Review*, vol. 73, no. 2, May, pp. 338–42.

Lall, Sanjaya and Sharif Mohammad (1983), 'Foreign Ownership and Export Performance in the Large Corporate Sector of India', *Journal of Development Studies*, vol. 20, no. 1, October pp. 56–67.

Lall, Sanjaya *et al.* (1983), 'The New Multinationals', *The Spread of Third World Enterprises*, New York: John Wiley and Sons.

Lavergne, Real P. and G.K. Helleiner (1985), 'US Transnational Corporations and the Structure of US Trade Barriers: An Empirical Investigation', in UNCTC, *Transnational Corporations and International Trade: Selected Issues*, New York: ST/CTC/54.

Maex, Rudy (1983), *Employment and Multinationals in Asian Export Processing Zones*, Working Paper no. 26, Multinational Enterprises Programme, Geneva: International Labour Office.

McCulloch, Rachel and Robert F. Owen (1983), 'Linking Negotiations on Trade and Foreign Direct Investment', in C.P. Kindleberger and D. Audretsch (eds), *The Multinational Corporation in the 1980s*, Cambridge: The MIT Press, pp. 334–58.

Nayyar, Deepak (1978), 'Transnational Corporations and Manufacturered Exports from Poor Countries', *Economic Journal*, vol. 88, no. 1, March, pp. 59–84.

Newfarmer, Richard (1983), 'Multinationals and Marketplace Magic in the 1980s' in C.P. Kindleberger and D. Audretsch (eds), *The Multinational Corporation in the 1980s*, Cambridge: The MIT Press, pp. 162–97.

Oman, Charles (1983), *New Forms of International Investment in Developing Countries*, Paris: OECD, Development Centre.

OECD (1983), *Investing in Developing Countries*, Paris: OECD.

Radetzki, Marian (1982), 'Has Political Risk Scared Mineral Investment Away from the Deposits in Developing Countries?', *World Development*, vol. 10, no. 1, January, pp. 39–48.

Reuber, Grant L. *et al.* (1973), *Private Foreign Investment in Development*, Oxford: Clarendon Press, for OECD Paris.

Safarian, A.E. (1983), 'Trade-Related Investment Issues' in William R. Cline (ed.), *Trade Policy in the 1980s*, Washington: Institute for International Economics, pp. 611–37.

Tsui, Kai-Y (1987), *A Social Cost–Benefit Analysis of Export Processing Zones in Some Asian Countries*, Phd dissertation, University of Toronto.

United Nations Centre of Transnational Corporations (UNCTC) (1983), *Transnational Corporations in World Development, Third Survey*, New York: UNCTC.

United States International Trade Commission (USITC) (1984), *Imports Under*

Items 806.30 and 807.00 of the Tariff Schedules of the United States, 1979–82, USITC publication 1467, Washington: USITC.

Usher, Dan (1977), 'The Economics of Tax Incentives to Encourage Investment in Less Developed Countries', *Journal of Development Economics*, vol. 4, no. 2, June, pp. 119–48.

Vernon, Raymond (1982), 'Codes on Transnationals: Ingredients for an Effective International Regime', Harvard Business School, mimeo.

Wallich, Henry C. (1984), 'Insurance of Bank Lending to Developing Countries', *Group of Thirty, Occasional Papers*, no. 15, New York.

Wells, L.T. (1983), *Third World Multinationals*, New York: MIT Press.

Westphal. L., Y.W. Rhee and G. Pursell (1979), 'Foreign Influences on Korean Industrial Development', *Oxford Bulletin of Economics and Statistics*, vol. 41, no. 4, November pp. 359–88.

Williamson, Oliver E. (1975), *Markets and Hierarchies, Analysis and Antitrust Implications: A Study in the Economics of Internal Organization*, New York: The Free Press.

13. Uncertainty, Information and the Economic Interests of the Developing countries

INTRODUCTION

The 'economics of information' has achieved 'take-off' within the last decade. Theoretical treatises proliferate on the previously neglected implications of informational imperfections and asymmetries for the functioning of markets, competitive or otherwise. This recent work has been additional to that associated with the older literature on game theory, bargaining, and negotiation, in which information and misinformation play important roles. It has wrought a potential revolution in the 'conventional wisdom' concerning market economies:

> . . . the traditional paradigms of competitive markets, with perfect information and markets equilibrated by the mythical Walrasian auctioneer, are not only not directly applicable, but may be seriously misleading. (Stiglitz, 1979: 344) . . .
>
> for at least certain important situations, the conventional full information paradigm is not even a good approximation; markets with even a little bit of imperfect information may look distinctly different from markets with perfect information. At the same time, there are undoubtedly situations where the traditional theory will suffice as a good approximation. The relative domains of the alternative theories remain a subject for discussion. (Stiglitz, 1977: 391)
>
> . . . clearly the traditional presumption of *caveat emptor* has no basis within welfare economics, when information is costly. (Stiglitz, 1979: 344)

At the same time there has emerged a technological revolution in the realm of information storage, retrieval, transmission and processing. New low-cost electronic information processing systems and telecommunications networks have already vastly changed the information scene as far as both market and non-market transactions around the world are concerned; and their full social and economic impact has yet to be felt.

Transnational corporations are among the most important users of new information technology. Much of their use of these systems can be interpreted as the replacement of markets – with their informational and other imperfections, only now being fully comprehended in terms of pure economic theory – with more efficient non-market relationships. Non-market information flows now take place across international boundaries without their notation or enumeration; since statistics for transborder data flows are still highly imperfect it is impossible to say more than that these flows are already substantial and are rising rapidly. So are the rather more 'visible' associated international transactions in information services, including consulting, data processing, software packages, data access and the like. Governments and international organizations are struggling to keep abreast of these rapid developments and to puzzle out their implications and potentialities.

While the debate on a code of conduct for technology contracts has persisted for many years, international trade in information and information-related services has not, until quite recently, received the same degree of attention – at least from economists. There is a great deal of discussion these days, however, about international trade in services and the need for an agreed international regime (in the US view, freedom) for it. Information and information services have become matters for high foreign policy.

In recent discussions on transborder data flow, it has become evident that not only are these particular flows unrecorded – and most certainly not in the balance of payments – but it is not even evident on what basis one might do so. How should they be valued, if at all? How should intrafirm data flows be treated? Should they be recorded only when payment is actually made for them? If so, this would be a breach of the conventional practice in respect of goods trade. At present it seems that only 'services' related to information are recorded in the balance of payments at all, and then quite imperfectly. It is likely that many intrafirm services are totally omitted from the accounts since the firm does not always conceive of itself as trading (within itself) the services of its own employees.

The implications of *either* the new theoretical understanding of the role of information in markets *or* the revolution in information technologies, alone, would justify some major effort to analyse afresh the developing countries' interests in the global economic and political system. Together, these changes both in perceptions and in realities present them with an enormous and complex challenge. What *do* we know now about the role of information in the markets, negotiations and other transactions of greatest interest to the informationally weakest in the world economy – the developing countries and individuals, firms and governments within them? What *do* we now need to know about structures of information flows? What *are* developing countries' interests and possibilities in the new information technologies and the policy debates on transborder data flows and so forth to which they give rise? What is likely to be the most efficient approach to policy-relevant research – detailed analyses of specific cases (markets, firms, institutions, countries, and so on), or a search for more generally applicable principles and objectives, or both?

INFORMATION 'PROBLEMS' AND THE DEVELOPING COUNTRIES

What exactly are the 'problems' associated with imperfect information in the effective functioning of markets or hierarchical planning systems? In the rich new literature of the economics of information it is possible to distinguish several different types of information imperfection. These can be grouped as follows:

1. uncertainty (incomplete information) about the future;
2. 'inherent' uncertainties and deficiencies or asymmetries in information about the present, about which there is little that can be done, notably in the realm of product quality;
3. informational deficiencies or asymmetries about the present which are 'unnecessary' in the sense that it is possible, at a price, to remove or at least reduce them by 'searching' and/or 'advertising'.

Uncertainty about the Future

'Expectations' are formed on the basis of the information available in the present and recent past and its processing according to different rules and with varying degrees of efficiency. While everyone suffers from this uncertainty, it is *not* the case that everyone suffers equally, since different 'expectors' possess different access to databases and varying capacities to process their contents. A recently popular strand of economic modelling attempts to reduce the importance of such uncertainty (and its differential impact upon different actors) by assuming that all economic actors possess and employ rationally all available and relevant information. In consequence, the price system can be assumed to incorporate efficiently all available information. 'Rational expectations', then, are seen as those based, in one way or another, upon prices. But even these crude modellers have been forced, in their efforts to bend reality to fit their models, to grapple with the possibility of lags in the conversion of information into price signals and the facts of substantial 'noise' (random error) and frequent 'surprises' (unforeseen events). Keynes pointed out that:

> Despite being flimsy, without solid foundation, and subject to sudden and violent change, present conditions and majority opinion have long been generally assumed to be serviceable guides to the future. (Keynes, 1936: 147–64)

Decision makers in 'remote' parts of the world, however, may not have access even to such rudimentary guides as information on present prices, let alone other conditions or opinions. In volatile commodity, financial and foreign exchange markets the effects of even slight delays in the receipt of information may be disastrous.

Evidence concerning the capacities of specialists to forecast such market phenomena as exchange rates, stock prices, commodity markets and the like is mixed at best. One clear conclusion, however, seems to be that some forecasters are a good deal worse than others (Levich, 1980). Another is that futures prices are not particularly good predictors of future spot prices; on the other hand, they are usually at least as good as readily available alternatives.

Whatever the other possible attributes of futures markets they do provide an insurance service to those with fears of unforeseen developments. Risks can obviously be covered via insurance contracts as well. They can also, as will be seen below, be shared by means of appropriate terms of contracts.

Apart from the possibility that 'insiders' or the better-informed may be better predictors of the future, there exists the further possibility that they may, in some circumstances, even be able, through their knowledge, to influence it. There is probably greater and more universal interest in the functioning of futures or contingency markets and the possibility of their creation where they do not exist, however, than in the perfection of forecasting methods or devices for market manipulation.

'Inherent' Deficiencies or Asymmetries in Information

The new economics of information has been particularly concerned with cases of imperfect information in which prices serve not only to clear markets but also to convey signals as to quality. Quality uncertainty may, to a substantial extent, be 'inherent' in the sense that increased search efforts may uncover very little further information concerning it. In the apparently upside-down world of quality uncertainty, which proves disconcertingly frequently to be the real one, higher prices can generate increased demand, and lower prices can result in lower sales. Buyers may have acquired, through their search activity, virtually complete price information; but, particularly with 'experience' products and 'one-off' purchases, they may still be *unable* to acquire anything like the same degree of completeness of quality information. In such circumstances, low prices may be taken as signals of low quality. Sometimes they are correct signals in that respect. Sometimes, however, they are not, in which case those picking up the incorrect signal are losing the opportunity of a bargain. Low prices may therefore be seen by buyers as involving greater variability of quality – high-risk, high-return opportunities – to be set against the higher prices of more certain products such as, for instance, those associated with larger firms or better-known brands.

These informational problems may directly impede developing countries' entry into world markets in which they have not been selling before. The quality of their products, particularly manufactured ones, may be regarded by buyers as uncertain; the lower are their prices, the greater may be buyer resistance.

Imperfect information is also said to generate lender resistance to developing country financial instruments in world credit markets. In such circumstances, higher-risk premiums may be totally ineffective in overcoming the problem and, conceivably, could even make it worse. The 'herd behaviour' of private banks' lending to particular developing countries suggests highly imperfect information on the part of bankers and reliance upon signals such as the behaviour of other market participants. So does the behaviour of speculative international capital flow.

To some degree, these credit market problems flow from an informational deficiency on the part of the lenders which is exemplary of a wider class of market problems: those of 'moral hazard' and 'adverse selection'.

Insurance contracts and markets generate incentives for altered behaviour (greater risk-taking or the knowing encouragement of the contingency against which insurance has been obtained) on the part of the insured. This is the well known 'moral hazard' problem. Since (where there is an equal degree of risk aversion) those facing the greatest risks are those most interested in insurance, when the same premiums are charged to all insurers there will be 'adverse selection'. An insurance company able to discriminate among parties with varying degrees of risk – that is, one with sufficient information for this purpose – will charge higher premiums to higher-risk insurers. If it cannot do this, and even if, to some degree, it can, it may choose not to offer contracts to those quite willing to pay higher premiums because their very willingness to pay these high rates is evidence of their very high risk and increased moral hazard; thus there may be an upper limit to the price at which the insurance company is willing to contract.

That banks may not offer credit to willing borrowers (say, in developing countries) above the maximum risk premium over the market rate of interest can now be understood. Similarly, employers may not hire willing workers below some minimum salary, or will oppose or even refuse to go along with efforts to smooth out salary structures. In all these examples there is assumed to be asymmetric information: the advantage rests with the individual purchaser of insurance, borrower or worker, and the problem is seen as that for the relatively ill-informed firm that, in the absence of alternatives, uses 'market signals' for the acquisition of its information.

Probably of even greater importance is 'inherent' informational asymmetry of the opposite kind: the relatively ill-informed buyer or seller in the developing countries facing the relatively well-informed businessmen (and governments) of the industrialized countries. The dangers from the provision of misleading or incomplete information in environments within which there are few checks or balances are demonstrated most dramatically in the infamous case of baby formula milk sales in the less developed countries. In another case, the newly TV-oriented Samoan society was found in the mid-1970s to consume enormous quantities of highly advertised Pepto-Bismol 'in a society where no incidence of intestinal or digestive ailments had previously been visible'. There is evidence that in the industrialized countries less educated, lower-income and lower-status consumers are generally more susceptible to misleading advertising. While firm evidence is lacking, it seems reasonable to hypothesize that consumers in less developed countries are more likely to form their 'tastes' on the basis of misinformation than those in developed countries and without the same capacity to process the information coming to them from advertising (James and Lister, 1980: 83–4).

The problems of developing country purchasers are not simply those of easily duped consumers. Governments and firms also face major informational problems as buyers. For developing country purchasers, the informational situation is frequently analogous to Akerlof's (1970) classic analysis of the market for 'lemons'. This is particularly the case in the markets for differentiated products like machinery, consulting services, turnkey projects and the like. Those who sell high-quality products are reluctant to sell in the open world market at some kind of 'average price' which includes that for low-quality products. The seller of superior goods and services *knows* that his are superior and will not be adequately valued in a market in which 'lemons' are also to be found, and in which the inevitably less well-informed are unable easily to tell the difference. The cautious (or informed) buyer is willing to pay higher prices for higher quality and seeks to avoid the risk of the 'lemon' market in which the good and bad are interspersed. There are some signs – firms' reputations, brand names and so on – to guide the inherently or otherwise ill-informed; but they typically involve oligopoly 'rents' which poor purchasers sensibly seek to avoid. The poorest and the least informed tend to look for bargains on the 'used car markets' of the world; and they, like used car buyers, are frequently 'ripped off'. Quality uncertainty is central to their problems. The low-quality goods (and businessmen) drive out the high-quality ones on open markets. Not only, then, are there direct costs to the cheated purchasers from quality misrepresentation by sellers but, more importantly, there are social costs, deriving from the driving of some legitimate business out of existence.

Sellers of goods clearly can have an interest in *restricting* information by concealing defects in that which they are selling. Competitors will equally clearly gain from exposing such deficiencies; to some degree, where there is competition, the dangers of incomplete information distorting the selection processes of the buyers may thus be reduced.

Information deficiencies on the consumers' end of market relationships have generated considerable interest both in the courts and in the 'consumer movement'. The courts in the USA and UK have recognized 'unfairness' and 'unequal bargaining power' as grounds for declaring unenforceable or illegal certain contractual provisions which have been voluntarily entered into. Followers of traditional economic doctrine are frequently uncomfortable with the concept of 'unfairness' in voluntary exchange and find reasons for questioning such legal approaches (Klein, 1980).

In a world of effectively functioning and competitive markets, the selling firms would be disciplined by the market to be truthful in the information they supply and to offer prices which are commensurate with quality. But if markets provide this kind of textbook discipline they do so only 'on the whole'; it would be folly to rely upon them for this purpose in specific transactions. Badly informed consumers may buy inferior products at excessive prices either because of their own inadequate search, because of the inherent difficulty in acquiring information, or because of misleading sales activities on the part of sellers. Time, effort and expenditure to be spent upon search activities are a function of the opportunity cost of the relevant inputs and the expected return from search activities. The risks of being deceived vary with the nature of the product being purchased. 'One-off' transactions are riskier than those which are expected to lead to further purchases: purchases from small unknown firms are riskier than those from 'established' firms with reputations to protect: standardized products are less risky to the purchaser than complex or highly differentiated ones.

The smaller the economy, other things being equal, the greater the likelihood of 'one-off' transactions, the longer it will take to 'learn' about the relative merits of different products, and the less information can buyers generally be expected to possess. When small economies are also geographically or communicationally remote, the consumer problems are obviously multiplied. If suppliers of information appear, to sell information to those who are patently undersupplied with it, similar consumer problems apply to these suppliers as well.

Potential Response to Informational Deficiencies or Asymmetries

Both buyers and sellers face information uncertainty. The buyer attempts to reduce his deficiency by search. The seller attempts to acquire information by 'marketing' activity, which consists essentially of the collection, use, and selective supply of information. Those who provide information, through advertising for instance, may be able to charge higher prices for identical products because they know that they are thereby reducing their buyers' search costs. A conscientious searcher can often therefore avail himself of cheaper prices. Price dispersion can exist because of imperfect arbitrage which is itself the result of search costs. The advantage taken by a seller of an ignorant buyer would be at a maximum when he perfectly discriminates among each of his buyers, charging each that price which he can, on the basis of his unique demand elasticity (which is in part a function of his degree of ignorance) (Salop, 1977); this is presumably easier to justify when the product being sold is a complex and differentiated one, such as a used car.

Some transactors perform much 'better' whether in markets or hierarchies, than others. Differences in abilities may derive from differential costs of becoming informed. While it will generally be agreed that greater search activity will always generate more information, and thereby probably improve the quality of decision-making and/or the confidence in these decisions, it does not necessarily follow that investments in search are always 'profitable'. In the first place the (marginal) cost of search must be taken into account. Second, the marginal return from increased information may be small: the extra information gleaned through expanded search may be too small to justify any change in the information possessor's actual behaviour.

There are many ways of acquiring information. Some is 'emergent' and can be acquired simply through waiting, although by the time one has waited it is sometimes too late to employ it productively. Some may be acquired through international non-market sources and some may be purchased. The market transactions in information give rise to the same sorts of questions as have arisen in the discussion of markets for technology.

If information were freely available to all, no one would pay for it. If prices fully reflect all available (at least publicly available) information, then there would be little point in paying for it either. The existence of private specialized information companies, even in highly competitive markets such as those for foreign exchange, suggest that 'insiders' *can* acquire extra information (at a cost which is less than the marginal return from it). Barriers to entry may make it possible for high returns to be earned by those who produce it under monopolistic or oligopolistic conditions: these barriers could include scale economies, or its underpricing by firms that also sell other services (Salop and Stiglitz, 1977).

Information may be offered on direct sale terms; it may be either project-packaged or process-packaged. As in the case of technology, we still know remarkably little about the channels through which information and information-related services actually flow; or their relative costs and advantages or the potential for better channels in terms of cost, quality or other criteria. Nor do we as yet know much about the buildup of indigenous information systems, either in practice or in potential.

APPROACHES TO INFORMATION POLICY FOR THE DEVELOPING COUNTRIES

Where there is a high degree of uncertainty, either because of limited access to potentially available information or because of inherent uncertainty (about the future, for instance), there is an evident extra need for flexibility and the capacity to switch from one type of activity to another. Similarly, where there is an unusually high degree of risk aversion, which characterizes those individuals, firms or countries at the margin of survival (physical, economic or political), it may be worth paying a high premium to reduce the potentially disastrous effects of 'surprises'. Among the unfortunate ironies of the Third World is its typical rigidity of production and decision-making structures in the face of the unusually high premium, because of limited information and high risk aversion, on flexibility. Where the avoidable costs of 'switching' are high it may pay to invest considerable sums in improved information acquisition. These circumstances also explain the developing countries' keen interest in international 'buffering' schemes to reduce their uncertainty concerning commodity prices, foreign exchange earnings, terms of trade, exchange rates, and so forth.

Information-related disadvantages of developing countries in international economic relationships can be addressed in different ways. First, there can be efforts to alter the legal and institutional infrastructure of international exchange through the introduction of codes, guidelines, agencies and the like which relate to the provision of increased information by informed transactors, generally increased transparency, and at least a minimum of monitoring and enforcement by disinterested parties. Second, there can be increased use of contracts in which the risks are shared more equitably than they are when some transactors possess more information than others. Third, and more fundamentally, there can be efforts directly to increase information and information services within the developing countries themselves. These alternatives will be addressed in turn.

Improved International Legal and Institutional Infrastructures

Within nations there are frequently 'consumer protection' laws of various kinds. These, like antitrust laws which are likewise designed to 'soften' the functioning of 'free markets', tend to be both more developed and more enforceable in the developed countries than in the less developed countries. Similar laws or the principles lying behind them might be applied either within those less developed countries with the capacity to enforce them or at the international level (probably through the device of 'codes') or both.

Among the informational devices available for the purposes of consumer protection are:

- laws or codes requiring truth in the provision of information by the seller (or, put the other way, the prohibition of false claims);
- laws or codes requiring the provision of more complete information ('disclosure') – for example, warnings as to health hazards, the establishment of uniform and easily understood measures of particular product characteristics (a 'metric');
- the prohibition of some kinds of information or claims;
- the provision at public expense of increased information about product attributes, prices, and so on.

Such remedies of informational deficiencies which operate to 'improve' the flow of information to purchasers (or for that matter to sellers) obviously depend upon effective communication: 'uncomprehended information that is ignored produces no benefits'.(Beales, *et al.*, 1981: 411). In the case of the less developed countries 'effective communication' may be particularly difficult. Even in the American context, it has been observed that messages 'must be consonant with the information processing capabilities of the target audience . . . and must consider the limitations of the medium in which it will be placed'. (ibid: 413).

In this area, as in others, it is possible that developing countries might seek exemption from 'disclosure' requirements; but, so far as basic standards are concerned, this would probably not be in their interest. (This is not to say that they would not gain from the restriction of some other kinds of information, such as that on export crop prospects.)

Whether any of these sorts of measures could be agreed at the international level or, if agreed, actually enforced, is an open question. Certainly in the foreseeable future any such schemes seem rather unlikely. On the other hand, gross violations of accepted Northern standards in advertising and marketing on the part of Northern-based transnationals (if perhaps not on the part of local firms) may be susceptible to 'control' by Northern public opinion.

Altered Distribution of Risks in Contracts

Informational deficiencies may also be attacked via policies not dealing directly with information at all: for example, the regulation of product standards and/or prices; the regulation of the terms of contracts (through the requirement of warranties, for instance); price stabilization and so on. Broadly speaking, this second category of policy alternatives seeks to alter the distribution of risks with respect both to the unknowable future and to quality dispersion, information on which may be asymmetrically available.

Market transactions are usually assumed to be 'non-contingent', in the sense that an agreement is made to buy or sell at a point in time or over a period, regardless of what new circumstances may develop in the interim, or of subsequent satisfaction with the original contract. The transaction costs involved in detailed provisions relating to all manner of future contingencies create an obvious disincentive to their use. But the presence or absence of such provisions has clear implications for the carrying of risk (Heal, 1977; Spence, 1977). 'Non-contingent' terms of contracts may include implicit provision for risk within the conventionally-defined 'price' – for example, risk premiums charged on loans to 'less creditworthy' borrowers.

Political bargains are more often of a contingent character than are economic contracts: 'if these events occur, then these arrangements and reactions will follow'. Where longer-term or particularly comprehensive treaties or agreements are negotiated, there is frequent resort, however, to an 'escape clause' (or several of them) in order to preserve the legalities while permitting contingent observance of their terms:

> ... complete, fully contingent, costlessly enforceable contracts are not possible ... Rather than the impersonal marketplace of costlessly enforceable contracts represented in standard economic analysis, individuals in most real world transactions are concerned with the possibility of breach and hence the identity and reputation of those with whom they deal. (Klein, 1980: 356)

Since the possible contingencies are so many, and since it is often difficult to prove a breach of contract, a common option for the transactors is simply to 'renege on the transaction by holding up the other party, in the sense of taking advantage of unspecified or unenforceable elements of the contractual relationship' (ibid). If this prospect is understood in advance, again, the terms of a contract may implicitly reflect it, even if they appear to be 'non-contingent'.

A conscious effort could be made to reduce risks for more informationally deficient transactors through encouraging the reduction of uncertainty surrounding the eventual effects of contracts. This could be done by greater use of Bisque clauses in financial contracts, explicit inclusion of contingency arrangements or performance bonds in commercial contracts, the use of basket currencies for the denomination of contracts, and the like. There is a considerable history of efforts to stabilize certain commodity prices and, more recently, to offset fluctuations in export earnings and even some of those in import requirements. In all such schemes, however, there remains the question of who is to bear their cost and ultimately, therefore, the question of whether improvements will be truly 'additional'. As has been seen, 'better' terms of contracts in the sense of reducing uncertainties may be offset by worsened prices. Increased compensatory financing may be at the expense of some other kind of finance for generally the same set of beneficiary countries.

The Development of Indigenous Information Systems

A third policy set is much more fundamental: measures designed directly to improve the information and the information handling capacity of the informationally most deficient. These can be undertaken by the international community; by groups of countries allied by regional, sectoral, functional, political or other interests; or by individual national governments or firms. They can relate to forecasting, quality and price dispersion, and a wide variety of other types of information. Transnational corporations may play an important positive role in this area. And it is in this area that the new information technologies, if they can be appropriately and effectively harnessed, may be of great significance.

Scale economies in the collection, processing, storage and transmission of information have always been at the centre of discussions about informational adequacy on the part of economic and political actors. The relative disadvantages of small and medium-sized firms in world markets – whether importing or exporting – have long been attributed in large part to their relative weakness in information. To overcome this weakness, the traditional remedies have been the formation of large-scale trading houses (or marketing boards), the use of the information networks of the international financial institutions with which small actors are associated, the purchase of information from specialist firms in the relevant sectors and so forth. Governments have frequently tried to assist informationally weaker national firms in international trade through the services of commercial attachés, trade missions, export promotion bureaux, statistical services and the like. Above all, if scale economies are important, is the need for cooperation among small actors for the purpose of reducing cost. This is evidently an area for major potential gain, particularly for the smaller countries, through economic and technical cooperation with other developing (or even developed) countries.

CONCLUSION

According to some, the revolution in telecommunications and informatics is generating a potential 'sea change' in the relative informational advantages of small and large actors. If there is the potential for virtually immediate access to all manner of market and other data through cheap and reliable satellite communication systems it may no longer be economic in the future for firms to try to develop their own (decreasing cost) information networks. The comparative informational advantage will then rest with those with the capacity to process and interpret broadly available information; and that may be much less a function of scale than the capacity to develop an information network is. Small-scale 'software' firms should be able to thrive internationally as, to some extent, they already do within the industrialized countries. Opportunities for developing countries may exist in this arena much more than in the hardware portion of the new information sectors: India, for instance, was exporting informational software well before it was able to sell hardware competitively abroad. The key questions would then be those of what may be the most useful forms of indigenous or custom-made 'software' for developing countries, and where they are to come from.

In the meantime, the developing countries must obviously work with what is at hand. What are the sensible next steps for developing countries of different economic structures and different levels of overall development? While it may be possible for newly industrializing countries to hire 'senior information systems executives' at internationally competitive salaries, many other developing countries are not so fortunate. In many countries the issues have as yet scarcely been posed.

The uncertain decision-maker seeking to make the best use of his restricted amount of information is highly dependent upon his own 'communication system' (Shubik, 1971). What information does he most need? Where does he now get his information? What is its quality? What does he pay for it? What measurable difference does it ultimately make to him?

To get at these issues, and thus to be able to consider improved alternatives, one must know much more about global information channels; the technology they employ; their degree of centralization and market structure characteristics; the possible biases in them; their costs and the principal factors influencing them; the capacities of users to employ what they channel; and the gaps in what they offer in relation to already perceived needs. These are empirical questions which are likely to vary among sectors, countries, firms and time periods; and they are likely to be changing rapidly. The structures of current information flow for use by developing countries, whether through markets or other institutions, present a potentially rich field for social scientific research. Those who can employ such research to understand and eventually to help to shape a more equitable use of information in international transactions will make a truly rich contribution.

REFERENCES

Akerlof, George A. (1970), 'The Market for 'Lemons': Quality Uncertainty and the Market Mechanism', *Quarterly Journal of Economics*, vol. 89, August.

Beales, Howard, Richard Craswell and Steven Salop (1981), 'Information Remedies for Consumer Protection', *American Economic Review*, vol. 71, no. 2, May.

Heal, Geoffrey (1977), 'Guarantees and Risk-Sharing', *Review of Economic Studies*, vol. XLIV, no. 3, October.

James, Jeffrey and Stephen Lister (1980), 'Galbraith Revisited: Advertising in Non-Affluent Societies', *World Development*, vol. 8, no. 1, January.

Keynes, John Maynard (1936), *The General Theory of Employment, Interest and Money*, London: Macmillan.

Klein, Benjamin (1980), 'Transaction Cost Determinants of 'Unfair' Contractual Arrangements', *American Economic Review*, vol. 70, no. 2, May.

Levich, Richard (1980), 'Analyzing the Accuracy of Foreign Exchange Advisory Services: Theory and Evidence' (and 'Comment' by Michael Dubin) in Richard M. Levich and Clas G. Wihlborg (eds), *Exchange Risk and Exposure, Current Developments in International Finance Management,* Lexington: D.C. Heath.

Salop, Steven (1977), 'The Noisy Monopolist: Imperfect Information, Price Dispersion and Price Discrimination', *Review of Economic Studies*, vol. XLIV, no. 3, October.

Salop, Steven and Joseph Stiglitz (1977), 'Bargains and Ripoffs: A Model of Monopolistically Competitve Price Dispersion', *Review of Economic Studies*, vol. XLIV, no. 3, October.

Shubik, M. (1971), 'Information, Rationality and Free Choice in a Future Democratic Society' in D.M. Lamberton (ed.), *Economics of Information and Knowledge*, London: Penguin.

Spence, Michael (1977), 'Consumer Misperceptions, Product Failure and Producer Liability', *Review of Economic Studies*, vol. XLIV, no. 3, October.

Stiglitz, Joseph (1979), 'Equilibrium in Product Markets with Imperfect Information', *American Economic Review*, vol. 69, no. 2, May.

Stiglitz, Joseph (1977), 'Introduction, Symposium on Economics of Information', *Review of Economic Studies*, vol. XLIV, no. 3, October.

14. The International Information Industry and the Developing Countries*

INTRODUCTION

In order for individuals, firms or nations to profit fully from exchange they must have adequate information to permit them to assess the available alternative terms and forms of exchange. Developing countries are notoriously ill-equipped in this respect, and their relative disadvantage shows vividly in their limited capacity to assess the appropriateness of the prices with which foreign suppliers or buyers present them.

Political independence in the Third World, and the more recent attempts to delink economic relationships – through nationalizations, the exercise of greater control over exports and imports, unpackaging, and so on – alter, in a fundamental way, the organization of the relevant information flows and processing systems. Whatever their other characteristics, colonial relationships in the realm of economics offered 'internalized' rather than arm's-length, market-type forms of informational (and other) organization. The move 'from status to contract' in North–South relationships implies a need for the development of new informational systems and means of interaction. Where developing countries are now independently buying or selling on world markets they must develop effective means of search in the manner of any arm's-length shopper or seller. Where intrafirm trade still persists in their international transactions, such search is required instead for the purpose of monitoring or controlling transfer pricing.

At present, information flows to the developing countries' decision-makers through a wide variety of channels and media. It arrives through 'in-house' collection and communication on the part of overseas commercial representatives, attachés or agents; it is assembled through trade

* I am grateful to Robin Murray and Reginald Green whose comments on an earlier version have considerably sharpened the argument; neither are to be implicated, however, in the contents of the present chapter.

journals, specialized consultancies, the services of brokers and dealers, the messages of salesmen and foreign aid or trade bureaucrats and various informal contacts. Rarely is its assembly and dissemination systematized on an ongoing basis as it typically is in large commercial enterprises (Strassman, 1976; Nanus, 1978). The basic informational resources – in the form of libraries, data banks, and the like – available to the poorest countries are typically hopelessly inadequate, frequently taking the exclusive form of published sources arriving sporadically by sea mail to understaffed libraries. For those 'in the trade', published sources, even 'hot from the press', are typically too obsolete to be useful for daily decision-making. The telephone and other telecommunications, while more expensive, are frequently *essential* instruments of communication.

It is necessary to assess the capacity of the informationally weak to acquire, usually at arm's length, and to process the information which they now require to make independent decisions which are in their own interest, rather than in the interests of the total information (and other) systems of which they were previously part. Difficult decisions must be made on how much, and in what ways, to spend in order to improve the informational 'efficiency' of national decision-making.

INFORMATION, MARKETS AND ECONOMIC THEORY

Intrafirm trade is partly the product of the peculiarities of economic transactions which are made under conditions of informational uncertainty, and of imperfections in markets for information. There are thus strong pressures working against 'delinking' and in favour of internalized international trade; they can be expected to encourage intra-firm trade in newer Third World-based firms as well as in the old-fashioned transnationals. In order both to understand the difficulties of shifting to more arm's-length economic relationships, and to assess the possibilities for the mobilization of information for the control of transfer pricing where internalized trade remains, it is important to understand the economics of information.

Until very recently the study of information and knowledge has occupied 'a slum dwelling in the town of economics' (Stigler, 1961: 171). It should not therefore be surprising that the implications of information economics and politics for the poor of the world have received so little attention. In no part of the current debate over global political and economic problems is the importance of information more dramatically evident than in the search for new forms of mutually agreeable relations between transnational corporations and poor nation states.

The information industry can be defined in different ways. Marschak (1968) regards it as that which provides the services of 'inquiring, communicating, deciding'. Inquiring is a matter of data-gathering or production; communication involves means of encoding, transmission through a variety of channels of differential speed, reliability and cost, and decoding; deciding has to do with the software which renders what is available usable by decision-makers. Broad definitions would include virtually all white-collar employment, and in particular, the educational system. In one study, employing a broad definition, it is estimated that the information industry accounts for over 40 per cent of US employment (Porat, 1977). It is at the very centre of the notion of 'post-industrial society'.

Information and knowledge can take many different forms. Considerable attention has been devoted in recent years to the developing countries' dependence upon imported knowledge in the form of technology; and to the imperfections of technology markets, the inappropriateness of much of what is available to them and the need for developing increased indigenous technological capacity. Rather less attention has been devoted, however, to the more general question of *market* information' or 'commercial intelligence', upon which the effective functioning of arm's-length systems of exchange depends; this, at a time when increased resort to arm's-length exchange is an accepted part of Third World aspirations. The latter kind of information is obviously relevant to the control of transfer pricing.

This type of information cannot be entirely separated from knowledge of the underlying technical change, demand shifts and the like. The distinction between 'market information' and other types of knowledge is nevertheless a real one. A consideration of the economics of market information must address such matters as the economics of alternative organizations, and the economics of search, as well as the peculiar properties of information markets. Political-economic analysis must obviously extend still further to include interest articulation, power and other organizational issues.

Fully informed, rational economic man still can be found in elementary economics textbooks where 'his cool, consistent mind quickly and costlessly scans the myriads of alternatives facing him' (Shubik, 1967: 358). In popular mythology, his principal habitat today is in large business organizations and, above all, in the transnational corporations. But, increasingly, theorists are investigating models of a more realistic world in which one typically finds instead 'the uncertain decision-maker acting under severely restricted conditions of information embedded within a communication system upon which he is becoming increasingly dependent' (Shubik, 1967: 361).

Market information is not a free good, available to all. It can be considered as a product like any other which can be acquired at a cost – either by 'making' it oneself or by acquiring it from another. In the standard literature on the economics of search (Stigler, 1961) it consists of information on the range of available price alternatives in a real world in which, because of transactions costs of various kinds, the 'law of one price' is all too rarely encountered; and assumptions as to the distribution of prices and the costs of searching lead to decision rules for both buyers and sellers on how much to search or how much information to offer through advertising. Matters become more complex when the searcher does not even know the degree of price dispersion, for then he cannot know how much to search; the ignorant – for example, the tourist in a foreign land – can expect to pay more when he buys and receive less when he sells. But market information involves much more than this static and undimensional fact of price dispersion. Prices and their degree of dispersion are constantly changing in response to innumerable influences upon demand and supply; market information therefore becomes obsolete very quickly. More important still, information as to the likely (though obviously still uncertain) future state of prices becomes a necessary input to market decision-making. Even better, if one possesses the capacity to process it independently, is information concerning the major underlying influences upon future market behaviour, for this permits one to make one's own judgments independently of others' possible biases or 'opportunistic' behaviour. Information of this more qualitative kind is clearly much more difficult to quantify or even theorize about.

Of equal importance to price information, particularly when goods are not homogeneous, is information as to the *quality* of items to be acquired. Search must therefore take place on the intensive (quality) margin as well as on the extensive one. In some instances, the suitability of goods to the buyer can only be tested through use; such products have been termed 'experience' (as opposed to 'search') goods (Nelson, 1970).

Among the means of reducing qualitative informational uncertainties in a complex world are the development of 'customer relationships', brand loyalties, 'reputation' and 'goodwill'. In conditions of great informational uncertainty, cautious buying (or selling) behaviour is understandable: the familiar – in terms of existing relationships, geography, language and the like – may be chosen even when the cost, objectively speaking, appears high. As information improves, the breadth of shopping (and marketing) increases. Thus what geographers call 'information space' (Törnqvist, 1977: 156–7), the nature of information networks, can play an important role in the determination of the direction of both domestic and international flows of goods and services. The internalization of trade inside firms is a major device for reducing informational uncertainty.

Those who do not themselves obtain information in the volume or form they require in the course of their general activities must acquire it from others. While such acquisition does not always occur on markets, it is analytically helpful, as in the case of technology, to consider it as if it did. Information markets, like technology markets, have peculiar properties.

1. Information is not an exhaustible product – that is, it is not 'used-up' through employment or dissemination. Many can possess it at the same time. Its provision to others, even if transactions costs are zero, may nevertheless involve one in losses, and there may be private advantages in not sharing it. On the other hand, substantial costs may also be sensibly incurred for the provision of information to others – for example, through advertising. (Indeed, there may be advantages in passing on *mis*information; and that fact necessitates a greater capacity to assess information acquired from 'external' sources.)
2. The cost of transmitting information which has already been produced (transactions cost) is not zero and can be expected to vary greatly between different types of information and different means of transmission. Transmission systems have their own factor-intensity and scale requirements, and it is likely that the lowest-cost systems require substantial capital inputs and scale. The latter create barriers to entry to certain transmission systems, and it follows that different actors will have differential access to low-cost media.
3. The returns from the production of information are generally not fully appropriable; that is, it is often possible for others to realize gains from the use of information which you 'produced' without your being able to obtain a share of them. There are no laws or conventions, such as those governing patents and trademarks, which protect intellectual property rights in this area. It follows that great quantities of information are transferred through low-cost or even totally non-commercial channels, sometimes quite informal ones. (Some kinds of information are not easily transferred, such as those learned best by doing; and others are successfully kept secret.)

4. Information is a product of extremely rapid obsolescence, an attribute which also impedes its effective transfer among unrelated decision-makers.
5. Like technology, its quality is impossible to judge accurately until one possesses it; many of those with the 'best' supplies are themselves, consciously or unconsciously, biased about its content. Given the advantages to be gained from the conscious provision of misinformation, one must be particularly careful about its reliability.
6. Information is frequently only available (at reasonable cost) in packages or indivisible lumps which, not being tailor-made, include goods and services other than those actually sought. These indivisibilities may relate to the size of the information package itself, to the packaging of the required information with goods or other purchases, to the minimum period of time over which it is to be offered, and so on. It is often a by-product of some other activity.
7. On the supply side, the production of information seems likely to be characterized by economies of scale, economies of experience ('learning by doing'), and positive externalities; the cumulative effect of acquiring information over wider areas and over longer periods of time is to render one better at acquiring more. 'Since the cost of collection of information is (approximately) independent of its use (although the cost of dissemination is not), there is a strong tendency toward monopoly in the provision of information: in general, there will be a 'standard' source for trade information' (Stigler, 1961: 220). Where information is not supplied by independent specialized firms, these influences promote oligopolistic tendencies in the industries dependent upon it.
8. Still on the supply side, the production, storage and processing of information is highly skill-intensive and capital-intensive.

Incomplete information, and resulting risk and uncertainty, have become central to major theories of economic organization, both at the macro- and the micro-level. At the macro- or societal level, the debate between advocates of central planning and decentralized market systems has long centred on questions of data collection and distribution. Hayek, in the pre-computer age, believed that the sheer size of the data collection, communication and processing requirements for effective centralized decision-making made it unfeasible, whatever other merits or demerits it might have. Markets are themselves, he argued (Hayek, 1945), the most efficient and effective information systems. Needless to say, the new technologies of the electronic age today require a different formulation of such arguments. The efficiency with which macro-systems of economic organization employ available data for the purposes of allocation of resources continues to be a matter for (pure) economic theorizing. These investigations have not as yet adequately addressed the implications for 'social efficiency', (in which 'efficiency' is defined not in terms merely of Pareto optimality but in terms of income distributional objectives as well), of the *differential and asymmetric* access to information of actors within the system.

At the micro-level, the modern theory of the firm itself, and certainly the theory of mergers and vertical integration, have been built substantially upon assumptions with respect to the availability and quality of information. In a symposium on the frontier of the 'economics of internal organization' its organizer remarked on the 'striking' fact that all of the papers were 'critically concerned with information in some form or other' and could be regarded as explorations into 'a variety of informationally constrained resource-allocation problems and institutional responses that characterise firms, organizations, and groups' (Spence, 1975: 164). The replacement of the market through integration or merger takes place, among other reasons, as a result of 'transactional failures' in markets (Williamson, 1971), failures traceable primarily to problems in the processing of information. Dunning (1977: 403) refers to them as 'cognitive imperfections' (see also Malmgren, 1961; Marschak, 1968; Williamson, 1971; Hirschleifer, 1973 and Spence, 1975).

According to these theories, in circumstances of great complexity and uncertainty there may be limits to individuals' or small firms' capacities to receive, store, retrieve and process information faultlessly, or to transmit information to one another effectively ('bounded rationality'); in such circumstances internalization of what would otherwise be arm's-length transactions or 'learning by doing' may be the most effective means of organizing activity and realizing scale economies.

Moreover, where there may be reason to doubt the total veracity or completeness of information being supplied by one's (arm's-length) source, particularly where 'small numbers bargaining' rather than active competition (which is to some degree an automatic 'policeman') is found, it may be necessary to internalize one's information sources to prevent what has been termed 'opportunism' (that is, 'an effort to realise individual gains through a lack of candor or honesty in transactions' (Wachter and Harris 1975: 258–9). Internalization may also reduce the incidence of 'information impactedness' stemming not so much from opportunism as from inherent difficulties of specifying contractual arrangements.

Both the cost of information and its quality may be influenced by the institutional arrangements through which it is collected, communicated and processed. In general, modern micro-theory concludes, 'A situation in which anonymous agents deal with an impersonal market is not conducive to efficiency with imperfect information' (Spence, 1975: 171). Internalization of transactions through merger or integration is the mechanism through which private actors seek to overcome these problems in a market economy. Governmental institutions and planning systems are obvious alternative means of organizing information assembly and use in order to seek more efficient overall outcomes.

At the international level, the potential for governmental institutions is limited by the weakness of the world 'political system'. The transnational corporations are far ahead of governments in their utilization of the most modern information systems. They possess the capital, skill and scale to produce, transmit and process information with maximum efficiency, and they have long since overcome the major imperfections of market exchange by internalizing their informational (and other) flows.

IMPROVED INFORMATION FOR DEVELOPING COUNTRIES

There is a clear need for the development of better systems of market information for the use of the developing countries, particularly the poorest and weakest among them. But the basic characteristics of the information industry, its markets and its present institutional manifestations, severely challenge the ingenuity of developing countries seeking to improve their access to international market information. On the one hand, the development of an indigenous informational capacity faces, especially in its early stages, the disadvantages of small scale, limited experience, and limited positive externalities, together with its need for substantial capital and skill inputs. These constitute significant barriers to entry. On the other hand, to acquire information through arm's-length purchase is to face the difficulties of quality assessment, rapid obsolescence, inappropriate packaging, others' market power and probably high cost. Whether information is to be 'made' or bought, the difficulties of appropriating the product, the gains to be realized through its diffusion, and the potential for scale economies and positive externalities, all suggest the potential productivity of governmental rather than decentralized private activity in this sector.

Within individual developing countries there is undoubtedly some potential for improvements in existing systems for gathering and interpreting market information. By no means all information is firm-specific, sector-specific or ministry-specific; yet even within the same governmental system, it is frequently collected in parallel efforts through different sources in a wasteful and repetitious manner, without adequate domestic distribution or use. Information is often acquired at great cost from foreign sources when it is already readily available at home (or from cheaper foreign sources known to other domestic users). It may be possible to realize at least some scale and other economies through greater rationalization of existing information systems; and this is likely to involve conscious governmental policy to that end.

It is likely that the developing countries, especially the poorest, will still have to purchase many of their information requirements from abroad. This is as true of information required for the control of transfer pricing as of that for more efficient arm's-length shopping or marketing. The available sources of information for the possible use of developing countries are varied, and differ with the sector concerned. There are not many sellers of across-the-board information on market prices.

It may be worth considering a specific instance in which a private firm in the information industry at present does provide such *general* services to a number of developing country governments, from the standpoint of its 'efficiency' relative to possible alternatives.

The activities of General Superintendence, (actually Société Générale de Surveillance, SGS), on behalf of the countries which employ its services, illustrate some of the limitations of present market arrangements in the information sector. Here is a firm of substantial scale and experience, drawing upon considerable reserves of capital and (especially) skill, to provide certain limited packages of rapidly dating information to its clients. Specifically, it undertakes to check the quantity, quality and price of imports, the latter being compared with 'prices commonly charged for this product and related services in the applicable market and conditions'. The information it supplies consists of a 'yes' or 'no' on each shipment it inspects. In return for this service it is paid a fee averaging roughly 1 per cent of the value of the shipments. The quality and value of its services to these clients is extremely difficult to assess. Its reputation in the field of its specialized activity may alone be sufficient to deter large numbers of exporters from practices they might otherwise attempt to employ against ill-informed buyers, even if the quality of the information it actually provides is dubious. It could also be influenced by conflicts of interest, particularly where, as in the case of its relatively small African clients, it has more important interests and business relationships to protect.

Moreover, it does not begin to provide the full shopping information which buyers really require. In the first place, it confines its role to making comparisons with other shipments purely at the national market level. (British and American customs authorities are considerably more stringent in their assessments of the 'reasonableness' of prices for traded goods.) Second, it does not even transmit the market information it collects; it simply offers a dichotomous verdict (yes/no) on individual shipments. This modest price information is not typically sold to private clients since, significantly, they prefer to do their shopping themselves. SGS is unlikely to do more for their developing country clients because of their need to preserve the value of their information and their image of independence and objectivity. A commercial firm must, after all, seek to appropriate as much as it reasonably can from its investments.

What this service provides, then, is a generalized check upon some forms of 'opportunism' on the part of those with whom Southern buyers transact at arm's length, including foreign firms whose shipments are made on an intrafirm basis. The possibility of some opportunism on the part of the information firm itself remains, but it is presumably believed to be smaller. It does very little to improve commercial information of the more important sort, such as price information, which is at the core of the economics of search. Nor, therefore, does it provide an adequate information base for the effective monitoring of transfer prices.

The commercialization of information generates some obvious social inefficiencies. If a commercial firm in the information industry, such as SGS, learns that a *particular* exporting firm is unreliable or 'opportunistic' in its dealings with weaker trading partners, or that *particular* shipments are qualitatively flawed, or that the price dispersion with respect to a *particular* product in its particular 'applicable market' is thus, and so it never pays it to make this information widely available. Although the cost (whether private or social) of transmitting such information widely would be minimal and the social gains potentially great, it will not happen because there are no private gains to be appropriated from such a practice. Only those who specifically pay for the provision of such information will receive it, and even they will receive no more than is specifically required under the terms of their contracts. Thus, if a shipment of grain is found to be infested, the probable effect of the commercialization of the information industry will be to redirect it from a country which pays for its services to another which is less well serviced or informed; indeed, if the exporter himself knows of the infestation he may well redirect it in advance to countries which are not as well serviced by the information industry.

The cost of transmitting such information, once acquired, is seemingly very small. If a private firm does not do it – for reasons which are readily apparent – why do governments which have acquired it not do so? Once one client of the commercial information firm has paid its service charge, why should it not pass the resulting information on at minimal further cost to other interested and friendly parties? Could not at least some of the information be paid for only once, instead of – as in the case of SGS' eight African clients – eight times? In part, the answer may lie in the problem of the 'free rider': it is difficult to arrive at mutually agreed means of financing activities which are in everyone's interest when individual parties know they will derive benefits from the service anyway. In part, it may lie in the technical difficulties of transmitting relevant data, since certainly the problems of shipment-by-shipment checking will remain, and the supporting infrastructure for such information storage and transmission is weak or non-existent in Africa today.

Probably most important, however, is the fact that although SGS has information which, if widely shared, could be much more productively employed, it provides it only in a form (dichotomous decisions on individual shipments) which severely limits not only its use but also its transferability.

It is time, then, to consider how an alternative information system might work. Could the considerable expenditures (1 per cent of their total import value) undertaken by SGS' African clients be better employed in some collective information activity of their own? Or, if not, could the information that they already acquire at least be more effectively utilised in their common interest? What is at issue is not necessarily a matter of across-the-board import substitution of SGS so much as a matter of considering in which sectors and activities they are really best suited to supply their services.

Evidently SGS does not provide much price or market information to its African clients, although that information is certainly collected. A major positive externality of the policing function thus remains unrealized, essentially because of SGS' own business calculations. If buyers controlled the organization they would most certainly utilize all of these possibilities more effectively.

Cooperation and exchange of information among information-poor countries has gone much further in the exporting sector – through producers' associations and the like – than it has in importing. I do not mean to minimize the difficulties – both technical and political – of working out such new schemes for economic informational cooperation. Nor should one underemphasize the enormous headstart and genuine advantage enjoyed in these matters by large, experienced firms such as SGS. It may be that, for the present, one can do little better than to continue to employ them for many purposes. One suspects, however, that better terms might be negotiated through coordinated bargaining: African government business alone accounted for about 10 per cent of SGS' total turnover in the 1970s (*Financial Times*, 2 February 1979).

Further investigations of alternatives and the exercise of a little institutional imagination are certainly due in the informational sector. There can be no defence of unthinking adherence to the *status quo* in the face of its obvious and manifest limitations. The question in this specific instance is whether there may be scope for governmental action to take advantage of the potential for positive externalities and scale economies realizable through the exchange of information. By so doing they might begin to counter the advantage currently enjoyed by large, experienced commercial firms operating in quasi-monopolistic circumstances. More generally, failure to develop new information systems for the developing countries, to permit them more effectively to shop efficiently and to control transfer pricing, may mean not only the perpetuation of the inefficiencies and inequities of present international exchange but also their worsening, as a result of internationally unbalanced technical change in the foreseeable future.

REFERENCES

Darrow, Joel W. and James R. Belilove (1978), 'The Growth of Databank Sharing', *Harvard Business Review*, November–December.

Dunning, John H. (1977), 'Trade, Location of Economic Activity and the MNE: A Search for an Eclectic Approach' in Bertil Ohlin *et al.* (ed.), *The International Location of Economic Activity*, London: Macmillan, pp. 395–418.

Hayek, F.A. (1945), 'The Use of Knowledge in Society', *American Economic Review*, vol. 35, no. 4, September.

Hirschleifer, J. (1973), 'Where Are We in the Theory of Information', *American Economic Review*, vol. 63, no. 2, May.

Malmgren, H. (1961), 'Information, Expectations and the Theory of the Firm', *Quarterly Journal of Economics*, vol. 75, August.

Marschak, J. (1968), 'Economics of Inquiring, Communicating, Deciding', *American Economic Review*, vol. 58, no. 2; reprinted in D.M. Lamberton (ed.), *Economics of Information and Knowledge*, Harmondsworth: Penguin, 1971.

McHale, John (1976), *The Changing Information Environment*, Boulder, Col.: Westview Press.

Nanus, Burt (1978), 'Business, Government and the Multinational Computer', *Columbia Journal of World Business*, Spring.

Nelson, P. (1970), 'Information and Consumer Behaviour', *Journal of Political Economy*, vol. 78, March–April.

Porat, Marc Uri (1977), *The Information Economy: Definition and Measurement*, Washington DC: US Department of Commerce, Office of Telecommunication.

Shubik, M. (1967), 'Information, Rationality and Free Choice in a Future Democratic Society', *Daedalus*, vol. 96, pp. 771–8; reprinted in D.M. Lamberton (ed.), *Economics of Information and Knowledge*, Harmondsworth: Penguin, 1971.

Spence, Michael (1975), 'The Economics of Internal Organization: An Introduction', *The Bell Journal of Economics*, vol. 6, no. 1, Spring.

Stigler, George (1961), 'The Economics of Information', *Journal of Political Economy*, vol. LXIX, no. 3, June.

Strassman, Paul A. (1976), 'Managing the Costs of Information', *Harvard Business Review*, September–October.

Törnqvist, Gunnar (1977), 'Comment' in Bertil Ohlin *et al.* (ed.), *The International Allocation of Economic Activity*, London: Macmillan.

Wachter, Michael L. and Jeffrey E. Harris (1975), 'Understanding the Employment Relation: the Analysis of Idiosyncratic Exchange', *The Bell Journal of Economics*, vol. 6, no. 1, Spring.

Wachter, Michael L. and Jeffrey E. Harris (1975), *Markets and Hierarchies, Analysis and Antitrust Implications, A Study in the Economics of Internal Organization*, New York: The Free Press.

Williamson, Oliver E. (1971), 'The Vertical Integration of Production: Market Failure Considerations', *American Economic Review*, May.

Index